# 7a Max - Sco

## A GUIDE TO CLIMBS

by
Sebastien Rider and Topher Dagg

Second Edition
2015

Published by Rider-French Consulting Ltd. Scotland

Website : www.7amax.co.uk
Facebook : www.facebook.com/7amaxscottishsportclimbingguide

Copyright © 2015 Christopher Dagg & Sebastien Rider
ISBN: 978-0-9541906-5-1

Contains Ordnance Survey © Crown copyright and database right 2010
Contains Met Office data © Crown copyright, Open Government Licence
All photographs by the authors unless otherwise credited

Printed by Replika Press Pvt. Ltd.
Distributed by Cordee Ltd, UK. sales@cordee.co.uk +44 (0)1455 611 185

**Between the Deil and the Deep Blue Sea** (6c) on a breezy day at Arbroath. See p175

# Scottish Sport

## A Guide to Climbs from 2 to 7a+

Second Edition 2015

Sebastien Rider and Topher Dagg

# CONTENTS

**Rock Types**: Gn - Gneiss ; Sc - Schist ; Cg - Conglomerate ; Ss Sandstone ; D - Dolerite/Basalt ; V - volcanic intrusion ; Gr - Granite (see page 8)
**Grade Spread**: Chart only applies to 7a Max routes, see page 7 for colour code

# INTRODUCTION

Scotland is home to over 1500 sport routes of all levels of difficulty from French grade 2 to 9a. Sport climbing is found the length and breadth of the country, from somewhat urban locations in the Lowlands to remote crags of the northern Highlands. Due to its complex geology and topography, Scotland offers a great variety of sport climbing on sea-cliffs, mountain crags, quarries, and even man-made stone towers.

**7a Max** is aimed at the 'weekend' and visiting climber, and describes all of Scotland's crags with worthwhile routes up to 7a+; which surprisingly is the vast majority of the country's sport venues! According to the UK's leading climbing website, UKClimbing.com, over 90% of sport routes logged are up to 7a+. The focus on climbs up to 7a+ has allowed for the production of a guide that is especially tailored to those operating within these grades.

## USING THE GUIDE

Scotland's sport crags are grouped into several sections based on their location (see inside front cover). These include: Northern Highlands, Western Glens, Central Highlands, Angus and the North East, and The Lowlands. For each region, a summary of the essentials is provided along with area maps displaying crag locations.

Each venue has an introductory page complete with crag information, directions, maps, public transport information, and approach times. Icons show crag aspect, midge rating, and also specify if a cliff is accessible by public transport and bike and/or by car; in either case a time is given for the cycle or walk to the crag.

For smart phone users, QR codes on the introductory page can be simply scanned to display the crag location on your mobile's map or GPS app. Icons also show WGS-84 lat/long references for both the crag and parking locations, which can be used with your smart phone, satnav, or for browsing online mapping with *gridreferencefinder. com* or *streetmap.co.uk*. These sites can also convert lat/long co-ordinates into any format compatible with your particular device.

As an indication of the best crags to visit for one's given abilities, each venue has a bar graph summarising the number of routes at a particular difficulty (see example below). For every crag, maps show road approaches, parking areas, approach paths, and crag layouts where useful. Routes on every topo are described from left to right throughout and numbered using colours relating to the level of difficulty (below). See the inside back cover for full map and topo legends.

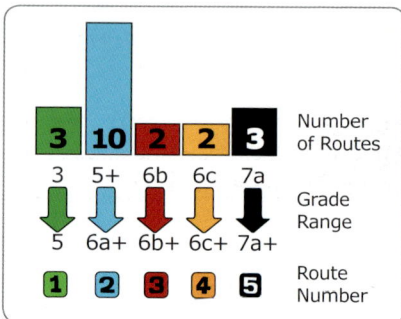

| | | | | | |
|---|---|---|---|---|---|
| 3 | 10 | 2 | 2 | 3 | Number of Routes |
| 3 | 5+ | 6b | 6c | 7a | Grade Range |
| 5 | 6a+ | 6b+ | 6c+ | 7a+ | |
| 1 | 2 | 3 | 4 | 5 | Route Number |

**7a Max** uses the well-established French sport climbing grading system, by which all British sport routes are graded. This grade is a single subjective rating indicating the overall difficulty of a route. Expect harder moves on short or cruxy routes than on longer or sustained routes of the same grade. Climbs are categorised numerically increasing in difficulty from 2 to 9. From numerical grade 6, each grade is further subdivided alphabetically with increasing difficulty from a to c. The '+' suffix indicates a hard route at the given grade.

The table below gives an *approximate* comparison beween four commonly used grading systems.

| French | USA | Australian | UK Tech |
|--------|-----|------------|---------|
| 3 | 5.3 | 10 | |
| 3+ | 5.4 | 12 | 4a |
| 4 | 5.5 - 5.6 | 13 | 4b |
| 4+ | 5.7 | 14-15 | 4c |
| 5 | 5.8 - 5.9 | 16-17 | |
| 5+ | 5.10a | 18 | 5a |
| 6a | 5.10b | 19 | |
| 6a+ | 5.10c | | 5b |
| 6b | 5.10d | 20 | |
| 6b+ | 5.11a | | 5c |
| 6c | 5.11b | 21 | |
| 6c+ | 5.11c | 22 | 6a |
| 7a | 5.11d | 23 | |
| 7a+ | 5.12a | 24 | 6b |

Seb enjoying the golden gneiss of
**Bovnahackit** (6a+)
Creag nan Cadhag - p73

# Introduction

## ROCK TYPE AND CLIMBING STYLE

*"Some rocks are gneiss, others are schist!"*

For the climber, the legacy of Scotland's ancient geological history is a plethora of rock types to climb on. Unlike in England or many European sport climbing cliffs, mainland Scotland has no bolted limestone. Each rock variety offers particular climbing characteristics such that success on one type is not guaranteed on another!

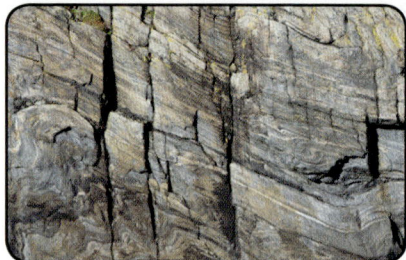

Those who have ventured outside the Peak District to the far northwest of the Scottish Highlands will know that God's Rock is actually **gneiss**! Due to its coarse grain, friction on this rock is superb. This is a very pleasant rock type to climb on and mainly located in the far northwest.

**Schist** is the most common rock type of the Scottish sport crags, and is predominantly found in the central and western Highlands. This metamorphic rock can be steep, and depending on the folding it has undergone, can vary considerably from crag to crag; expect anything from crimps, slopers, small pockets to sharp quartz crystals. Several of the schist crags seep in the winter months, but routes not affected by seepage can be quick drying. Schist is extremely slippery when wet – you have been warned!

Several sport Scottish sport crags, particularly in the north-eastern Highlands are **conglomerate** - sandstone interspersed with rounded and polished pebbles, or patatas (potatoes) as the Spanish call them. These crags are akin to Riglos or Montserrat in Spain, but somewhat shorter! The hardness of the sandstone matrix determines the quality of this rock, varying from solid to 'a little loose'; popping pebbles can be expected at some crags and occasionally some routes may even change grade. When solid this is an enjoyable rock to climb, usually involving face climbing with pockets, slopey pebbles and crimps. In climbing style, it could be said to be the closest thing to continental limestone in Scotland.

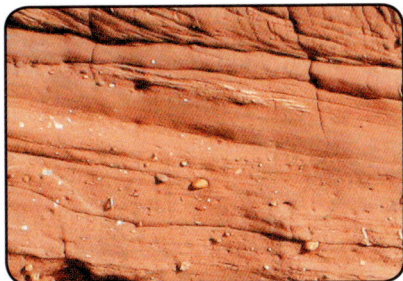

**Sandstone** is also a common rock in Scottish sport and is principally, but not exclusively, found in Angus. Depending on the variety, sandstone varies in climbing style between crags. Some sandstone crags, particularly when quarried, can be blank with 'reachy' climbing between horizontal breaks in the rock strata. Conversely, natural Torridonian Sandstone, such as at Glutton crag, is highly weathered and featured, requiring a variety of techniques to climb jamming cracks or fierce overlaps.

⚠️ Some sandstones and conglomerates become softer when wet or damp so are best avoided in such conditions to avoid potential damage.

Due to its many cracks, and the fact that it is extremely hard, **granite** is usually only home to traditional climbing. Scotland is home however to a few granite sport crags – mostly in Aberdeenshire. This rock is not typically steep but but makes up for this by often being rather blank and crimpy and with few foot holds.

**Dolerite**, and its finer-grained cousin **basalt**, are both volcanic rocks that are common in the Central Belt and on the Isle of Skye. The sport crags of these variable rock types can be 'blocky' or sometimes friable in nature. Some smooth basalts can be more challenging to climb when hot and humid and like schist this is another rock that becomes rather slippery when wet.

# Introduction

## SAFETY AND CODE OF CONDUCT

*"Climb if you will, but remember that courage and strength are nought without prudence, and that a momentary negligence may destroy the happiness of a lifetime."*
*- Edward Whymper.*

All types of climbing, including sport, involve an inherent risk of danger and even death. Sport climbing is often perceived as one of the safer genres of climbing. However, incidents due to equipment or rock failure, and/or climber error do occur and very occasionally are fatal. All personal climbing equipment should be regularly checked, and before each ascent it is prudent to do a 'buddy check'. For every climb it is the responsibility of the participant to check the integrity of all in-situ equipment and rock quality; the harsh Scottish climate and saltwater can cause rapid deterioration of both bolts and rock.

⚠ Treat with suspicion any bolts and hangers that show differential corrosion (below), as damage may not always be on the visible parts.

Sport climbing involves the shared use of climbing equipment, and more than often the crag itself. To ensure the preservation of all in-situ equipment and the climbing environment for other users, the following code of conduct should be adhered to by all sport climbing:

• Do not remove any lower-off carabiners or maillons
• Do not top-rope from fixed lower-offs; use your own carabiners to save wear on in-situ gear
• Do not lower off with another stationary rope left in place
• Leaving quickdraws in place does not give you rights to a route
• On harder routes quickdraws may be found left in place; remove if necessary but replace on leaving
• Try to avoid tick-marking holds; if absolutely necessary clean before leaving
• Report any in-situ gear and loose rock that is in a dangerous state. Internet forums e.g. UKClimbing.com are useful for this
• Do not disturb birds or livestock, especially during lambing season
• Take great care not to damage fence lines or walls, and leave gates in the state you found them, be that open or closed
• Take all your litter home
• If you need to defecate whilst at the crag, do so well away from the cliff, path or any watercourse. Dig a hole and carefully burn your toilet paper

# ETHICS OF SPORT CLIMBING IN SCOTLAND

*"Hilti also make angle-grinders!" - Anon.*

Scotland does not have a strong tradition of sport climbing, at least in the public eye. The national climbing ethic has always been adventurous trad, and with good reason. The land has a profusion of mountains, crags, and sea-cliffs of many different geologies that provide high quality, traditionally protected climbing, ranging from single pitch technical test-pieces to full day mountain outings. Modern rock climbing consists of several distinct realms including trad, sport, bouldering, dry-tooling and aid. Each has its own set of ethics, techniques, and jargon, often with limited degrees of mutual understanding. None should impose its own expectations and judgements on the others, as they are not cross applicable. Also, neither should any impose the physical effects of their passing on the grounds of the other.

Established bolting guidelines have historically been interpreted with varying degrees of strictness. For example, it cannot be doubted that Creag a Bhancair is a mountain crag, that Arbroath is all sea-cliffs, or that Brin was a long established trad venue. Under the original Mountaineering Council of Scotland (MCofS) guidelines, none of these crags would have strictly met the bolting criteria. These guidelines have now been revised to allow for the consideration of issues pertaining to each particular crag, and in attempt to address 'grey areas'. The present MCofS guidance suggests that within the Scottish climbing ethic, bolts are welcomed but only within these accepted guidelines:

**For established climbing venues...**
Bolts are unacceptable to the majority of Scottish climbers on established (documented) mountain cliffs and sea-cliffs, in both summer and winter. Established 'traditional' and sport venues would be expected to remain in their documented style. If a change in style is to be considered in the future (bearing in mind the above guideline on mountain and sea-cliff venues) then generally:
• Retro-bolting (the addition of bolts to established climbs without them) would only be considered with the agreement of the first ascensionist and after wide consultation with interested climbers at local and national level.
• Retro-trad (the removal of existing bolts) would only be considered with the agreement of the first ascensionist and after wide consultation with interested climbers at local and national level.

**For new sport venues...**
The development of new sport venues and climbs is welcomed within the context of a clear overall ethical framework.
• Mountain and sea-cliffs with a wild, remote character (also reflected in their surrounding environment) and adventurous nature are not suitable locations for bolts, either for the development of routes or their limited use in order to facilitate easy retreat: self-rescue and descent without fixed equipment are all

part of the adventurous nature of traditional climbs.

• Crags with good or adequate quality protection within strong natural lines (obvious routes) would be regarded as traditional venues. Crags where an overall lack of natural cracks for protection together with a lack of strong natural lines may be suitable venues for sport climb development as long as they could not be classed as wild mountain or sea-cliff venues.

• Bolts should be placed using current best practices.

Sport climbing clearly has its place in Scotland, but as a fairly recent development it could be said to be still 'finding its feet'. This genre of climbing needs to develop without conflicting with, or spoiling the challenges of traditional routes. One person's undeveloped sport crag is another's futuristic trad project, both of which would be celebrated by different sections of the climbing community. Our mountains and coastlines and their traditional climbs are something special, so let's not impact on the adventures of future generations.

## WEATHER AND CLIMBING CONDITIONS

*"How does the weather know it's the weekend?" - Captain Slackship and the Mezzanine Allstars.*

Owing to their location on the west of the European continent and proximity to the Atlantic Ocean, the British Isles are frequently the meeting point of several airmasses. The resulting fronts and fluctuations in air temperature give the country its characteristic variable weather we all know and love! Coming from the west and southwest, Scotland's prevailing weather is often created by warm and moist maritime air from the Atlantic Ocean. As this common airmass is lifted by the high mountains of the west, it releases its moisture as the rain we are all accustomed to. The result is a considerably higher rainfall in the mountainous west than the drier lowlands lying in the rain shadow to the east. Low lying areas in western coastal fringes, including the Hebridean islands, do often avoid the worst of this orographic effect and are consequently slightly drier than upland areas further inland. As crags in the drier climate of the east tend to be in condition more often, it can be wise to make the most of a good forecast in the west.

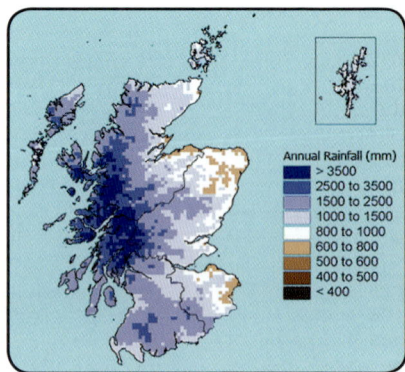

Annual Rainfall in 2011

The driest and sunniest months in Scotland are April to July and warmer maximum average temperatures (>10 °C) occur between May and October – these months are also the least windy. With frequent freezing temperatures,

December to March are the coldest months, with October to January being the wettest. As Scotland lies at a latitude comparable to Alaska, there is a large disparity between daylight hours in the winter and summer. In mid-summer there are more than seventeen hours of daylight in the northern Highlands. In stark contrast there are only seven hours of daylight to enjoy in mid-winter.

Some crags in this guide book are tidal. Tides ebb and flow twice in 24 hours with larger 'spring' tides at full or new moon and shallow 'neap' tides at half-moons. Typically a tide will take 6 hours to ebb or flow with around a half-hour 'slack' tide as it turns. Tides are easily predicted and tide times can be found on the BBC weather website, www.tidetimes.org.uk, or at any harbour office.

With a little knowledge of the characteristics of both the crags and the Scottish weather, an enjoyable days climbing can had in more conditions than one may think, even in mid-winter! In the depths of winter, crags which are southerly facing, low lying, and/or sheltered (if not seeping), will typically offer the best climbing conditions.

The aspect of each crag in this guide has been indicated such that this may be considered prior to a visit. It is worth noting that crags with overlying vegetation may seep for prolonged periods in the winter months. On occasions when the weather comes from an easterly direction, cliffs on the northeast coasts can become 'greasy' and unpleasant to climb on.

# BITING HAEMATOPHAGOUS NASTIES

*"Biologically speaking, if something bites you it's more likely to be female"* – Desmond Morris.

Midge
Photo: Narve Brattenborg (kronbladet.no)

The **Highland midge** is a mere 2mm in size but the females, which bite to amass the energy for a second hatch of eggs, are voracious creatures! As the presence of midges can seriously impact on one's visit, all crags in this guide have been given an icon to indicate the risk of any nuisance. The midge is widespread in the Highlands, living typically in damp boggy ground and occurs between April and October. They are typically active at dawn and dusk, and particularly on overcast, still, and damp days. Any breeze will keep midges at bay, as will bright sunlight... usually! Contrary to belief, in calm conditions midges can be found as high as mountain summits and by the sea.

Midge nets covering the face are effective against bites but impair vision. The moisturiser Skin So Soft™ applied liberally can effectively physically stop the insect biting, but it does not act as a repellent. Few, if any, repellents are 100% effective. If using DEET (Diethyl toluamide) repellents, keep them clear of climbing equipment as it can damage organic polymers. Some say bog myrtle (*Myrica gale*, below) can also deter the dreaded midge by frequently rubbing the leaves on exposed skin; it is fortuitously often found in the boggy midge habitat. A useful midge forecast map can be found at *www.midgeforecast.co.uk*

Although less of a pest than the midge, on sunny days in the summer months **horseflies** or 'clegs' (below) can at times be a problem. Unfortunately they are usually only felt after they have bitten, which can happen through thin clothing. The bite is large and care should be taken to avoid infection. If simply brushed away, the cleg will often return immediately to the same spot, so be ruthless!

**Sheep and deer ticks** (above) are common and can be picked up especially by walking through long grasses and bracken. Ticks harbour several blood borne diseases, the most serious of which is Lyme disease. Ticks become well attached on the skin and spend several days feeding on its host. Not all ticks carry Lyme disease but to reduce the risk of infection, ticks should be removed as soon as possible. This is best done with proprietary tick removers or tweezers, gripping the head of the tick as close to the skin as possible and pulling upward with a steady, even pressure. Be careful not to squeeze the tick's body or leave the stubborn head in, which can increase the chance of infection. Remember to check the backs of each other's legs! If you feel unwell or develop a 'bulls-eye' rash after being bitten, consult a doctor.

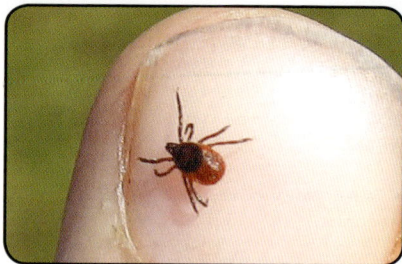

## ACCESS AND CONSERVATION

The Land Reform (Scotland) Act 2003 gives statutory access rights to most Scottish land and inland waters. As a consequence, access to the countryside is much less restricted than is the case in England and Wales. However, these rights can only be exercised if the privacy, safety, livelihoods of others, and the environment are respected. The Scottish Outdoor Access Code provides the following guidance on responsibilities to be taken by those accessing and managing land, or inland water:

- Take responsibility for your own actions
- Respect the privacy of others
- Support the safe and effective work of land managers
- Keep dogs under proper control at all times
- Take extra care if running an organisation, event or business
- Care for both the natural and cultural environment – take litter home

Some of the crags in this guide, including but not exclusively: Moy, The Camel, Glen Ogle, Rockdust and Princess Cairn, can be affected by nesting birds. Several birds, their nests, and eggs, are protected by the Wildlife and Countryside Act 1981, which makes it an offence to disturb any Schedule-1 bird; this includes most birds of prey e.g. peregrine falcons, golden or white tailed (sea) eagles, harriers, red kites and ospreys. Affected routes or crags may need to be avoided during the nesting season between 1st February and 31st July. Up-to-date bird bans are published by the MCofS:

Phone 01738 493 942
www.mcofs.org.uk/nesting-bird-warning.asp

## EMERGENCIES

In the event of a serious incident or medical emergency, contact the emergency services by dialling **999** or **112** and asking for the **Coastguard** or the **Police** (who can summon **Mountain Rescue**).

Give concise information regarding any injuries or medical condition. The crag location can be given using the WGS-84 lat/long coordinates shown on each crag topo. If at the Arbroath sea-cliffs, the number of the nearest new 'AS' posts can pinpoint the location.

Mobile phone reception, particularly in the Highlands, can be insufficient to make a phone call. In this situation a text, which only requires minimal bandwidth, may be sent successfully. Texts can be sent to 999 - the emergency SMS service. This requires your mobile to be previously registered and is simply done by texting 'register' to 999 and following the instructions that are received. Emergency texts should be answered within 3 minutes. If no reply is received, try again or find other ways of summoning help.

# HISTORY

*"After climbing a great hill, one only finds that there are many more hills to climb."* Nelson Mandela.

## 1980S - THE EARLY YEARS

Scotland, as with the rest of the UK, has had a long standing ethic of climbing by traditional means using leader placed protection and to this day the placement of bolts can still be contentious. As a consequence of this puristic ethos, sport climbing did not begin in Scotland until over three decades ago in the mid-1980s. Influenced by increasing sport climbing in the Peak District, Neil Shepherd and friends started it all in 1983 when they decided to place bolts at Legaston quarry in Angus. Thanks to the Scottish weather, Shepherd's **Driller Killer** (6c) was not climbed until the following year. Unsurprisingly, the use of bolts was not without disagreement, its hanger was removed by local Murray Hamilton and replaced by Shepherd on several occasions! Several more routes were soon added to the quarry with **No Remorse** (6c+). Eventually the routes stayed and sport climbing gained its place in Scotland.

In 1986, also inspired by sport further afield, Dave Cuthbertson and Graeme Livingstone decided to bolt the Tunnel Wall of Creag a' Bhancair in Glencoe, creating a **Fated Path** (7c+) with **Uncertain Emotions** (7b), respectively. Their bolts were not in fact the first on the crag; a few aid bolts had been placed in the early 1950s. Further routes were added over the following decades, the latest being **Vector Space** (7c+) by Dave MacLeod in 2011. Being so close to the mountains, bolts here were somewhat contentious. However, with every route a classic, Tunnel Wall is one of Scotland's finest sport crags. In the same year at Dunkeld, after several other leading climbers attempted to free the central buttress of Upper Cave Crag with minimal protection, Cuthbertson added more bolts and climbed **Marlina** (7c). The following year Livingstone linked a more direct version of Hamilton's **Fall Out** to the top of the wall, creating the one-pitch **Silk Purse** (7c+), now one of Scotland's most coveted classics.

In 1989 attention in Angus shifted to the overhanging main wall at Balmashanner quarry, where Shepherd went on to establish several lines, including the aptly named **Savage Amusement** (7b) and **Hell Bent for Lycra** (7a). Developments at this time also spread south to North Berwick Law quarry, where Rab Anderson added several mid-grade routes, mostly on its steeper main wall, and in doing so defied the **Law of Gravity** (7a). Good quality rock, amenable grades and proximity to Edinburgh ensured its continued popularity.

## 1990S - A COMING OF AGE

The 1990s saw a substantial surge in the development of Scottish sport climbing, but despite increasing acceptance, the potential to cause upset remained. In 1990, two bolted routes that appeared at Dumbarton Rock were promptly removed by Historic Scotland, who threatened a complete ban on climbing there. Two prominent climbers of the time, Andy

Gallagher and Cameron Phair looked elsewhere and began development of the very steep Dumbuck with **Awaken** (7c+) and the more amenable Dunglas where, in 1992, three easier routes were bolted, the best being Phair's **Airhead** (7a). The drill made a reappearance at Dumbarton in 93, where Phair and Gallagher established several classic lines, including **Omerta** (7c), **The Unforgiven** (7b) and after much effort by Andy, his well-named **Sufferance** (8a).

Angus continued to be a centre of sport climbing activity and in 1992 attention turned to the Pool Wall at Ley quarry. By 1994 most routes had been figured out, mainly by Shepherd and George Ridge, with one of the best climbs being Ridge's **Nirvana** (7a+). Sights were then set on the sea-cliffs of Arbroath where between 1992 and 1996 over fifty routes were developed, largely by Shepherd, Ridge, Jeff Ross, Neil Morrison and David Pert. Shepherd produced most of the original classics including **The E'Evil Dead** (6c), **Swindler's List** (6a), and **Silence of the Clams** (5+).

Further up the coast, Aberdeen based climbers wanted their own sport climbs but had to tread carefully as sea-cliff climbing in the area was staunchly traditional! Between 1993 and '94, Morrison and John Wilson began developments inland at Cambus O' May quarries. With Shepherd and Ridge enlisted for additional help, several routes were established on the main walls including the classic **Sun City** (7a+) by Morrison and **Heinous de Milo** (7b) by Shepherd. The Eastern

quarry was also developed but later stripped of in-situ gear after concerns over birds of prey. After the successes of Cambus O' May, Morrison and Wilson boldly moved to the Aberdeenshire coast in 1994, placing bolts on the sea-cliffs by Newtonhill. At the time, bolting of sea-cliffs was not in line with MCofS guidelines. As a result, a meeting was held in Aberdeen to draw up new guidelines for future sport developments. After constructive debate, Boltsheugh's routes were accepted and after additional routes were opened by local Tim Rankin between 2005-06, including **Rankin's Rain Games** (6b), it became the first of Aberdeen's own sport venues.

In the central Highlands, 1992 saw the beginning of developments in Glen Ogle by Paul Thorburn and Anderson, starting with the Diamond. Joined shortly after by Shepherd, Ridge, and other developers, a two year bolting frenzy ensued. They produced what was then Scotland's largest sport climbing venue with over 150 routes spread across 20 crags. Shepherd's 20m **Scaramanga** (7a+), one of the longer Ogle routes, and Anderson's **Metal Guru** (6c+) were some of the better mid-grade climbs. Shortly after its development, however, interest in Glen Ogle waned as more popular crags such as Weem sprung up. Nearby in 1993, spotted by Thorburn but largely developed by Anderson, Strathyre crag became home to several routes including **Electrodynamics** (7a) and **Static Discharge** (7b).

Further west, at the head of Glen Nevis, Cuthbertson, Malcolm Smith and Duncan McCallum bolted the first lines on Steall Hut Crag in 1993. It was no surprise that one of the UK's strongest climbers at the time produced Scotland's hardest route, **Steall Appeal** (8b) by Smith. Adding several quality routes to the crag, including easier routes on its left side, Dave MacLeod achieved Scotland's second 9a in 2012, **Fight the Feeling.**

The latter part of the 90s saw much attention go to the development of the now popular Weem crags in the forest above Aberfeldy. In the spring of 1997 Ridge, Shepherd, Colin Miln, Isla Watson and Jannet Horrocks produced over 35 mid-grade routes on several buttresses, including Shepherd's **High Pitched Scream** (7a) and Ridge's **The Screaming Weem** (7a+). At the end of the decade, between 1997-98, Miln and Watson went on to develop the crags east of Loch Lomond, including Stronachlachar, Wild Swans Buttress, and Crystal Crag. Route names like Watson's **Far From the Malham Crowds** (7a) at Crystal Crag and Miln's **My Own Private Scoltand** (6c) at Stronachlachar describe well the ambience of many Scottish crags. Towards the end of the 1990s, Miln, Watson, and Calum Mayland kept away from impeding **Millennium Madness** (5+) and bolted most the routes at Rockdust in Perthshire. A few routes were later added by Rab and Chris Anderson, including **Moulin Rouge** (6c).

Shepherd, having by now developed a keen eye for a classic, re-visited The Camel by Loch Duntelchaig in 1997. Over the following decade some of the best sport routes in the country came

into being, including Shepherd's sought after route **The Stone of Destiny** (6c+). The harder classic routes there were the works of Dave Redpath with **Ubuntu** (8a) and **Death is a Gift** (8a) by local Andy Wilby. Back on the east coast and close to home, in 1998 Shepherd and Pert found Elephant Rock. Having discovered the rock was better than it looked, Shepherd, along with Morrison and Wilson, put up almost thirty routes; Shepherd's **Tale of the Tape** (6a+) and **Hanger 18** (7a) became the crag classics.

## 2000S – SPORT GOES NORTH OF THE GREAT GLEN

The development of Scottish sport climbing was equally productive in the new millennium, particularly in the northern and western Highlands. In 2000 on the south-west coast, starting with the pleasant **Jerusalem** (6a+), Redpath and Michael Tweedley began developing the crags at Tighnabruaich. By 2006 several routes were added across the grades including **Apollo** (8a+) by MacLeod. Over in Angus, the warm summer of 2001 spurred the beginning of a second wave of new routing at Arbroath. Nearly a further fifty routes were added, including Ross's classic **The Siren** (6c), making Arbroath Scotland's largest sport venue.

In 2001 sport climbing was to arrive on the gneiss of the far north-west largely due to the efforts of Paul Tattersall and Colin Meek who began bolting routes on the steep Am Fasgadh. **Bog Talla** (7c) was one of the first routes and is still a classic. This was followed by the development of Creag nan Luch in 2004, again for the most part by Tattersall. Numerous classics were established including **Toss** (6c+) and **Superblue** (7b+). In 2007 Tattersall started his next project, Grass Crag, where thirteen mid-grade routes were established. In the same year Kuhjo was also bolted, mainly by Tattersall with the **Wicked and Weird** (7a+) being enjoyed by many. 2007 also saw developments begin at Goat Crag. Over the years, Tattersall, Meek, Wilby, Thornburn, Murdoch Jamieson, and Ian Taylor added several good routes there; among the best being the stunning **Mac-Talla** (7a+) by Meek. Starting in the same year the usual suspects, along with Martin Moran developed the routes on Creag nan Cadhag to produce, after some cleaning, **Battle Axe** (6c) and **Axe Grinder** (7a+). Meanwhile, keeping close to home, Tattersall took to the beach at Melvaig and had some fun with **Beach Balls** (6a+). Drills kept whirling out west between 2008-13 with Meek opening up fine routes, including **An Sinnoch Mor** (6b), at Creag nan Ord and Tattersall putting up, amongst other climbs, **The Otter Final** (7a+) on Creag na Oisean.

In 2002 the Aberdeenshire coast saw the return of the drill, in the hands of Rankin. Close to home in Portlethen, the short but steep Sportlethen came to be, his test piece there becoming **The Portlethen Terrier** (7c+). Rankin went on to develop much of the sport on the coast. In the five years that followed, he added routes to Boltsheugh, and opened several at Clashfarquhar, home to **Spice of Life** (7b+), and Ridge's abandoned project crag The Keel with **Titanic** (6c+) up the left of the prow.

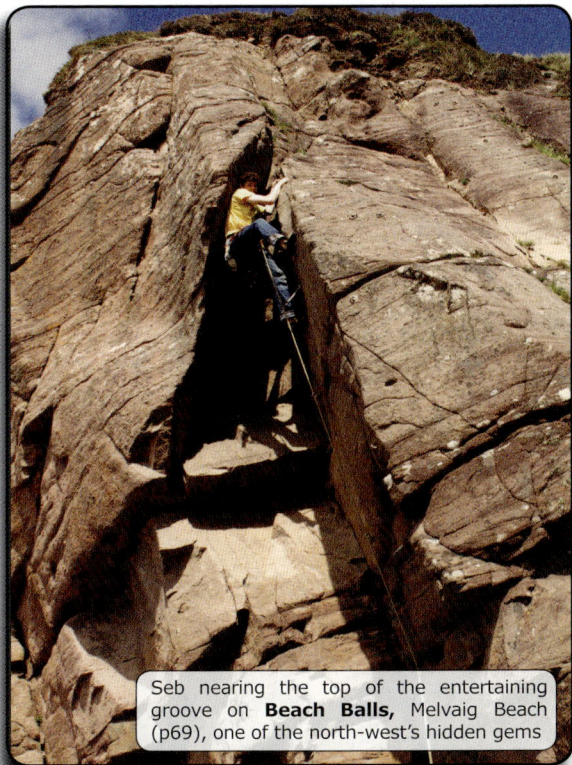

Seb nearing the top of the entertaining groove on **Beach Balls,** Melvaig Beach (p69), one of the north-west's hidden gems

Back in central Scotland, in 2003, after considerable consultation, Scott Muir bolted twenty five lower-grade routes on what proved to become the popular beginners crag of Bennybeg. In 2004-05 Muir subsequently developed Dunira with **Glen Bolt'achan Big Guns** (6c) and Lower Lednock, producing popular mid-grade routes including **Black Magic** (6b+) and **Cauldron of Fire** (6a+). Unfortunately Lednock's bolts were removed in 2007 when it came to light the crag's development had included retro-bolting of trad lines. As a trad venue the crag did not prove popular so it was eventually agreed the bolts could be replaced, which was done in the spring of 2013 by the SMC. In 2006-07, due to the largely unprotectable nature of the crag, John Watson decided to retro-bolt his routes with Graham Harrison at Ardvorlich. A number of routes were bolted including Watson's **The Groove** (6a). Except for Muir's crags and Ardvorlich, the schist of central Scotland saw much less development in the new mtillennium, most new routes being fill-ins at existing crags.

Over in the south-west, 2004 saw the discovery of the Anvil at Loch Goil by Tweedley, a huge boulder with three overhanging faces. This proved to become a significant crag where leading Scottish sport climbers put up several hard routes, the latest being Scotland's first 9a, **Hunger** by Smith in 2010. Further north Tom Ballard independently developed Black Rock near Arisiag, and Ranochan Wall and Cat's Eye Crag by Loch Eilt between 2006-08. Several routes were developed including the good **Swan Lake** (7c) at Cat's Eye and **Black Jack** (6b) at Black Rock. Sadly the in-situ equipment deteriorated before the crags became known to the wider climbing community.

In 2005, Muir continued bolting with the addition of the easier routes on the left wall at Balmashanner, before starting developments at the now sizeable Rob's Reed. Let in on the secret, in 2006 further routes were then added by Shepherd and Ken Edwards. The crag generated quite an interest and by 2010 a total of sixty routes had been developed. The secondmost extensive project in Angus, largely the work of Shepherd and Edwards, with the help of Ian Macdonald and Ronald Henderson, was the bolting of Kirriemuir quarry in the warm winter of 2007. By 2011, with a number of additions by Mark Cashley and the Hendersons on the right side of the quarry, eighty routes were ultimately established, creating one of Scotland's most popular sport crags.

2007 saw advances on the abundant conglomerate of the north-east Highlands, where at Moy the classics **Little Teaser** (6b), **The Dark Side** (6c), and **The Ticks Ate all the Midges** (7a), were established on the fine Teaser Wall by a secretive Wilby. Further north in the same year, close to home Simon Nadin brought sport climbing to Loch Fleet at Silver Rock, producing some steep routes including **Silver Darlings** (7a+) and **Champ at the Bit** (7a+). In 2008, Anderson followed by developing nearby Creag Bheag. By 2013 twenty four routes were added, creating a popular crag in the area.

Back south, between 2008-09, Watson and Colin Lambton added more routes at Dunglas to produce another good sport climbing venue in the vicinity of Glasgow. In Glasgow's outskirts in 2010, prior to his sad passing, Willie Arrol let the climbing community know of his bolting project at the Blantyre towers. He had found a new function for the disused railway viaduct stanchions; providing climbers of the city with local test pieces to train on, including the esoteric classic **Ivy League** (7b).

Towards the end of the decade Rankin was still developing new crags on the Aberdeen coast, . In 2009 he put up climbs in the very steep Orchestra Cave with Ali Coull. Classic test pieces were added with **Basson** (7a+) by far the easiest there! Attention then turned north of Aberdeen to Red Wall Quarry, and by 2012 over 10 routes had been figured out, mostly by Rankin, but the hardest line of the region, the True Finish (8c) of Dracula would fall to Gordon Lennox.

# 2010 TO PRESENT – DEVELOPMENT AND CONTROVERSY CONTINUES

As in the previous decades, new developments continued in the northern Highlands and on the Aberdeenshire coast. Bolts also appeared and some quickly disappeared in the Central Belt! Interest in Moy continued until 2014 where further routes were added by, among others, Taylor and Andy Nisbet. The crag literally came out of the woods and is now another of Scotland's premier sport crags. Again in secret, and inadvertently crossing an existing

trad route, Wilby started bolting good testing lines on the steep Crag One of Brin Rock in 2011. The finest climbs being **Pink Wall** (7b) and **The One and Only** (7a).

In 2012 Seb Rider investigated the sport potential of Creag an Amalaidh, above Loch Fleet. Along with fellow local Gregor Callum and Topher Dagg, fifteen routes were bolted. After a breakdown, a second and larger **Dirty Jenny** (5+) had to be carried up by torchlight, after which late-night drilling produced The **Great Rock and Route Swindle** (6b+) and **Sleekit** (6b). With a great deal of 'cleaning' a second pitch was added to Dirty Jenny to create **Ithaca** (5+), a 50m adventure up the full length of the crag and currently Scotland's longest sport route! Nearby, Anderson put up four routes at Torboll between 2011-12 and further routes were added in 2013 by Rider and Callum, **Riding the Rainbow** (6b) becoming a favourite.

In the north, Ullapool finally got its own sport crag in 2013, courtesy of the Cunningham family and Ian Taylor. Glutton crag had been previously explored for trad climbing but was deemed too short and dirty. After persuasion from his children Andy took to developing the crag for sport. 24 routes came into being including the photogenic **Rehab Roof** (7b). In the same year, Taylor and Wilby added Goat in the Woods just 'round the corner' from Goat Crag, the classics being **Evil Eye** (6c) and **Drill Bit Taylor** (7b+). Between 2013-14 Tattersall continued his bolting campaign to produce eight testing routes at The Perch including **Ornette** (7a+).

# Introduction

In the autumn of 2013, attention was given to the overgrown and abandoned Balgone Heughs, near North Berwick, which had been partially bolted decades before by Gordon Bisset. After much cleaning by Jamie Sparkes, he and Rider re-bolted and added new routes to the crag making a brittle but good addition to the central belt, with **Heughvenille Antics** (6c+) and **Heuthanasia** (7a+) proving popular.

Just as it was in the beginning, the latest sport developments have proved to be divisive. In 2013, after many calling for its retro-development and having approval by some first ascensionists, bolts finally appeared at Farletter crag in Strathspey. However, objectors promptly removed the bolts, resulting in a heated debate and an uncertain future for Farletter sport!

In 2013-14, EICA instructor Neill Busby cleaned and added several new sport routes at Ratho quarry, a traditional dolerite crag with three pre-existing sport climbs. There was much dispute due to the retro-bolting of some trad lines, most notably **Pettifer's Wall** (E4), which was promptly de-bolted with the exception the lower-off. Round the corner at Craigpark quarry Sparkes developed a handful of routes in 2014 starting with **Park Life** (6b+). Meanwhile on the Aberdeenshire coast, Danny Laing was **Up n Aboot** (6b) providing a good addition by bolting the slabs at North Glash quarry crag near Peterhead. Further north, Rider and Callum started 2015 by unearthing a 50m conglomerate monster at Loch Fleet. Updates on 7amax.co.uk

## HELP TO MAINTAIN OUR SPORT CRAGS

Developers personally incur significant financial costs. They are, however, rewarded with the satisfaction of the first ascent of a new route. Such an impetus is not there however for the maintenance and re-bolting of routes. Consequently, an increasing amount of Scotland's in-situ hardware is starting to show signs of neglect and disrepair. Indeed this was highlighted in 2013 by a bolt failure at Boltsheugh. The maintenance of Scotland's sport climbs with more durable modern equipment will not only require funds but also knowledgeable and willing volunteers to carry ouy the installation.

If you enjoy Scotland's sport climbs on a regular basis you may wish to contribute to the **7a Max** bolt fund or other informal bolt funds that exist. Alternatively, you may also volunteer to help re-equip routes. For more information on bolt funds or to volunteer visit **www.ukboltfund. org**, or contact the MCofS. For more information on the **7a Max** bolt fund or how to help, visit **www.7amax.co.uk**. 10% of the proceeds of this guide are donated to the **7a Max** bolt fund. With your support, the fund has been able to contribute to the re-development of Balgone Heughs and maintenance of the crags in the far northwest

# The 7a Max Top 30 Routes

Here for your enjoyment is the official, and yet entirely subjective, **Top 30 7a Max** Scottish sport routes. This is not simply a list of all the 'classics' but a flavour of the best routes across the country and across the full grade-range. Tick them all and award yourself a macaroon!

| Route | Page |
|---|---|
| **Lady Willoughby** *4+* <br> Bennybeag | 128 |
| **Smee Day** *5* <br> Kirriemuir | 184 |
| **Lippo Suction** *5+* <br> Glutton Crag | 54 |
| **Deil's Heid Route** *5+* <br> Arbroath | 175 |
| **Tain Spotting** *6a* <br> Creag Bheag | 43 |
| **The Groove** *6a* <br> Ardvorlich | 93 |
| **Sharp Practice** *6a* <br> Cambus O'May | 139 |
| **Fat Eagles Fly Low** *6a+* <br> Glen Ogle Sunny Side | 103 |
| **Tale of the Tape** *6a+* <br> Elephant Rock | 156 |
| **Jerusalem** *6a+* <br> Tighnabruaich | 94 |
| **The Deil** *6b* <br> Lower Glen Lednock | 122 |
| **An Sinnoch Mor** *6b* <br> Creag nan Ord | 74 |
| **Sleekit** *6b* <br> Princess Cairn | 48 |
| **Black Jack** *6b* <br> Arisaig - Black Rock | 80 |
| **Little Teaser** *6b+* <br> Moy Rock | 34 |
| **High Voltage** *6b+* <br> Rob's Reed | 188 |
| **21st Century Citizen** *6b+* <br> Rockdust | 135 |
| **Evil Eye** *6c* <br> Goat-in-the-Woods | 59 |
| **The Siren** *6c* <br> Arbroath | 174 |
| **Glen Bolt'achan Big Guns** *6c* <br> Dunira | 121 |
| **Toss** *6c+* <br> Creag Nan Luch | 63 |
| **Heuvenile Antics** *6c+* <br> Balgone Heughs | 217 |
| **Stone of Destiny** *6c+* <br> Creag nan Clag | 27 |
| **Kamikazi** *6c+* <br> Ratho Quarry | 219 |
| **The One and Only** *7a* <br> Brin Rock | 29 |
| **High Pitched Scream** *7a* <br> Weem | 115 |
| **Persistence of Vision** *7a+* <br> Dumbarton | 225 |
| **Axe Grinder** *7a+* <br> Creag nan Cadhag | 73 |
| **Immaculate Conception** *7a+* <br> Ranochan | 85 |
| **Mac-Talla** *7a+* <br> Goat Crag | 57 |

**5** **Look out for the highlighted route icons**

Topping out into the sun on the amenable classic
**Silence of the Clams** 5+, Arbroath (p170)

# NORTHERN HIGHLANDS

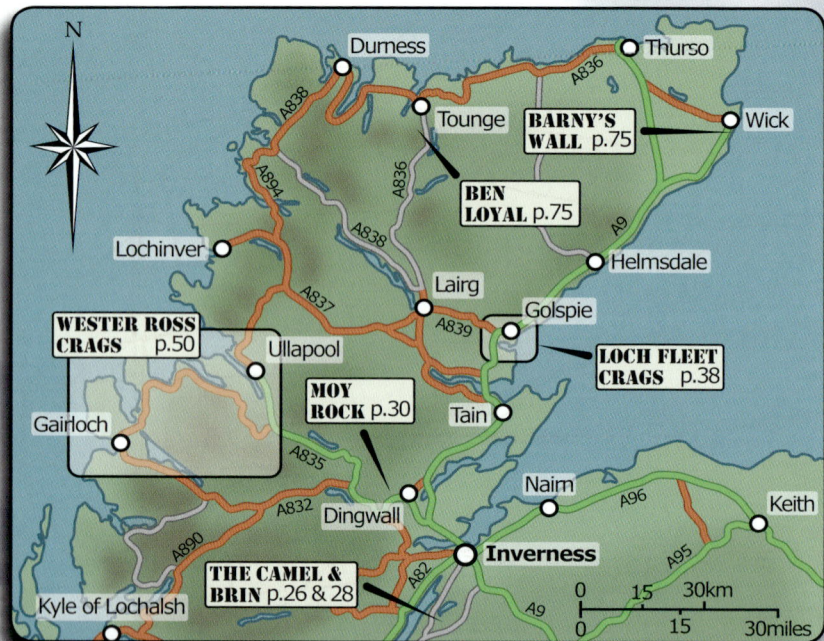

N

Durness
Thurso
Tounge
Wick

**BARNY'S WALL** p.75

**BEN LOYAL** p.75

A838
A836
A894
A836
A9

Lochinver
Helmsdale

Lairg
A838
A837

Golspie

**WESTER ROSS CRAGS** p.50

**LOCH FLEET CRAGS** p.38

Ullapool
A839

**MOY ROCK** p.30

Tain

Gairloch
A835

Nairn
A96
Keith

A832
Dingwall
A95

**Inverness**

A890
A82
A9

**THE CAMEL & BRIN** p.26 & 28

Kyle of Lochalsh

0    15    30km
0    15    30miles

For most, the remote crags of the far north are a long journey away. However, the northern Highlands are arguably home to Scotland's best mid-range sport climbing...if the weather and midges allow it! The venues are typically tranquil with picturesque outlooks and often an abundance of wildlife. One will frequently see birds of prey in the area including the elusive and majestic Golden Eagle. Intrepid sport climbers that make the voyage will undoubtedly be rewarded and despite the latitude, climbing can be had all-year round.

The west is wild in character and sparsely inhabited. The area has above-average rainfall but is home to some spectacular lochs and beaches. It also boasts a unique and ancient mountain-scape, with the Lewisian gneiss crags being the oldest rocks in Europe. Due to the deer (a hazard on the roads!), there are typically few trees and large expanses of open moor, so bring your wellies!

In contrast, the east is softer in nature. It is home to rolling hills and fertile farmlands, and the climate is considerably drier. The region's crags are predominantly conglomerate and gneiss, and tend to be somewhat higher than average.

Seb enjoying the *patatas* on **Pebbledash** (6b)
Moy Rock - p 33

# The Camel

57.32909 -4.32635

57.32927 -4.32251

The Camel, formally known as **Creag nan Clag**, is a striking conglomerate outcrop south of Inverness. The lines are few but are long and of exceptional quality, making a visit worthwhile. The routes lie on the north-facing side of a gully and are shaded most of the day, but are steep enough that they may stay dry in rain. Winds are often funnelled past the crag, and whilst this may be chilly, it can also provide respite from the summer midge. The cliffs are protected as an SSSI due to lichen and birds, thus no further developments should take place.

From the A9 near Daviot take the B851 down Strathnairn until a small right turn as you enter East Croachy. About four miles down this single-track the crag becomes obvious on the left. From Inverness follow signs to Dores (B862). At Dores take the B862 to Fort Augustus for three miles taking the second left for Loch Ruthven Nature Reserve. Park at a pull-in by a path end below the crags.

Topher grappling with the **Stone of Destiny** (6c+)

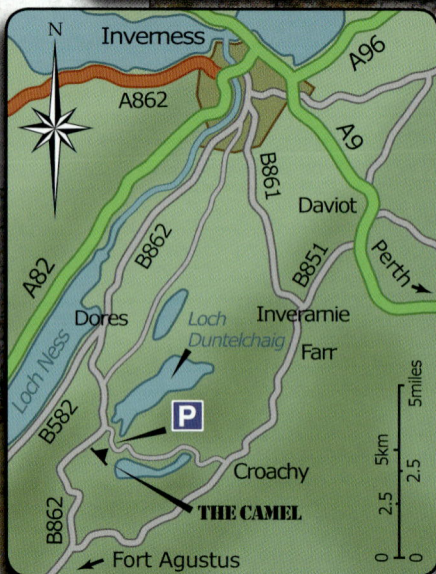

Schedule 1 legally protected birds often nest in this area. **If birds are present, there is a climbing ban between Feb and July.** Even outwith these dates, please don't climb near birds and leave any nests in peace. For the latest access situation check with the MCofS. (see p15)

**1 Inverarnie Schwarzenegger**
$7a$** (25m) The leftmost line of resin bolts is sustained until near the end

**2 Stone of Destiny** $6c+$*** (27m) The eye catching line, up to the projecting 'Stone' (passing this is the crux) to finish under the capping roof; a classic!

**3 Paralysis by Analysis** $7a+$*** (25m) Just right of the 'Stone', this line is steep, sustained, and difficult to read; a good test-piece

**4 There's Sand in my Pants** $6c+$* (25m) The large fissure that hangs in the centre of the face is gained with difficulty, then followed with a traditional feel to a lower-off shared with **3**

**5 Final Straw** $7a$*** (30m) Another high quality line with good exposure. A hard start leads to the hanging ramp, which is followed to a tricky groove and finishing overhang. Stepping left at the ramp gives you **Eyeballs Out** 7b***

The next routes are some the best of their grade in the country: **Giza Break** 7b+**; **Death is a Gift** 8a***; **Ubuntu** 8a** (**The Gift Link** 8a+*** starts up Death is a Gift then finishes up Ubuntu)

**6 Two Humps are Better than One** $6b$* (23m) The ramp line provides the easiest route on the cliff, but the first bolt may seem a little high for a warm-up!

**7 Over the Hills and Farr Away** $7a+$* (20m) The right-most route starts easily and then attacks the steep wall above trending rightwards

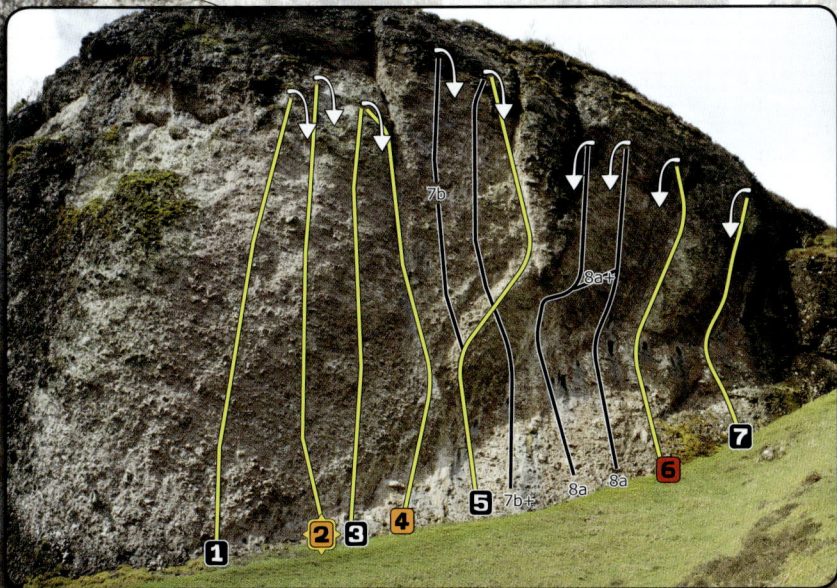

# Brin Rock

57.33405 -4.22668
57.32514 -4.23175

Brin Rock is a collection of good quality gneiss crags and boulders, positioned on the sunny south flank of Creag Dhubh. The area has long been known for its bouldering and trad, and only recently has the central steep section of Crag One been bolted.

Approach from north or south via the A9, turning onto the B851 near Daviot. The crags come into view just before the village of Croachy. Park on the rough verge, past the entrance of Achneim House B&B but just before the Steadings Hotel. Walk down the road toward the B&B. Cross the bridge and immediately skirt right onto a track to a field; from its top left corner a path up can be found. Follow this northwest until an old fence line on the right leads you up the blunt ridge line avoiding a boulder-and-heather struggle below the crags! The path will bring you out at the highest point of the crag, next to the first two routes.

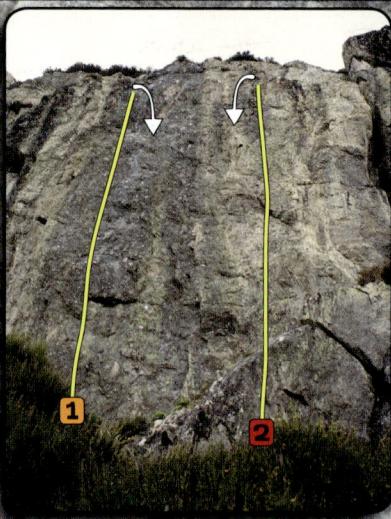

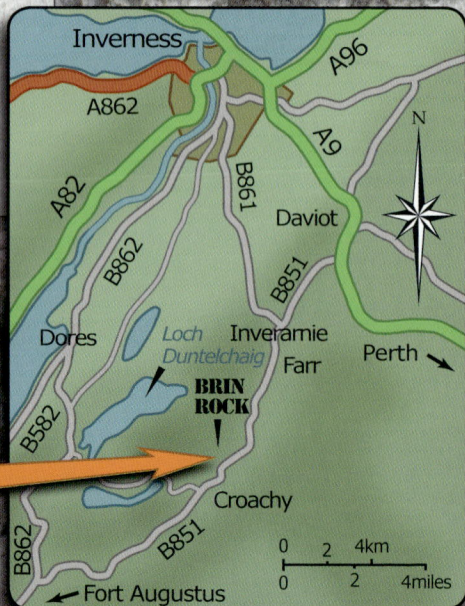

 15 mins

0 0 1 2 6

The first two lines lie on a small square face 100m left of the main buttress, and are encountered first on the approach.

**1** **The Path** *6c* (12m) Climb the bulge to the slab, and a lower-off in the notch

**2** **Gillette** *6b* (12m) Pass the shield to gain the face

There is then a series of broken crags before Crag One, with its distinctive hanging arête. The first routes are in a smaller triangular recess left of the arête:

**3** **Snow on the Ben** *7a* (15m) From the ledge, the left line

**4** **Despicable Me** *7a+*\* (15m) The right line on the small face shares a lower-off with **3**

The left side of the arête holds the steep testpiece **Pink Wall** 7b\*\*\*

Scramble up the rope to find the clean, vertical main face.

**5** **Snake in the Grass** *7a+*\*\* (16m) Start up Whinging Consultants (7b+\*\*) then step right to finish up **6**

**6** **The One and Only** *7a*\*\*\* (16m) The crag classic, featuring immaculate face climbing

Right of the face is a series of scoops containing an E2 trad line, and five sport lines, including:

**7** **Captains of Crush** *6c*\*\* (12m) A short line up the scoops

**8** **Vagisil Overdose** *7a+*\*\* (26m) An imposing route. Start on the left side of a large tooth, climb to a scoop, then exit right to climb the left edge of the slab in excellent position

**9** **Secret Garden** *7a*\* (12m) The rightmost route, with a bouldery start into a crack. Finish beneath the slab

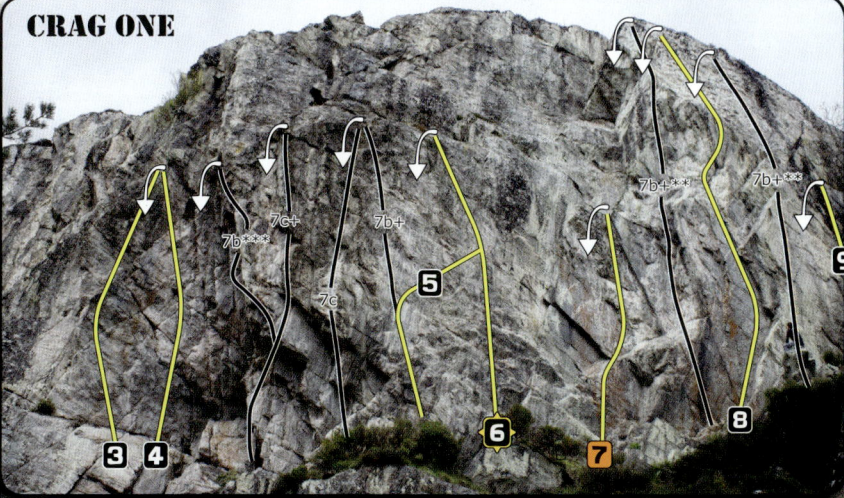

CRAG ONE

7b\*\*\* 7c+ 7b+ 7c 7b+\*\*\* 7b+\*\*\*

**3** **4** **5** **6** **7** **8** **9**

# Moy Rock

57.55942 -4.517074

57.55837 -4.515615

Having emerged from behind a stand of forestry, the conglomerate escarpment of Moy Rock is becoming one of the most popular sport climbing locations in the Highlands due to its proximity to Inverness; its south facing aspect; a proliferation of mid-grade routes; and generally excellent rock quality. As with all recently developed conglomerate crags however, some pebbles may pop, so belayers are advised to wear helmets.

This crag is often the nest site for several protected species of bird, especially in early summer. Please check the current status with the MCofS, and comply with any ranger notices at the cliff base.

Topher discovering that **The Ticks Ate All the Midges** (7a) - p34

**6 20 5 7 8**

5 mins   30 mins

Follow the A835 (Inverness-Ullapool) 3 miles west from the Maryburgh roundabout (by Dingwall) and look for a forestry gate just as the crag comes into view on the north side of the road. Park with care by the gate or on the road verge, but **do not block the gate**. Be aware also when parking or pulling off that this is a very fast road. The path cuts left from the gate up some steep ground to reach the Seer Wall in a few minutes. The closest rail station is Dingwall (4.4 miles).

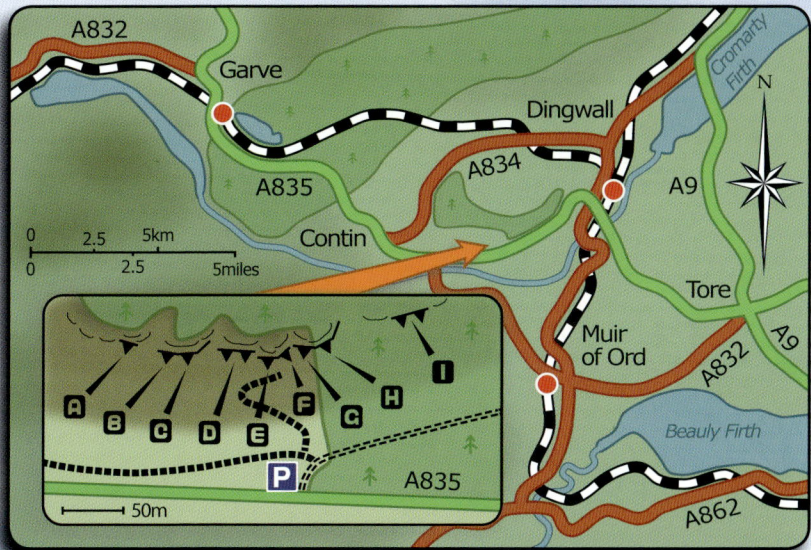

**A WEST BUTTRESS**
**B HERRING WALL**
**C RAVEN'S WALL**
**D TEASER WALL**
**E SEER WALL**

**F THE SLABS**
**G PEBBLE WALLS**
**H FORBIDDEN WALL**
**I EASTERN WALL**

# Moy Rock

## A. WEST BUTTRESS

The left-most buttress on the ridge holds a prominent holly tree behind a flake.

**1** **Eldorado** *6a*** (24m) Just left of the main buttress is a recessed wall. Start right of the groove. Follow the wall up past a recess, over the bulge and head left into the chimney

**2** **Holly Tree Groove** *6a** (18m) A pleasingly technical route. Scramble up the right side of the flake to belay from beside the holly tree. Climb a shallow groove in the wall just to the right

**3** **Conglomarête** *4+** (25m) This climbs the arête to the right of **2**, tending to its right side. The start is best direct, but easier on the right

## B. HERRING WALL

Immediately to the right of West Buttress is a tall wall with several prominent grooves and ramps. There is often an owl's nest on this crag, so please observe any warning signs.

**4** **Moy Racer** *6a* (14m) Start just left of the dirty pedestal. A tricky start soon eases

**5** **The Herring** *6c+** (15m) A pumpy route with an awkward bulge at half height

**6** **Fighting off the Vultures** *6a+** (20m) A more sustained outing up the tallest part of the buttress. Climb just to the right of a loose groove, finishing at chains just under the roof. High in grade

**7** **The Old Man of Moy** *6a+**(18m) A steep and pumpy route up the middle of the crag, good for warming up!

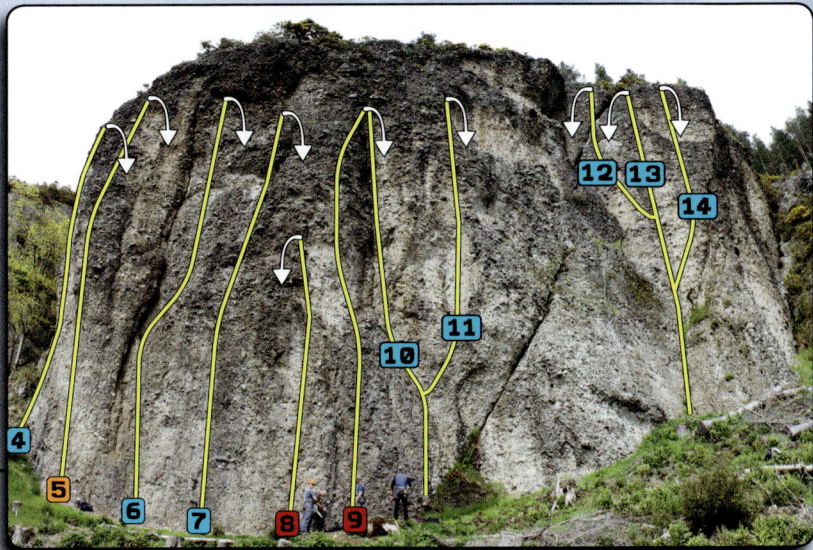

**8** **Moy Bueno** $6b$** (14m) A shorter route on the wall left of **9** finishes at the bulge

**9** **Pebbledash** $6b$** (20m) A line of old ring bolts up the groove and rib, with a crux bulge that seems to go on longer than it should!

**10** **Corvus** $5$+** (22m) The corner groove at the right side of the wall holds some interesting bridging manoeuvres. Steep but with good holds

**11** **Scoopy Doo** $6a$+* (20m) The hanging groove right of **10**

## C. RAVEN'S WALL
To the right of the corner there is a wall and arête.

**12** **Raven's Nest** $6a$+** (25m) Start as for **13** and head left at the 7th bolt

**13** **Black Streak** $6a$+** (25m) Start up the easy groove and then directly up the steep wall

**14** **Pyramid** $6a$+* (25m) Start as for **13** and head right at the 5th bolt. Interesting route finding

## D. TEASER WALL

This clean eye catching wall was the first to be bolted and still holds the local classic test pieces. It is found just left of the narrow ascent path and climbing generally starts above the wide ledge which is reached easily. It is common to belay from the path to avoid any possible falling rocks; this is conglomerate after all!

**1** **Match if You are Weak** 6c+** (18m) A very sustained and interesting line, starting above the knotted access rope. The name gives a clue to the crux

**2** **The Dark Side** 6c*** (20m) Good climbing with a crux at the last bolt, which is often skipped by fading arms in sight of the chain!

**3** **Little Teaser** 6b+*** (20m) Clean face climbing straight up the middle on interesting holds, with a sting in the tail. Make use of that half-way rest!

**4** **Pulling on Pebbles** 7a+** (20m) Technical and powerful with a difficult mid-section through the bulge

**5** **The Ticks Ate All the Midges** 7a*** (25m) A long route with a short sharp mid-height crux, before skipping round the left edge of the overlap to good holds - low in the grade

**6** **Cloak and Dagger** 6c+** (25m) Start just up the gully, and strike directly up through the overlap - pumpy

The wide chimney/crack on the right is called **Pudding Chimney** (S) and was first climbed wearing big boots in 1968.

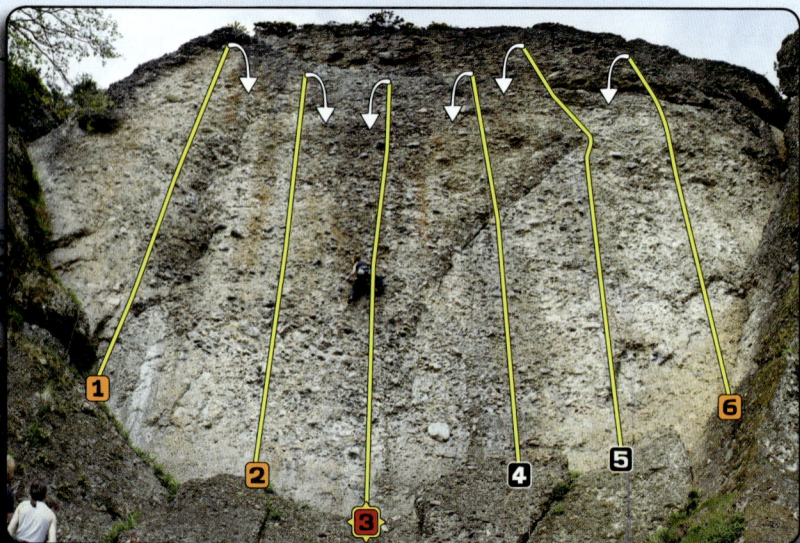

# E. SEER WALL

At the top of the ascent path is a striking wall with an obvious cave near the top.

**7** **One Man Went to Moy** 7a* (10m) Fingery vertical climbing on the wall to the bulge and then up the pale groove. Keep right to keep with the original line and claim the full tick

**8** **Burning Barrels** 6c* (10m) The slightly bulging grey wall to the right of **7**

**9** **The Seer** 7a+** (12m) The central, smooth-looking, slab. There are two extensions above the chains. The left hand is 7b*, while rightward to the excitingly located chains is **The Fear** (7b+**)

**10** **Constant Flux** 6c* (15m) Follows the slabby rib and bulges right of The Seer. So named as holds frequently embark on solo careers. Helmets on!

# Moy Rock

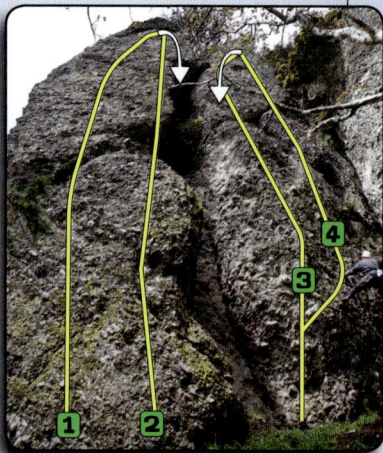

## F. THE SLABS

Just around the corner right of Seer Wall lie a set of easy slab routes on two broken pillars.

**1** **Easy Slab** 4+* (25m) Although un-inspiringly named, this route provides good exposure in the upper section

**2** **Ankle Biter's Delight** 4+* (24m) Follow the right edge of the slab (dyno start optional!) to finish as for the previous route

**3** **Ephemeral Artery** 4+* (23m) Climbs the left edge of the next slabby pillar, with the hardest moves gaining the first bolt

**4** **Venus Return** 4+** (23m) Start and finish as for **3** (or sneak in from the corner) but branch right at the first bolt to climb the slabby face

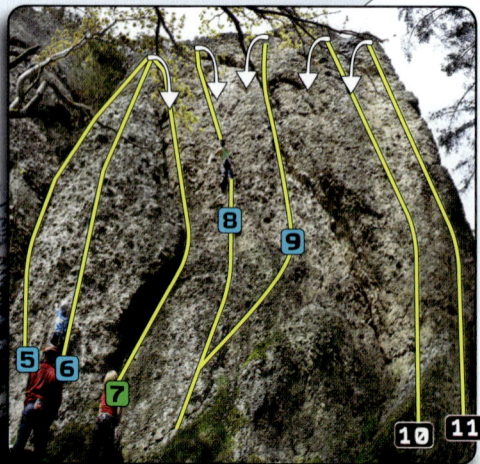

## G. PEBBLE WALL

On the right side of the gully lie a good selection of steeper routes.

**5** **Moy Soldiers** 5+** (17m) Climbs the left side of the arête

**6** **Pebble Party** 6a* (17m) Climb the face of the flake

**7** **L-Plate** 5* (17m) The corner line right of the previous route, sharing its finish

**8** **The Fly** 6a+** (15m) The excellent sustained wall

**9** **Magnifascent** 6a+* (23m) Climb to the 2nd bolt of **8** and move right into the crack

**10** **Silver Fox** 7a* (20m) A rising right to left line, above the crack, starting direct

**11** **The Clansman** 7a+** (20m) A few metres right of **10**. A bouldery start leads to a ledge, a pumpy middle and a late crux

## H. FORBIDDEN WALL

Follow the path right from Pebble Wall to find a shady steep wall, with a low overlap.

**12** **Round the Bend** 6a (29m) Start up the right-slanting ramp to the arête and follow this on the right. **60m rope needed!**

**13** **Hidden World** 6a+* (32m) Climb to and through the gap in the overlap, and finish up the left facing corner. The right-hand start lowers it to 6a. **60m rope needed!**

**14** **Forbidden Forest** 7a* (12m) Strenuous moves through the bulge

**15** **It's Rock Jim But Not as We Know It** 6c+* (12m) The central line. Strenuous up and right through the bulge then left to a good hold and a sustained finish

**16** **Collywobbles** 7a (12m) A harder start to **15** up the green wall and joining at the 4th bolt

## I. EASTERN WALL

70m further right along a good path.

**17** **Robert the Bruce's Spider** 6a** (17m) The clean slabby face on the left end of the buttress

**18** **Don't Look Down in Anger** 6a+** (20m) Starting at a tree stump, climb the blunt arête, finishing right

**19** **Curse of the Strong** 6b** (21m) Climb past the left of a shallow ledge and follow a diagonal crack to reach a break (crux). Finish left to lower-off of **18**

**20** **Summer Solstice** 6a+*(24m) 3m right of **19**, climb straight up passing right of the narrow ledge, to a lower-off below the overhang

Further right there is 'Ave It (7b**) and...

**21** **I Did it Moy Way** 6b+* (12m) Start from a pedestal, climb the crack and pull rightward onto the wall

**22** **Red Setter** 6a* (25m) Just right of the pedestal, climb the flakes and move right onto the wall and finishing slab

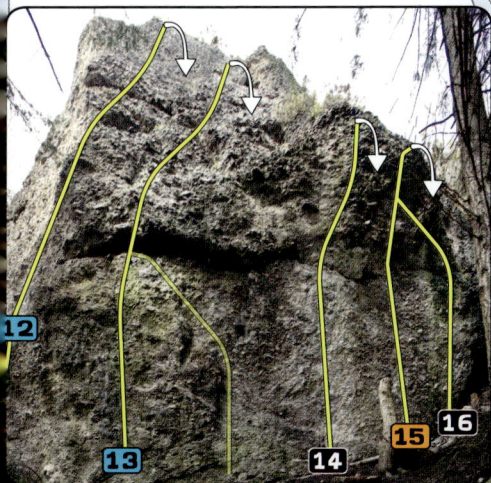

# Loch Fleet Crags

Greg soaking in the view on the
second pitch of **Ithaca** *5*+ (p.49)

The area surrounding Loch Fleet is of outstanding natural beauty. Paradoxically the unique alderwood owes its existence to Thomas Telford's manmade causeway and sluice gates, built in 1816, which stops the sea one mile short of its original high water. The estuary is home to a plethora of wildlife including deer, osprey, estuarine birds, seals and the Atlantic salmon waiting to run the river Fleet. The area has a strong crofting tradition and the huge statue keeping a watchful eye is that of the Duke of Sutherland who led the Clearances in the area during the early 1800s.

A journey to this part of Sutherland will be rewarded with pleasant climbing on serene crags with picturesque outlooks. Due to the un-protectable nature of the conglomerate in this area, significant rock climbing did not start until the arrival of bolts in 2008. There are now just under sixty good quality sport climbs spread over four crags – plenty to while away a weekend. As an alternative to climbing, the nearby Highland Wildcat Mountain-Biking Trails in Golspie are some of the best in the UK. If overnighting, a great place to stay is the unique youth hostel in 1st class railway carriages at Rogart station: www.sleeperzzz.com

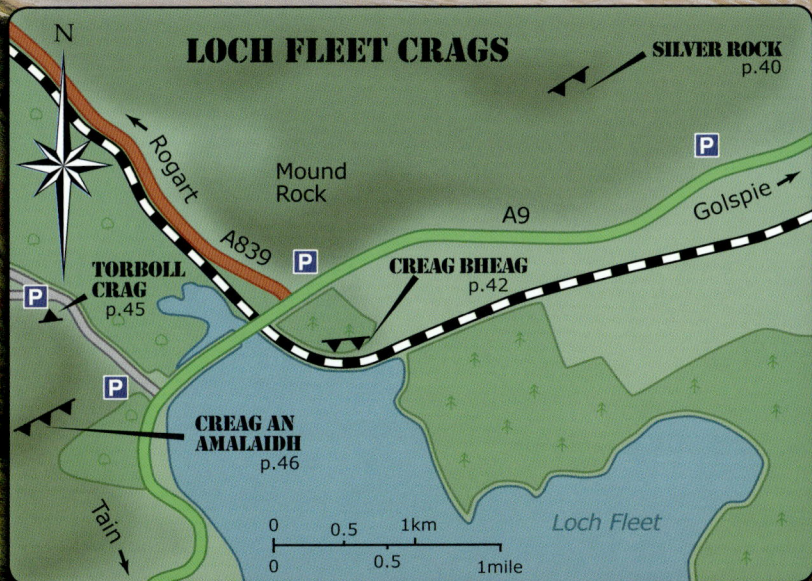

LOCH FLEET CRAGS

N

Rogart

A839

Mound Rock

A9

Golspie →

SILVER ROCK
p.40

TORBOLL CRAG
p.45

CREAG BHEAG
p.42

CREAG AN AMALAIDH
p.46

Tain →

Loch Fleet

| 0 | 0.5 | 1km |
| 0 | 0.5 | 1mile |

# Silver Rock

57.96947 -4.036098

**P** 57.96669 -4.018278

While not having the number of routes of Creag Bheag (p42), Silver Rock makes up for it with a stunning position, beautiful rock and routes that pack a vicious punch. The conglomerate rock is very compact and glacier-polished, producing an unusual limestone-esque overhang and fewer generous holds than one might expect. The crag faces south and catches whatever breeze there is, which is a blessing in the midge summer but can be chilly in winter.

Topher getting his teeth into
**Champ at the Bit** (7a+)

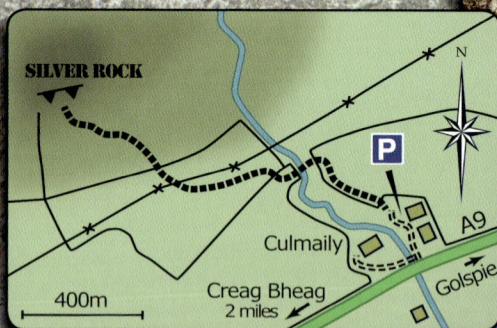

SILVER ROCK

N

**P**

Culmaily

A9

Golspie

400m

Creag Bheag
2 miles

Approach via Culmaily Farm; 2 miles from the Mound junction and 1 mile from Golspie (nearest train station). The farmer requests you don't park on the roadside verge but considerately at the back of the white cottages behind the farm. Start in the field left of the farm and follow a tractor path leftwards towards the crag. Cross a stream (use the log but take care not to damage the fence) and head uphill towards a pylon. The gate in the deer-fence to the open hillside is used to reach the obvious crag in a steep 20 minutes.

**2 2 1 4 3**

20 mins · 30 mins

The first route is at the far left of the crag.

**1** **Extreme Lichen** 3 (7m) The slab near the fenceline

**2** **High School Blues** 4 (10m) 15m right of the first route is another slab. The crack is 'Czech Connection' (VS)

**3** **Fleet of Foot** 5+ (10m) Right of the trad crackline. Climb the bulge to the start of the upper slab

The rest of the routes start around the sloping rock shelf in the centre of the crag.

**4** **Ag Rippa** 6b+* (20m) Easy slabs lead to a strenuous bulge, and an upper slab with its own bulge

**5** **Sans Per** 6c+* (16m) Start up the slabby groove then head right through the bulge to a ledge and a final bulge

**6** **Silver Darlings** 7a+** (12m) A bouldery start on pockets leads to a ramp and a notch in the overhang

**7** **Champ at the Bit** 7a+** (10m) A vicious start leads rightwards to better holds and respite before the overhang

**8** **Ground Clearance** 6c** (10m) Start just over the 'bad step'. Steady steep climbing leads to an interesting finale over the capping bulge

**9** **Dashed Pebbles** 7a** (10m) Continuously steep climbing on rounded pockets and a crux mono, passing the overhang to its right

**10** **Trust in Me** 6c* (10m) Start up a short hanging groove then move up right to black ledges and some tricky moves to gain the slab
Stretching left from the 2nd bolt via two pockets to join **9** is **T.B.C.** (6c+)

**11** **To Infinity and Beyond** 5+* (14m) A dirty slabby route accessed by a mossy grade 3 solo. Lower off to the path to avoid having to reverse this!

# Creag Bheag (The Mound)

57.95416 -4.058422

57.95857 -4.063407

Creag Bheag is a small, accessible conglomerate crag with a good selection of easy to mid-grade climbs on pockets and pebbles. It provides a good sheltered, sunny alternative to higher crags, although the tables are turned in summer when one might want to flee to higher ground and escape the dreaded midge. While some lines are prone to seepage, a day or so of sunshine dries it up nicely, making it climbable year-round. The very highest spring tides can affect the base of the crag!

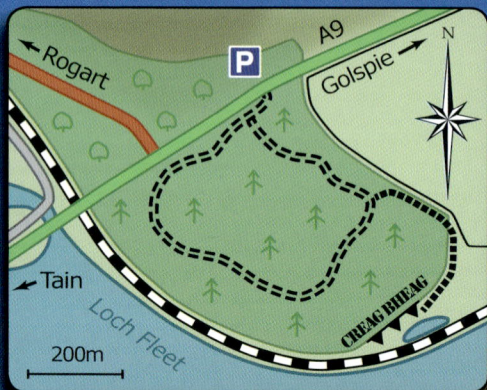

A9
Golspie →
Rogart →
P
← Tain
Loch Fleet
CREAG BHEAG
200m
N

Park in the layby on the A9 250m north of the Mound junction (to Rogart) and cross the road to the forestry track. Take the first left branch and enter the forest. When the track bends right, cut down left through the trees to the fenceline. Follow this round to the right to find the crag (10 mins). The nearest rail station is Golspie (3 miles).

1  2  3  4  5  6  7  8

**5** **16** **3** **0** **0**

10 mins    20 mins

**1**  **Manitou** $4+*$ (8m) This route lies by itself to the far left of the crag and follows easy angled steps

**2**  **Squelch** $5*$ (8m) 6m left of the main area. Climb the orange groove/flake to a small overhang

**3**  **Splat** $5*$ (8m) Juggy holds lead through a small bulge, then move left to the lower-off of **2**

**4**  **Gift Wrapped** $4+*$ (16m) A longer route, but the top section does not live up to the pleasant first half

**5**  **Tied Up** $5*$ (16m) A squeezed in little route. Climb to the heather ledge then step left into **4**

**6**  **Off the Rails** $5+*$ (15m) Climb the slab on pockets, pull through a small bulge and move right to finish

**7**  **Tain Spotting** $6a**$ (15m) The increasingly steep wall, passing the overhang to the right

**8**  **Turbine Charged** $6a+**$ (15m) Start up the nose of the ledge. A steep, sustained route up the pale pink wall

**9**  **The Mound** $6b**$ (14m) From the wide ledge, follow to the left of the faint white streak

**10**  **Fleet Street** $6b**$ (14m) A technical outing up the right side of the white streak, finishing as for **9**

**11**  **Jailbird** $6b**$ (13m) A pleasant route with lovely pockets, passing a large cobble to pull through a double-bulge

**12**  **Blade Runner** $6a+$ (13m) At the right end of the ledge keep left of the strong white streak

# Creag Bheag (Continued)

Creag Bheag topo on previous page

**13** **Jibe Test** 6a+* (14m) Right of the white streak, an easy start leads to a steep sting in the tail

**14** **Crazy Horse** 6a+* (14m) Climb to the break, then pull steeply through the right end of the bulge

**15** **Above the Line** 6a** (14m) A less pumpy but more technical route

**16** **Pickpocket** 5+** (13m) A sustained route via the pod

**17** **Twintrack** 6a** (13m) Continually interesting and steeper than its neighbours

**18** **Glug** 6a* (13m) A meandering route but on good holds

**19** **Pablo's Pebble** 6a* (14m) Just to the right of the black streak, then trending rightward to the lower-off

**20** **Vincent's Lug** 5+* (14m) Juggy climbing through the bulges to a lower-off shared with **21**

**21** **Life's a Beach** 6a* (14m) Through the bulges to an easier finish and shared lower-off

**22** **Edge of Reason** 6a (14m) The arête left of the wide crack, passing through overhangs

**23** **The Pebble Parlour** 6a (11m) On the right of the wide crack, through a low overhang to easier ground

**24** **The Bheagining** 6a+* (11m) The rightmost line, through the overlap. Shares both lower-off and character with **23**

Topher pulling through the crux of
**Jailbird** (6b) - p43

57.95735 -4.093761

This small roadside crag lies just north of Creag an Amalaidh on the edge of SSSI protected alderwoods. The cliff faces north so is slow to dry and may be damp in winter, but does get late evening sun in the summer.

Take the minor road signed for 'Lochbuie' at the south end of the Mound causeway. Follow this for about 600m until the crag appears on the left by a small fork in the road. Park with consideration at the junction, or the passing place just before the crag. Please do not drive over the soft verge. See map p46

**1 Riding the Rainbow** 6b** (12m). Steeper than it looks! Climb straight up to the embedded stone with a tricky reach. Continue to the break and bulge

**2 Mr Happy** 6b+** (12m). Good and increasingly difficult climbing leads to the break. Go straight up the bulge above trending left to finish as for **1**

**3 Sport Secrets** 6a+* (13m). Climb the left side of the slab to a right-trending groove. Follow this clipping bolts on the left before moving back to climb the left side of the bulgy arête

**4 KG Max** 6a+** (15m) Follow the slanting crack, then the white streak up the wall to a ledge. Finish up a bulging corner

**5 The Turbinator** 6a+** (15m) Straight up the wall, past a small overlap, to the ledge and finishing through the bulge above

**6 Veggiemight** 6b* (15m) Starting inside the gully, climb straight up the wall to a ledge and finish through the bulge with difficulty

**7 Mr Angry** 6a* (10m) Follow the white streak to finish on the ledge

# Creag an Amalaidh

57.94949 -4.096851

57.95187 -4.082795

Turn off the A9 onto the Lochbuie road at the south end of the Mound causeway (white house), and park by the cattle-grid. As with all the crags in the area, the nearest train station is Golspie (4 miles). Follow small 'paths' south from the road up through the birch woods, then diagonally up the slope to the crag. The crag catches the morning sun, dries quickly, and is sheltered from the worst of the prevailing wester-ly winds. The left hand sector can seep in wetter months.

Red Kites nest on this crag. Please avoid disturbing the birds by not climbing **Ithaca** if they are present.

N

P

TORBOLL
(P45)

Lochbuie

P

A9

CREAG AN
AMALAIDH

Cambusmore

200m

A    B    C    D

APPROACH

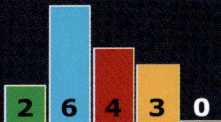

2 6 4 3 0

20 mins    45 mins

The sizable crags of Creag An Amalaidh (Princess Cairn) have surely caught the eye of many climbers driving north up the A9. Sitting high above Loch Fleet, it offers a fine vista over the loch, the Mound causeway and south to the Cairngorms. The rock is a good solid conglomerate, ranging from very compact to blocky, producing slightly slabby walls and fierce overlaps. Uniquely the crag offers an adventurous two pitch excursion up its full height...a must do!

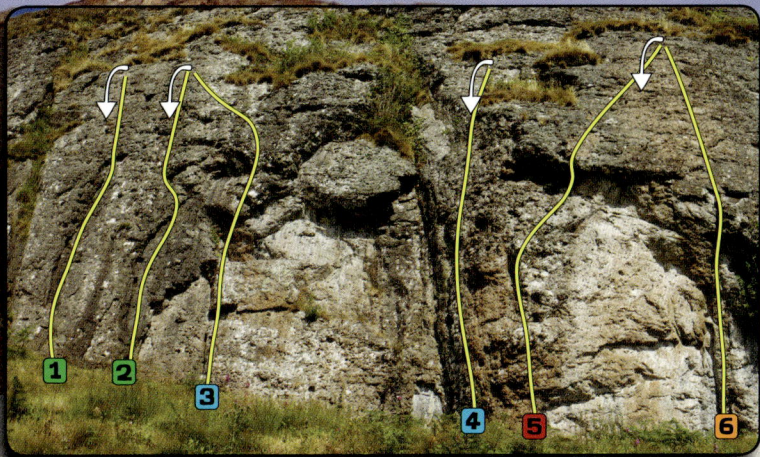

# A. SECTOR HEATWAVE

The furthest left area is defined by a short pale wall split by a deep crack

**1** **No More Routes** 4+* (10m) Ascend the shallow right hand curving corner to its end and then continue straight up to trickily gain the lower-off

**2** **Our Routes** 5** (10m) Climb the curved flake to near its end and then head straight up. A pleasant route

**3** **Moonbow** 5+* (10m) Head up the crack to get established on top of the block. Pull through the double overhangs with interest before trending left to the lower-off of the previous route

**4** **Hogmanay** 6a* (11m) Bolted and climbed on the day! Initially use the cracks left of the bolts before heading up the wall above to reach a hanging groove, which is climbed to an exit on the right

**5** **Get Out My Garden** 6b* (12m) Pull up steeply on the arête left of the bolts. Surmount the overhang slightly right to gain the slab which is climbed trending right to reach the lower-off of **6**

**6** **Heat Wave** 6c** (12m) Good climbing and sustained to the slab. Climb up nice pockets to a tricky sequence through the overhang. The slab above provides a little respite before the finish

# Creag an Amalaidh

## B. MAIN WALL

10m right of Sector Heatwave is a striking double overhang and a steep slab to its right.

**7** **The Moonlighting Meerkat** *6c*** **
(10m) Make tricky moves into the left-most hanging corner, pull up to the nose on huge but spaced pockets and finish up right to the lower-off

**8** **Badass Honey Badger** *6c+*** **
(10m) Start up the flake then span left to a handrail; cut loose and make a tricky rockover onto the slab. Launch through the upper overhang to glory

**9** **The Great Rock'n'Route Swindle** *6b+*** (13m) Start up the corner to a small ledge, trend left over space with good holds, rockover by thin moves onto the delicate slab and finish up the groove to the niche

**10** **One in the Eye for the Duke** *6a*** (13m) Follow the face right of the arête, step through a small bulge, then join **9** at the groove

**11** **Creative Commoners** *6b*** **
(16m) Start up the S-flake, pull through a bulge into a curving corner, then make thinner moves left, then back right to a lower-off under the hanging block

**12** **Sleekit** *6b**** (16m) A more sustained companion to the previous route, starting up the face on small holds, then finding a way through the headwall on pockets and slopers

## C. ITHACA
20m right of the main wall is a tall slabby pillar containing one unique route.

**13** **Ithaca** *5+*** (50m) A long adventurous route up the whole face. Best with 60m rope to allow a two-abseil descent, but there is an additional abseil point on P2 for those with shorter ropes. Can be topped out (but no anchors) : walk south past the summit to find a path leading down the left of the crag

**Pitch 1 -** *5+* (22m). Previously 'Dirty Jenny'. Climb straight up the slabby pillar to a stance on a ledge
**Pitch 2 -** *5* (28m) Go up and right across the groove (some loose pebbles) and climb a blunt arête to a heather ledge. Climb up and left to the lower-off

## D. TEUCHTER'S SLAB
About 75m right of Ithaca are two routes just right of a large overhang above a slab.

**14** **Teuchter** *6a** (10m) Clip the first bolt and climb up the slab. Go awkwardly rightwards to the second bolt and straight up to skirt round the right of the big overhang to finish in the slab above with ease

**15** **Incomer** *6a* (10m) Climb the V-groove with short lived difficulty to reach the slab above. Easy climbing leads to the lower-off of the previous route

# Wester Ross

The spectacular mountainous area to the south of Ullapool contains a substantial amount of the celebrated Lewisian gneiss and Torridonian sandstone, both providing excellent sport and traditional climbing aplenty. In this sparsely inhabited region, wild camping is rarely problematic, so long as livestock are not disturbed.

Should you require the social warmth of an evening, pubs may be found in Ullapool and Gairloch. The Ceilidh Place in Ullapool is a good live music venue. More off the beaten track are Melvaig Inn and Badachro Inn, both renowned for their hospitality. Ullapool has a large supermarket and Gairloch a smaller one; both villages have fuel stations. Many stores close on a Sunday in these parts, particularly in the winter months, so take care not to be stranded without supplies!

If you fancy a personal guide to the area or some instruction, look up the friendly guys at **GoFurtherScotland.co.uk** who have developed many of the crags in this section, and so have exceptional knowledge of all the climbing in this area.

The view eastwards to Loch Maree and Tollie Farm, with Creag nan Luch hidden in shadow

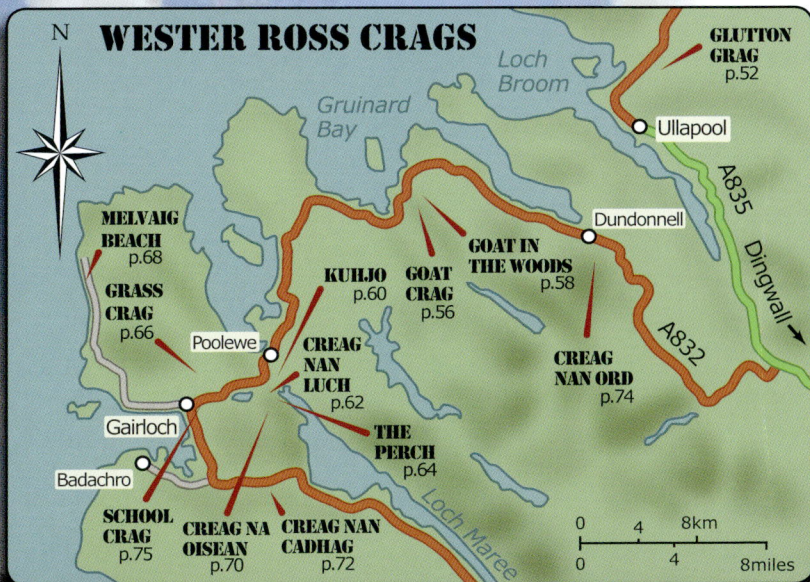

# WESTER ROSS CRAGS

N

Loch Broom

Gruinard Bay

**GLUTTON GRAG**
p.52

Ullapool

A835

Dundonnell

Dingwall →

**MELVAIG BEACH**
p.68

**GOAT IN THE WOODS**
p.58

A832

**GRASS CRAG**
p.66

**KUHJO**
p.60

**GOAT CRAG**
p.56

**CREAG NAN ORD**
p.74

Poolewe

**CREAG NAN LUCH**
p.62

Gairloch

**THE PERCH**
p.64

Badachro

Loch Maree

**SCHOOL CRAG**
p.75

**CREAG NA OISEAN**
p.70

**CREAG NAN CADHAG**
p.72

| 0 | 4 | 8km |
| 0 | 4 | 8miles |

# Glutton Crag

57.94679 -5.142641

57.95040 -5.147768

Ullapool's own sport crag appeared in 2013 largely courtesy of Andy Cunningham and sons. It offers a mixure of slabby and overhanging Torridonian Sandstone, akin to its trad neighbour Ardmair. The rock is very rough, harsh on both ropes and hands (especially in jamming cracks!) but with excellent friction. The right side holds the steeper routes and also dries faster as it catches the sun from mid-afternoon.

The exposed aspect gives fantastic views across Ben Mhor Coigach and the Summer Isles. Its NW orientation does allow some shelter from the prevailing winds, which can be a good or bad thing depending on the midges!

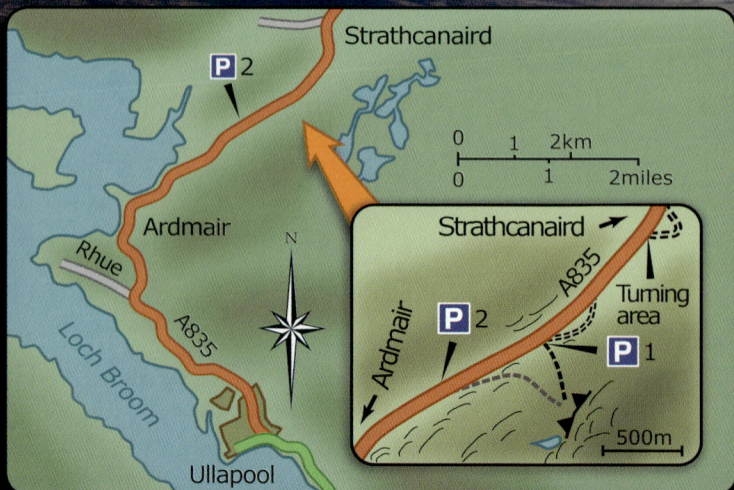

2 7 4 4 2

20 mins

The crag is just under 5 miles north from Ullapool along the A835. Cars can be parked on the southern verge at the east end of the Glutton straight (**P**1), but as this is a fast road, it is recommended any turning be done 0.7 miles further along. From the parking, where the old road can be seen, climb steeply uphill on a 'path' following marker wands to the crag. The approach has been described as "vertical bog" so bring suitably waterproof footwear and avoid the holes!

If preferred, it is possible to cut a slightly longer, but drier and less steep, line diagonally up the slope from a proper parking place (**P**2) at the west end of the straight.

The view from Glutton crag over Strathcanaird to Ben Mhor Coigach

# Glutton Crag

## LEFT SIDE
Slabs, cracks and some overlaps, the left side takes a little to longer to dry.

**1 Freek** 6a+** (12m) Takes the pleasant crack to gain the right side of the arête

**2 Wot a Waist** 6c* (18m) Climb the open groove then take the bulging arête starting on its right side

**3 Obesity Link** 6a* (18m) Follow **4** as far as the corner, then top out leftwards onto the final slab of **2**

**4 May Contain Guts** 6b+* (18m) Climb up the nice diagonal crack to the hanging corner, then step right and make airy moves up the wall to the LO of **5**

**5 Liquid Lunch** 6b* (18m) Easy climbing leads to a right facing crack and corner to the top

**6 Lippo Suction** 5+** (18m) Climb easily to the overlap, step right (crux) to gain a flake and shallow 'V' groove to the top

**7 Gastric Groove** 6b** (18m) Gain the overhang and make a tricky move into the slabby open groove above

**8 Swingfly** 6b** (18m) Swing up onto the pedestal and take on the roof above (crux) to easier slabby climbing

**9 Cloudcult** 6a** (16m) Start up the short hanging groove and gain the slab above

**10 Heartbeat** 5** (14m) Climb the obvious groove to a lower-off at its end

**11 Coronary Corner** 5+* (13m) Follow the obvious 'V' groove onto the slab

# RIGHT SIDE

Continuous with the left side, this section holds steeper, harder routes and some projects.

**12** **L is for Looser** $6c$+* (15m) Ascend the roofed wall for 2 bolts then take a left to pull onto the slab and LO. Finishing directly wins you the 7b testpiece **Rehab Roof**

**13** **Blobin** $7a$+ ** (12m) Follow the right edge of the roofed wall then head rightwards to skirt the roof to the LO

**14** **Flashmob** $7a$** (14m) Climb steeply to the arête, pull onto the steep slab and climb a final overhang to gain the LO. The start has some soft footholds

**15** **Wolverine** $6c$** (15m) Start on the pedestal and climb through a weakness in the overlaps, then through the overhang to a groove and LO

**16** **Fruit and Fibre** $6c$* (11m) Climb up the detached block to the overhang and capped groove exiting rightwards to the LO

**17** **Lust** $6a$+* (9m) Start under the overlap then follow the thin crack to a recess before the top

**18** **Greed** $5$ (7m) Climb the flake to the notch and LO

**19** **Neigh Burgers** $5$+ (6m) Far right, start in the recess and climb the wall above leftwards to finish as for **18**

# Goat Crag

57.86332 -5.432858

57.86504 -5.436909

This extensive, steep crag lies above the river and coast of Gruinard Bay. It holds some of the country's finest lines on perfect compact gneiss. The crag is popular with the local climbing community for good reason. The beach nearby is a pleasant place to camp and swim after success up the hillside.

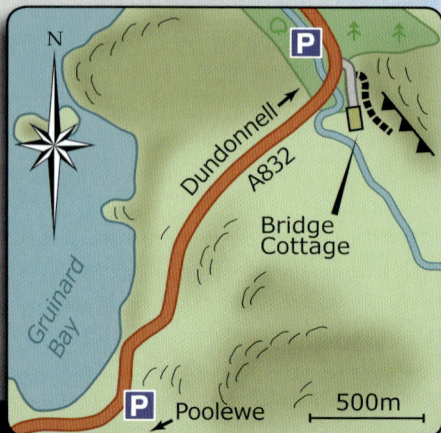

Approach from the A835 Ullapool road, turning at the Braemore Junction onto the A832 and passing Dundonnell. The spectacular Corrieshalloch gorge at the junction is worth a look, if only to dream of a winter cold enough for it to come into ice-climbing condition!

Just before Gruinard bay comes into view, park just downstream of the bridge and walk up the access road to the cottage. Cross the fence at the stile and cut directly up the slope to the crag (15 mins).

5 minutes walk to the right (southeast) of Goat Crag lies **Am Fasgadh**, which deserves a mention as the first crag to be developed in the area. While most routes are 7b-8a+, there is a lone **Bat Day** 6a at the left end of the crag, and the rightmost lines are (L-R):

**B-Movie** 7a* (10m)
**The Shield** 7b*** (15m)
**Scorchio** 7a** (15m)
**Teasle** 7a** (15m)
**The Groove** 6c* (15m)

While these routes are generally just warmups for the main events, it's definitely worth a visit if you are nearby.

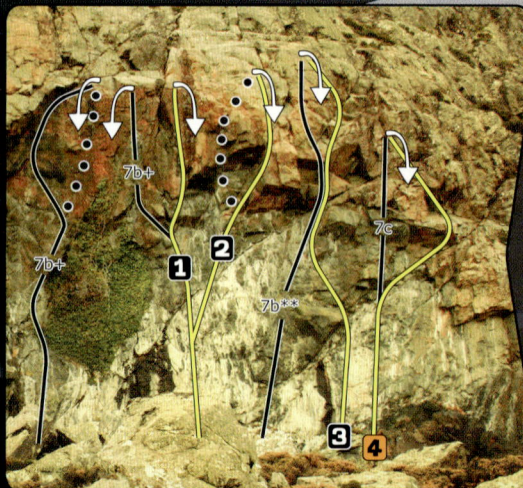

15 mins

**1** **Snow Flake** $7a$+*** (15m) Just to the right of the ivy, trend left to gain and follow the giant flake with a well positioned rest

**2** **Batman and Robin** $7a$+* (15m) Start as **1**, but continue upward, taking the right hand line through roofs. High in the grade, some say 7b

**3** **The Penguin** $7a$+* (15m) Climb right of a triangular nose and weave through the roofs via a niche

**4** **Bamboozle** $6c$ (15m) Gain the tallest point of the white wall, pass the roof to the right, and finish back left

**5** **King George** $7a$* (15m) A direct start to **6**, up a steep initial wall

**6** **Tom Paine's Bones** $6c$* (15m) The steep start resolves into much easier climbing up the arête. Or start from the right at a more consistent 6a+

**7** **Teepee** $6a$+** (20m) A fine and sustained natural line up the steep blocky corner, breaking right at the top

**8** **The Combo** $7a$** (20m) A linkup of the easier sections of two adjacent 7b's, skirting the roof to the right

**9** **Mac-Talla** $7a$+*** (20m) Local test piece and one of the best of its grade in the country. Sustained and interesting wall climbing at the top of the grade

**10** **Hydrotherapy** $6c$+*** (25m) Another high quality line, both steep and technical, following the steep groove onto the hanging slab in a fine position

**11** **Between the Monsoons** $6c$+** (25m) Starting up white streaked rock, gain the leftward groove with difficulty and finish as for **10**

**12** **Cloudburst** $7a$* (20m) The groove leads to broken overhangs

**13** **Caberfeidh** $6b$** (15m) A good shorter warm-up, finishing at the base of the smooth face. Or it's 7b* to the top

**14** **Fidgey Muckers** $7a$** (25m) A good climb starting up the broken pillar right of **13**

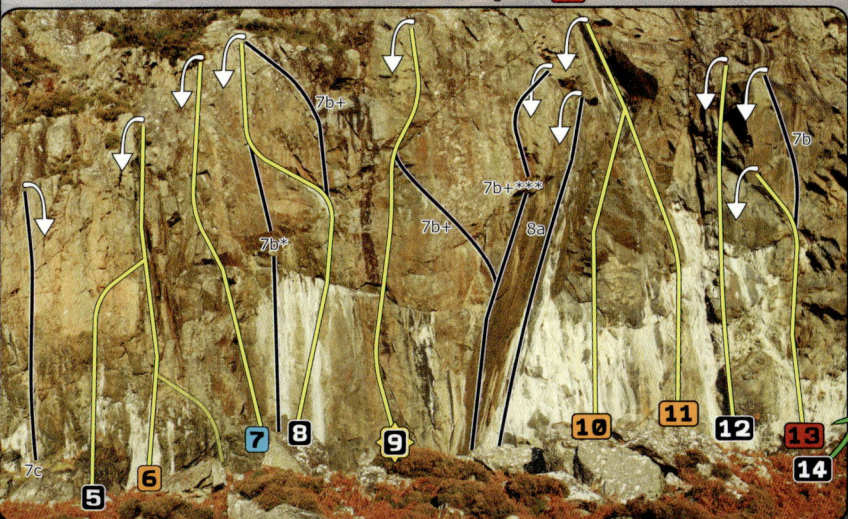

# Goat-in-the-Woods

57.86834 -5.431980

57.86504 -5.436909

A subsidiary crag north-west of the larger Goat Crag. It overlooks the surrounding woodlands and Gruinard Bay. Gruinard Island, now decontaminated, was famously the site of weaponry testing with Anthrax in the 40s. The routes are short and steep on nice clean gneiss. The sunny aspect makes the crag climbable in winter, but the crag does seep somewhat after rain needing a day or so to dry out.

Park as for Goat Crag where an old forestry track heads up into a pleasant beech woodland. Follow a path through the woods up and leftwards to a firebreak. Walk uphill along the break, past its highest point and on to the bottom of the slope. From here cut right into the wood on a faint path following an old fence. After 50m a small stream is reached. Follow it leftwards for 20m, then head right to reach an old mossy track, which is crossed to find a faint path leading off rightwards up the hill to the crag.

Gruinard Bay

Poolewe
A832

P 100m

500m

Goat in the Woods

Goat Crag

**1 Evil Eye** $6c$*** (15m) A great sustained route straight up the left of the crag, and bearing right to the LO

**2 Boltaholic** $6c+$* (15m) Climb the lower wall to the steep bulge. Surmount this (crux) onto the ledge and climb the thin wall to the LO shared with **1**

**3 Death by a Thousand Bites** $7a+$* (15m) Takes the green hangers up and over the bulge to the wall above

The two routes tackling the steepest central section of the wall are **Drill Bit Taylor** 7b+*** and **Jungle Gym** 7b+**

**4 Pink it and Shrink it** $7a+$* (15m) Climb up to the narrower left end of the overhang, surmount this into a scoop and then climb up and right to finish

**5 Cote d'Or** $7a$** (12m) Climb to the overhang, just right of the white streaked rock, launch with belief through the big bulge, and up the wall directly above

The line breaking right from **Cote d'Or** at the roof remains a project at the time of writing

**6 Lemon and Co** $7a$** (12m) Climb up the right edge of the left facing corner, sneak out the right end of the roof and finish directly up a smooth headwall

**7 Midgens** $6a+$* (12m) Your best bet for a warm-up! Mantel up onto the ledge and climb the blunt arête to the LO

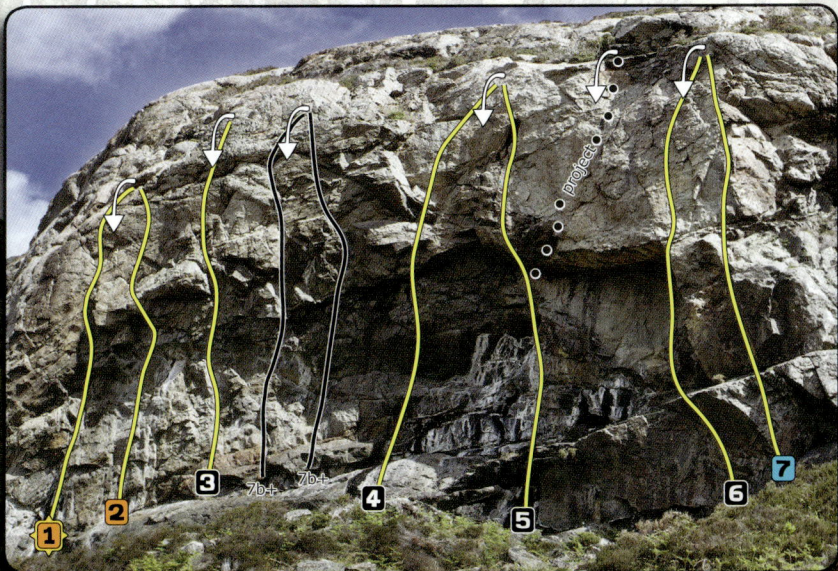

# Kuhjo & Clown Slab

57.75092 -5.592851

P 57.74983 -5.596442

This small set of gneiss crags lies on a wooded hillside that catches the evening sun. While steep, the crags tend to seep after rain, especially down the obvious grooves. The Clown Slab provides a good bolted beginners area. Park at the water treatment works just north of the Tollie Farm turnoff (space for 2 cars) and walk directly east down a steep wooded slope and across a flat boggy area.

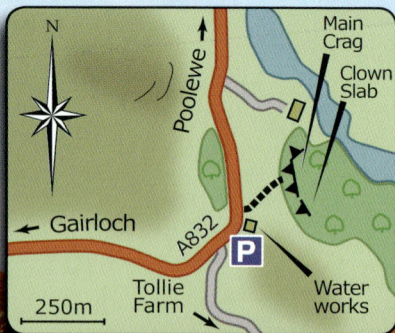

N
Poolewe
Main Crag
Clown Slab
Gairloch ←
A832
P
Tollie Farm
Water works
250m

## WEST FACE

The short dark face around the left arête of the crag.

1. **Whittled into Kindling** 6c (6m)
2. **Slave Trade** 6c (8m)
3. **Cowskull** 7a* (10m)
4. **Spiderman** 6c* (8m)

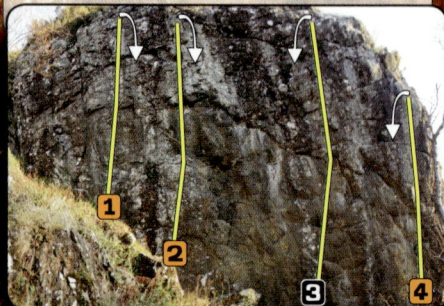

## MAIN FACE

5. **The River Gods** 6a** (10m) Ste right from the crack and grovel up the groove
6. **Eco** 6c* (12m) Short and cruxy
7. **Polluted Planet** 6c* (13m)
8. **Wicked and Weird** 7a+** (15m
9. **Don't Kick the Bolt** 6a* (12m) The wide corner, breaking out left
10. **Cocohead Arête** 6b** (10m) Pleasing balancy climbing, marred on by the ledge
11. **The Green Solution** 6c* (9m A snatchy, technical slab

10 mins

**4** **2** **1** **6** **2**

## CLOWN SLAB

Skirt 30m round the slope to the south-east of Kuhjo to find this small slab with a selection of easy lines (all 10m)

**12** Future's Bright *4*
**13** The Snatcher *4**
**14** Wonders of the Woods *4*
**15** Path to Power *5**

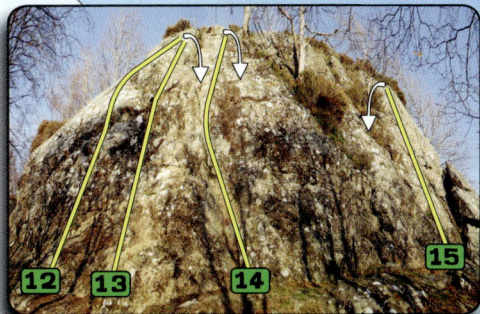

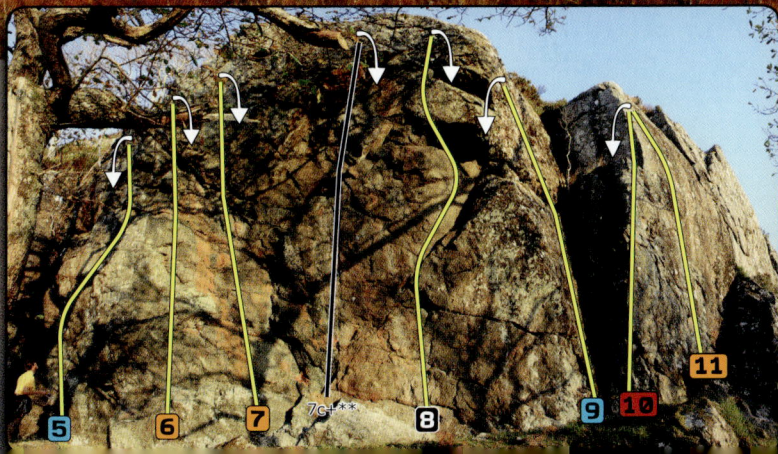

# Creag nan Luch

57.74326 -5.590409
57.74569 -5.590146

Creag nan Luch (meaning 'crag of the mouse') contains some of the best mid-grade sport climbs in the region. The rock is clean solid gneiss. Routes on the lower tier tend to be slabby and technical. In contrast the more intimidating upper tier contains steeper hard lines.

From the A832, 1 mile south of Poolewe, take the minor road signed 'Tollie Farm' for a 1/2 mile. Park just after the farm, then cross the fence by the stile and follow the track uphill (5 mins) to the lower tier. The upper section (p64) is another 10 mins uphill.

Just to the north of the crag, 200m rightwards from the stile on the approach, is a slab. Currently it holds a single line, **Red Mouse** *5* (12m) to the left of the gully, with potential for more routes.

10 mins

# LOWER TIER

**1** **Pumpernickel** $6a+$ (25m) At the far left end of the crag. A tricky start leads to an easy slab

**2** **Old Snapper** $6b+$* (15m) Follows the groove, starting from the left

**3** **Hairdubh** $6c+$* (18m) Just left of the hanging crack. A hard start leads rightward onto a smooth wall

There follows a project up the smooth wall, the flake-crack of **Superblue 7b+***, and then the wall of **Shottabeena** 7b+**

**4** **Astar** $6a+$** (20m) The left-leaning S-shaped line of flakes crosses Shottabeena and sports a pumpy finish. High in the grade

**5** **Ni Dubh** $6b$** (20m) Start as for Astar then finish right of the overhang

**6** **Toss** $6c+$*** (20m) The superb left-hand slab line, thin and technical throughout, finishing left of the flake

**7** **Walkaway** $7a+$* (20m) The right hand slab line, desperately thin

**8** **Alice in Wonderland** $6b$* (25m) Follow the blunt arête left of the gully, the tree is optional

**9** **Psychopomp** $6b$*** (20m) Excellent balancy climbing right of the gully. Low in the grade

**10** **So Phia so Good** $6b+$** (20m) Steeper and less obvious than **9**

**11** **Unfinished Business** $7a+$* (15m) A slabby start but a crimpy crux near the end

**12** **Mr Smooth** $6c$* (15m) The right-most line may often be wet

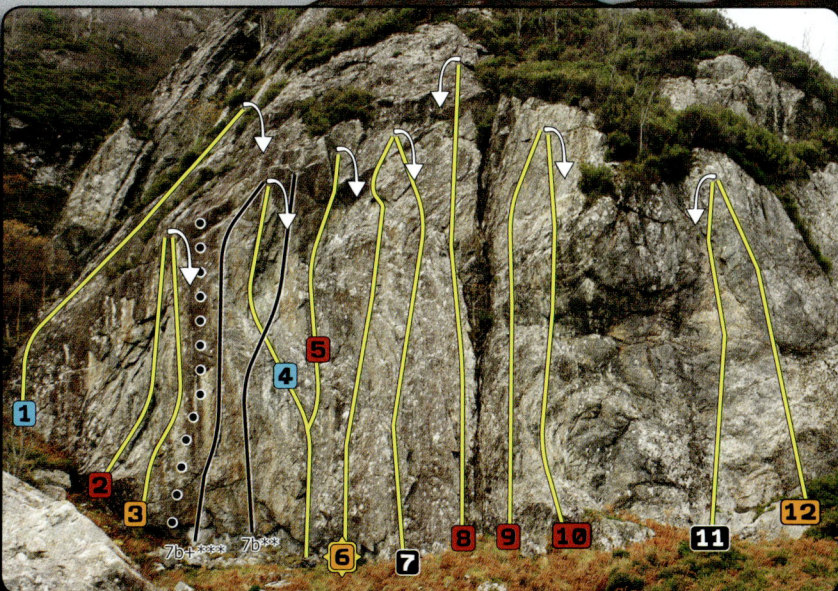

# Creag nan Luch (cont.)

A further 10 minutes steep heather-pulling and boulder-hopping up the right side of the lower crag brings you to the intimidating overhangs of the **UPPER TIER**. The leftmost routes lie up a steep gully/ramp with an in-situ rope for safety, and the contrast with the slabby, technical lower tier could not be more pronounced. The right side is less steep, with a mixture of slabs and overhangs.

**LEFT SIDE**

**13** **Little Leaf** *6c** (12m) A short, pumpy line high up on the left

**14** **King of the Swingers** *7a*** (25m) A fantastically positioned line leading diagonally right into space. Enjoy the swing!

**15** **Big Knives** *6c** (25m) An uninviting start leads across the line of **14** onto the headwall

**16** **Remember to Roll** *7a** (15m) Climb to a lower-off at half-height. Or it's 8b to the top!

**17** **Behaving Badly** *7a+** (25m) A sustained line up the left edge

**18** **Fighting on All Fronts** *7a+* (25m) Starts as for **17** but more direct with a crux around the sentry box

**19** **Happily Married** *7a+** (25m) A direct line through slabs and overhangs on slopers. Finish on the chain

**20** **The Power of Tears** *7a+** (25m) Start as for **19** but head right. Hard at start and finish

To the right of these, sharing a lower-off, lie two more slabby routes:

**21** **Troyka** *6b+* (25m)

**22** **Swallows** *6b+* (25m)

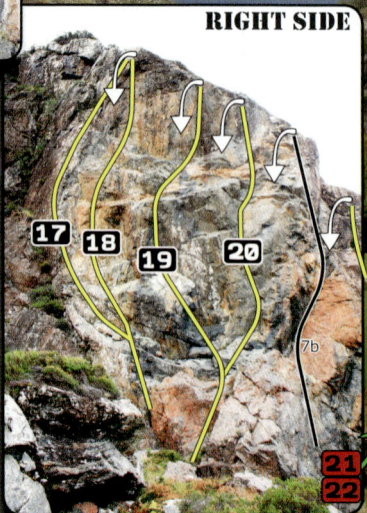

**RIGHT SIDE**

# The Perch

The aptly named Perch sits above the western end of Loch Maree and has a pleasant outlook. The crag is a very clean gneiss, which dries quickly and gives steep and crimpy climbing. Unusually, all the climbs start from a single small area, so there is little room for more than one party - two at a push!

57.74069 -5.582052

57.74202 -5.582973

Take the road past Tollie farm, as for Creag nan Luch, where the crag is visible straight ahead, and park at the road end at Tollie Bay. From the carpark a flat path leads into the woods towards the Tollaidh crags. Cross a small burn after about 50m and shortly after this strike uphill on a faint path past the lower crags to your left. On the left a gully with a rope handrail will be encountered. Pull up this and at the top go right at a tree and walk along the ledge to pick up a second handrail rope up a gully leading directly up to the crag.

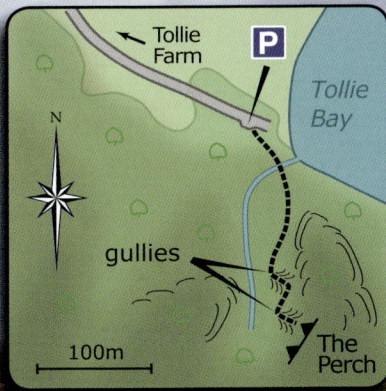

**1**   **Spanner's Away** *7a*** (12m) Climb the curving blunt arête at the left of the crag

**2**   **Ornette** *7a+**** (12m) Follow shallow grooves via a small overlap and finish up a shallow flake

**3**   **In Flew Bud** *7a+*** (12m) Take the first two bolts of **2** but then head right through the overlap to meet a wide crack. Finish on the right

**4**   **The Crazy Dude** *6c*** (12m) Climb the curving shallow groove to meet **3** at the bottom of the wide crack

The route tackling the bulge direct is **Riemann Zeta** 7b** and to its right is a project line called **Try Flying**.

**5**   **Bird Cage Blues** *7a*** (12m) Up the ramp. The clean bulging wall

**6**   **Chicken Run** *6c** (12m) The open groove at the right of the crag

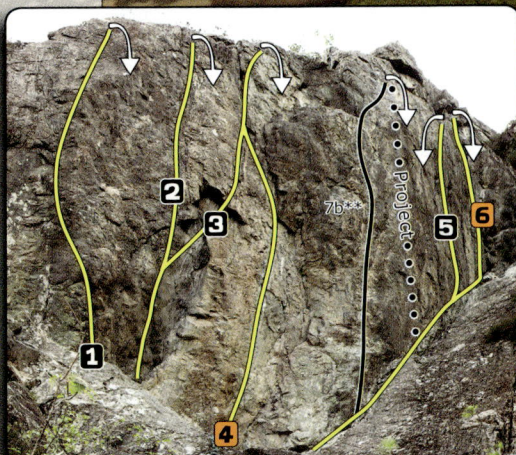

# Creag na Oisean

57.74096 -5.595788

57.74931 -5.597271

This striking open-book of clean gneiss is found on the other side of the hill from Creag nan Luch. Park at the start of the Slattadale path 100m uphill of the junction to Tollie on the A832 between Gairloch and Poolewe. Take the path south downhill before crossing the river and heading up the pleasant valley for approximately 1km. The crag, with its obvious corner will be seen on the left behind some boulders 50m uphill from the path.

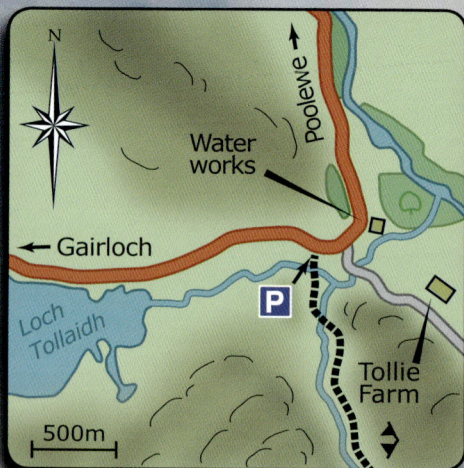

N

Poolewe

Water works

← Gairloch

P

Loch Tollaidh

Tollie Farm

500m

## LEFT BUTTRESS

To the left of the main crag is a pleasant off-vertical buttress of clean rock.

**1** **Little Dancer** $S+*$ (15m) Jug haul up the lower section to a crux on the pleasant slab and crack above. Surmount the capping bulge and go right to the lower-off

**2** **Old Degs** $S+*$ (14m) Similar to **1** with a crux on the higher slab. Resist the temptation to wander into **3**!

**3** **Cosets and Colonels** $S*$ (13m) Climb the right side of the crag going left to the lower-off after the break

20 mins

1 4 1 0 1

## MAIN BUTTRESS

**4 Stormy Monday** *5+** (15m) Follows the groove and crack to finish on the well positioned arête

**5 A Game of Towels** *6b* (15m) Easily up the slab left of the corner and finish up a steeper wall

**6 Oshan Toshan** *6a* (15m) Follows the big corner directly with continual interest. May become vegetated if neglected

**7 The Otter Final** *7a+*** (15m) A good sustained line up the steep left wall of the corner

Greg enjoying big views on **Little Dancer** (5+)

# Grass Crag

57.74645 -5.669242

57.73759 -5.668020

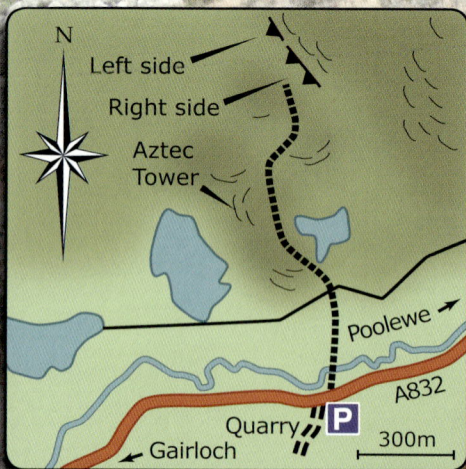

N

Left side

Right side

Aztec
Tower

Poolewe

A832

Quarry

Gairloch

300m

A fairly diminutive crag, but very quick drying and catches the evening sun with a fine view south over Loch Gairloch. The good quality gneiss provides generally vertical routes with small holds. The crag is split into two halves, with most of the routes on the longer right side.

Park at the quarry entrance on the A832 1.5 miles north of Gairloch. Walk for about a 3/4 mile over boggy ground behind the obvious trad escarpment of Aztec Tower, and passing to the left of a small loch.

Sophie on **Waiting for the Man** (6a+)

20 mins

# LEFT SIDE

**1 Like it Hot?** $7a$ (12m) A thin fingery crux leads to better holds. Low in the grade

**2 Waiting for the Man** $6a+$** (12m) Goey moves through the mid-height bulge lead to easier ground

**3 Side Flake** $5^*$ (10m)

**4 Sign of the Jug** $5^*$ (9m)

# RIGHT SIDE

**5 Joint Account** $6a$ (8m)

**6 Invest Wisely** $6a$ (8m)

**7 The Thinker** $6a+$ (8m)

**8 Constipated Miser** $6b+^*$ (8m) The thin slanting crackline

**9 The Dump** $6c^*$ (8m)

**10 Pants on Fire** $7a$ (8m)

**11 All the Arts** $6c^*$ (8m) Bouldery start to a sidepull

**12 Kick Ass Yoga** $6a+^*$ (8m)

**13 Third and Final** $5+$ (8m)

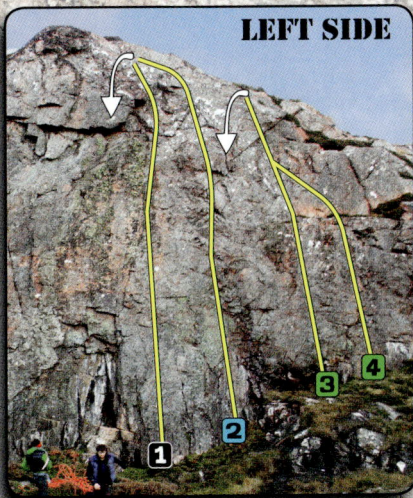

LEFT SIDE

# Melvaig Beach

7b+

7b+

1   2                                      3   4                        5

This remote beach north of Gairloch boasts views to the outer Hebrides and climbing on two sandstone buttresses. Needless to say this pleasant location is a good place to bring the family! The rock is quick to dry and nicely featured, but it can be a little sandy in parts. It is non-tidal and midges should be okay... most of the time!

From the A832 in Gairloch drive 8.3 miles north on the B8021 towards Melvaig to Aultgrishan. 20m after the small Aultgrishan sign park considerately by a sheep pen opposite a white cottage. Here a river runs in a small valley to the sea. Take either side of the valley on sheep paths to the beach. Once on the beach head south for just over 150m to meet the North buttress. The South buttress is just over 200m further south.

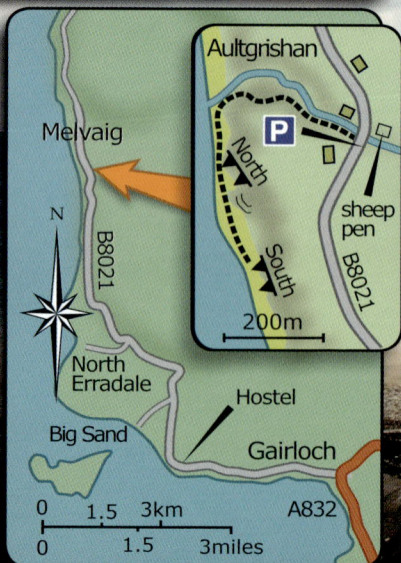

Aultgrishan

Melvaig

North Erradale

Big Sand

Hostel

Gairloch

A832

N

B8021

sheep pen

B8021

North

South

200m

0   1.5   3km

0        1.5        3miles

10 mins

## A. NORTH BUTTRESS

**1** **The Water Front** $6c$* (8m) Start up the hanging corner, then swing through the roof direct to a cracked headwall

**2** **Teen Town Trad** $6c$* (10m) Move up right from the corner to breach the overlap using cracks on its right end

**3** **Two Canoes** $6b$+** (10m) Climb the straightforward corner to a tricky crux near the top before finishing right of the arête

**4** **Queen Witch** $6a$ (10m) *Toprope only,* no bolts. Clip the lower-off from **3**

**5** **Sailing in a Big Wind*** $6b$ (10m) Follow the R/L slanting crack to the top

The final two routes on the clean, thin wall are both $7b$+

## B. SOUTH BUTTRESS

**6** **Morris Minor** $6a$** (8m) After a tricky move off the small ledge, wander up the wall on the left end of the crag

The clean front face holds two 12m routes at $7b$

**7** **Beach Balls** $6a$+*** (12m) Fun climbing up the obvious groove to the V notch. The last bolt is directly above on the left!

**8** **The Benniano Arête** $6b$+* (8m) Take the nose on the right of the crag using a pocket on the right side. The half-height lower-off is used for top-roping, with a extender over the rough edge

**9** **Power Rule** $5$ (10m) Climb the veg-etated slab on the right edge of the but-tress

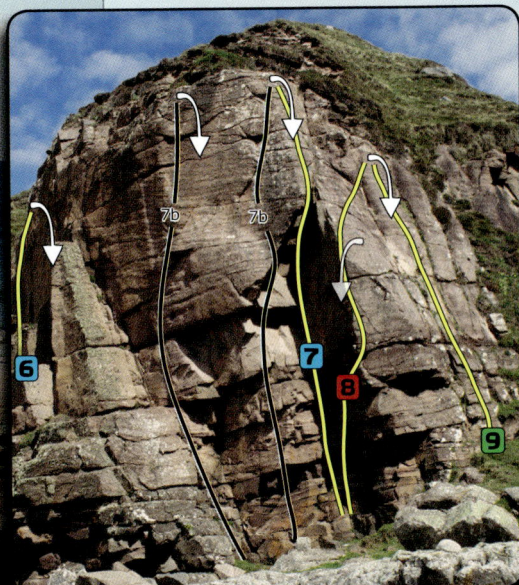

⚠ This is an actively eroding coastline, and so there is always a risk of newly loos-ened holds or rocks falling from the upper slopes.
Helmets shoud be worn and novices closely supervised.

# Creag nan Cadhag

57.68864 -5.585478

**P** 57.68978 -5.587114

This recently developed gneiss crag looks out over Am Feur Loch, on the edge of the Bad na Sgalag native pinewood restoration project. Neighbouring the excellent trad Stone Valley crags, the sport here has a similar feel, sometimes following crack lines or other natural features, although the harder routes tend to lie on the open faces.

Approach either from Gairloch (~6miles) or turn off the A835 at Garve and follow the A832. The crag is 13 miles from Kinlochewe and will suddenly appear on the left. Park by the road beneath the crag 200m from a cattle grid (or along by the hut) and cross the deer fence by the stepped strainer-post immediately down the bank. Once the fence is crossed, strike up the boggy slope to the crag (10 mins).

N

Other Parking area

Kinlochewe

A832

**P**

Gairloch

Cattle grid

250m

8a+***

7b+***

7b+**

1  2  3  4  5  6  7  8  9  10  11

**1 3 1 2 4**

10 mins

**1 Old Man's Beard** 6a* (22m)
Pass two ledges to climb the left side of the cleaned face on jugs

**2 Bovnahackit** 6a+** (22m)
Follow the rings up the lower crack, past the ledge, to fine climbing on the blunt arête

**3 Battle Axe** 6c** (15m) Face climbing up the leaning wall right of the arête

The three lines up the steep central face L/R are **Ronald Raygun** 7b+***, **Nuclear Nightmare** 8a*** and **Game Over** 7b+**. The central line has a lower-off at half-height for mortals:

**4 Nuclear Litemare** 7a** (10m)
Follow the groove until a step right leads to sidepulls and a lower-off

**5 The Deaf Violinist** 7a** (15m)
Up the right side of the central wall, prone to seepage

**6 Drip Drip Drip** 7a** (15m) An aptly named route that follows a quartzy crack through steep ground. Good if dry!

**7 Axe Grinder** 7a+*** (15m)
Start in the middle of the face, gain a ramp, and then a bulge to finish up a widening diagonal crack

**8 Ball Park Incident** 6c** (15m) A savagely technical start leads to a very 'trad' corner crack and a steep, juggy top

**9 Volturi** 6b+ (14m) Awkward moves up a capped groove, then right to the ledge and a short headwall

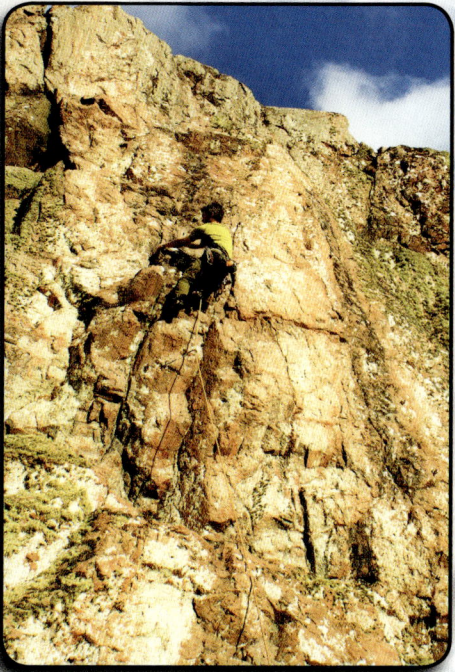

Toph on the appropriately named
**Old Man's Beard** (6a)

**10 Flying Scotsman** 5+* (12m)
Pleasant, balancy steps up the slab

**11 Born to Run** 5** (12m) A more obvious companion to **10**

# Creag nan Ord

20 mins

57.82865 -5.200594

57.83376 -5.194757

closed project

This tall outcrop of clean Torridonian sandstone lies on the hillside above Dundonnell, and beneath the flanks of the mighty An Teallach. While it only sports 4 routes at the time of writing, there is scope for more so be prepared for lines to appear. From the A835 between Inverness and Ullapool, take the A832 signed for Gairloch. 1 mile before the Dundonnell Hotel park on the right at the start of a patch of forestry. Follow a small track up the left side of the stream until the crag emerges on your left.

**1** **Guga** 6c+** (30m) An impressive and varied line taking the full height of the crag. Follow a line just right of the blunt arête, then pass rightward through a niche to gain the easier but delicate headwall

**2** **Siostan** 6c* (25m) Climb the slab and pull through the rounded roof, then up a short curving corner to join **1**

**3** **An Sinnoch Mor** 6b*** (25m) Follows a fine series of grooves up the centre of the crag before trending awkwardly left to meet the lower-off of **1** and **2**

**4** **Carnyx** 6a** (20m) The delicate rippled face right of the upper corner. Top-out to belay on a spike (no lower-off at time of writing)

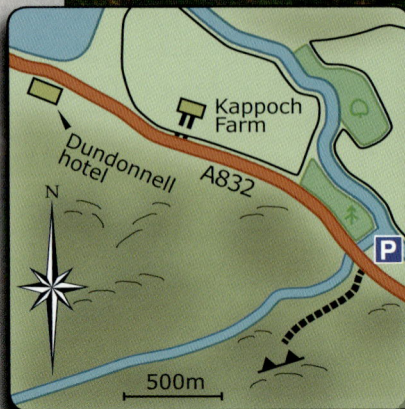

Kappoch Farm

Dundonnell hotel

A832

N

500m

# Other Minor Crags

## GAIRLOCH : SCHOOL CRAG (57.73360 -5.685639)

As the name suggests, this small gneiss outcrop is ideal for making your first leads. The angle is easy, the bolts frequent, and the climbing straightforward on fine, incut holds. It also catches whatever breeze there is in summer, allowing some respite from the midge and drying the crag quickly after a shower. No more excuses, get on the sharp end! The crag is right next to the A382, just after a cattle grid 0.4 miles north of the main junction in Gairloch. Park by the road literally at the base of the crag. Map on page 51. There are five 10m routes on the crag (left - right): **Starboard or Port** (4); **Ajay** (4); **Better than Maths** (4); **Ben Nevis** (4); **Allan Keys** (4).

## BEN LOYAL : CREAG DHUBH (58.41436, -4.381406)

While the upper crags of this mountain hold fine trad routes, there is one bolted line on the clean, north-facing, granite slab above the A838. Drive 30 miles north from Lairg to park beneath the crag at some concrete ruins (P 58.41426 -4.375151) and walk 10 mins uphill to the crag. **Friend or Foe** (6c*** 30m) cuts a fine line starting at an overlap and continuing straight up, linking pockets and flakes.

## WICK : BARNY'S WALL (58.42673 -3.073450)

Barny's wall is situated on the Powe headland by Wick and contains a handful of routes. There are also some small trad crags in the vicinity. The stone is Caithness flagstone: steep, friable in parts and crimpy. The crag is non-tidal although the projects may be affected by rough sea. A clip stick will be appreciated on some of the routes, and while the bolts are in good condition, the lower-offs are somewhat corroded.

From the A9 in Wick follow signs for 'Castle of Old Wick' which leads through housing to a single track road and the coast. Just before the coast is reached an old white tower will be seen on the right. Continue to the road end and parking (P 58.42669 -3.074709). Looking towards the sea, take the faint path to the left of the low wall. A big slab and the crag will appear to your left (2min).

At the left end of the crag: **Mystery Machine** (3+* 12m) climbs the wide stepped corner, **Da Ma Wick** (6a* 11m) follows the arête, and **Wicked** (6b* 11m) takes the flake to its right, finishing at the same lower-off. 20m to the right is an open project and another 20m further right again. Both are around 6c, crimpy and a little crumbly.

# WESTERN GLENS

Across the southwestern Highlands and Islands, traditional climbing prevails, with the mighty ranges around Glencoe and Ben Nevis dominating the landscape. Bolted crags tend to be few and far between. Hidden across this vast area, however, are some delightfully scenic sport venues, particularly those along the A830 to Mallaig. The region boasts the hardest routes in the country, courtesy of the Anvil and Steall Crag (p94).

Several areas are easily accessible as a day trip from Glasgow, whilst others provide an alternative to higher crags around Fort William should the weather be inclement on the mountains. Should conditions turn too wet to play outside, there are indoor walls in Fort William, Glasgow and Kinlochleven (p226) as well as many good climber-friendly pubs and cafes nestled amongst the picturesque glens.

Journey times throughout the southern Highland glens should not be underestimated as the roads can be busy and are often winding and indirect.

Seb basking on
**Black Jack** (6b)
Arisaig - p80

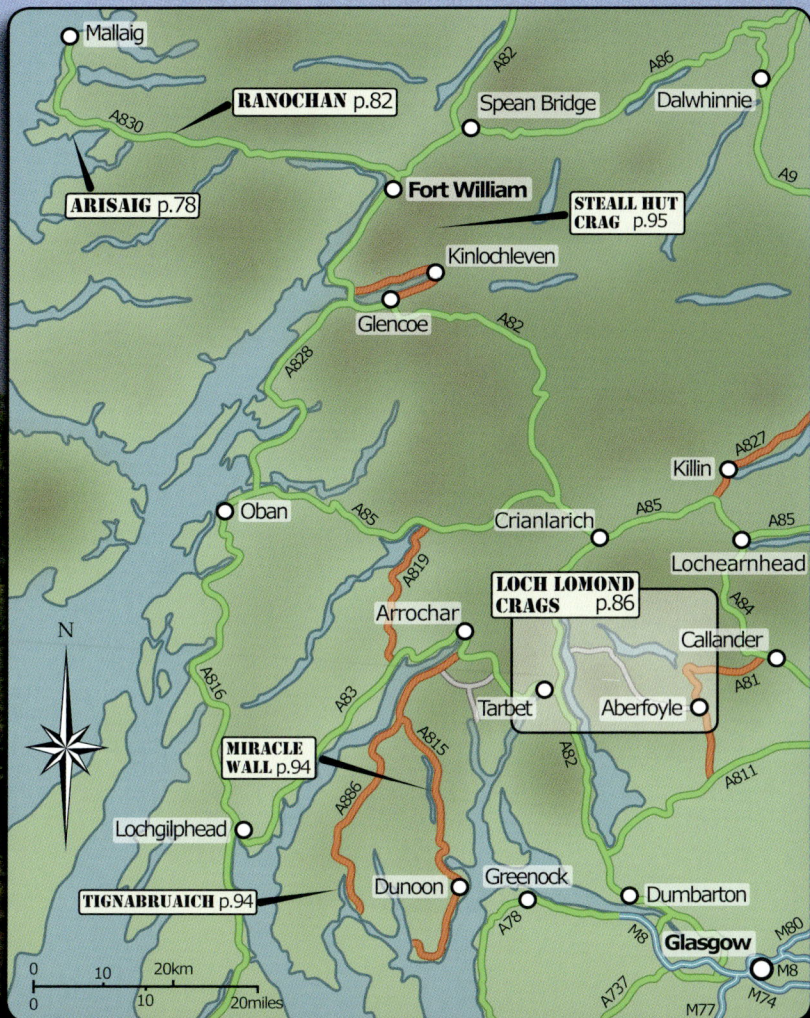

Mallaig

**RANOCHAN** p.82

A82

A86

Spean Bridge

Dalwhinnie

A830

A9

**ARISAIG** p.78

**Fort William**

**STEALL HUT CRAG** p.95

Kinlochleven

Glencoe

A828

A82

Killin

A827

Oban

A85

Crianlarich

A85

A85

Lochearnhead

A819

**LOCH LOMOND CRAGS** p.86

Arrochar

A84

Callander

A816

A83

Tarbet

Aberfoyle

A81

**MIRACLE WALL** p.94

A815

A82

A811

A886

Lochgilphead

**TIGNABRUAICH** p.94

Dunoon

Greenock

Dumbarton

M80

A78

M8

**Glasgow**

M74

0  10  20km

0  10  20miles

A737

M77

M8

N

# Arisaig (Black Rock)

56.88647 -5.815703

56.89199 -5.803469

The sizable **Black Rock** lies in a serene bay by the sea just south of Arisaig. The views from the crag and the setting are particularly nice. The main cliff is a basalt dyke and for the most part good rock, but suspect in places. The crag needs a few days to dry after prolonged rain. As with other basalt crags with closely packed lines, many linkups and variations are possible once the initial selection is exhausted. Not all are recorded here, just use your imagination!

Behind the main crag lies **Atonement Wall** (56.88729 -5.815456), a clean south facing slab of schist. To approach bushwhack your way uphill just to the right of Black Rock. A spiral shaped pinnacle will reveal itself in the trees; the crag lies in a chasm behind this.

⚠️ Treat some of the ageing gear with caution. Some anchors comprise of chains that must be abseiled from, or you can start a trend and leave a maillon or old carabiner to lower off.

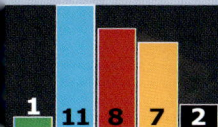

**1** **11** **8** **7** **2**

35 mins    15 mins

Drive west from Fort William towards Mallaig on the A830. 1.5 miles west of Beasdale station is a turn off for Druimindarroch. Take this road and turn sharply (second) left by the cottage. Follow the single-track down to its end (0.6 miles) where there is space for a car on the verge or on the shingle on the shore (may be tidal). This point is a 20 minute cycle from Beasdale train station (4 trains per day, 1 hr from Fort William). From here walk rightwards along the faint path on the shore, round the corner to follow the coast. The bay of the crag will eventually reveal itself. Waterproof footwear will be useful as the walk is wet underfoot.

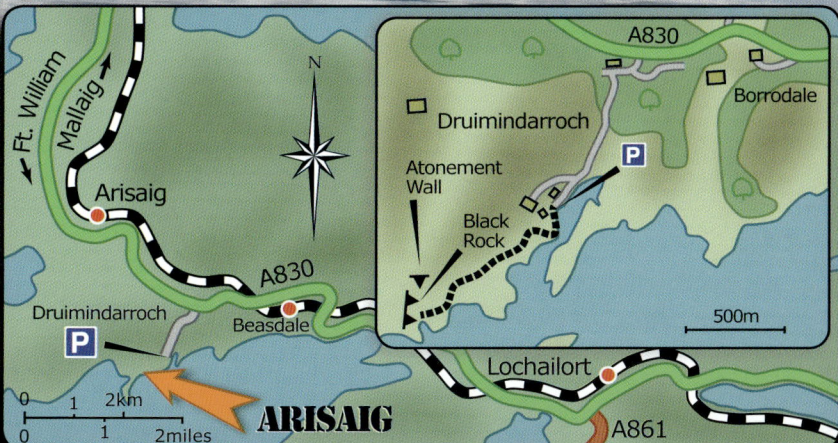

N

Ft. William
Mallaig
Arisaig
A830
Druimindarroch
Beasdale
Lochailort
A861

A830
Druimindarroch
Borrodale
Atonement Wall
Black Rock
P
P
500m

0  1  2km
0  1  2miles

**ARISAIG**

# Arisaig

## BLACK ROCK

**1** **Grey Edge** 6a* (10m) Climb the bulging arête on slopers to the slab above

**2** **Black Sabbath** 6b* (10m) Climb rightwards to a hanging boss, surmount the overhang and finish up the slab

**3** **Black Heart** 6b+* (10m) The right-slanting rails lead to a thrutchy finish

**4** **Black Adder** 6b** (10m) Great climbing in the lower half straight up to the lower-off of **3**

**5** **Black Beard** 6a+** (12m) Start up the black rock, go up to under the overlap and go right to the LO. High in the grade

**6** **Black Friday** 6a+* (12m) Easier climbing on the lower section leads via more testing crimps to the LO of **5**

**7** **Pot Calling the Kettle Black** 6a+* (12m) Left of the wee sapling. The tricky start eases briefly before a steeper finish

**8** **Black Pig** 6a+ (12m) To the right of the sapling. Follow the shallow depression to a steeper finish

**9** **Unfinished Business** 5 (10m) Straight up a shallow groove to single bolt lower-off. Vegetated but worthwhile

**10** **Black Dog** 6a+* (15m) Go up the left facing groove then head straight up to a crux finish and LO on the right

**11** **Black to Black** 6a* (12m) Start on the bulge right of the groove on jugs and continue up the wall on flatter holds

**12** **Black Death** 6a+** (14m) Follow a thin, slightly left-leaning crack and wall above to the crux and finish

**13** **Black as Bill's Mothers** 6a* (10m) Follow the thin vertical crack to the top, finishing on the right

**14** **Black Jack** 6b** (10m) Nice climbing through the left side of the overhang on pockets. Eases briefly before a pumpy finish right to the LO of **15**

**15** **I Can't Believe it's Not Black** 6c* (12m) Climbs the right side of the overhang via small holds to the wall above, past a block, to a sting in the tail

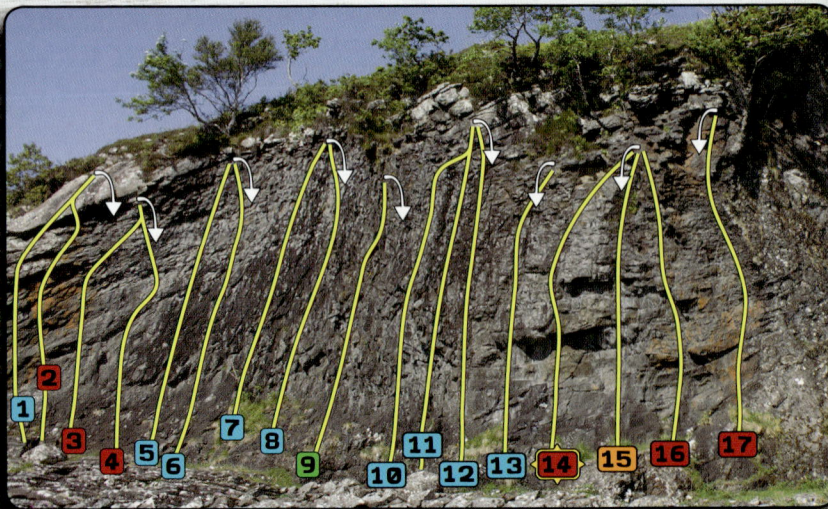

**16** **Black Seal of Approval** 6b* (12m) Takes the left side of the orange wall to finish up a blocky, left facing corner

**17** **Black Mamba** 6b* (12m) Start up the concave rock right of the orange wall to finish on a steep slab

The next routes are longer and start right of the large tree. This wall can be a little damp and mossy higher up but the routes are good.

The first two routes are in need of a clean and have no hangers. In the event of them being reinstated they are L-R:

**18** **Blackberry** 6c (20m)

**19** **Black is Back** 6c (20m)

**20** **Black Eyed Peas** 6c* (20m) Protruding bolt studs. Climb the bulge to reach a slab (rest). Thin moves gain an easier overlap to a tree lower-off (old tat)

**21** **Black Where We Belong** 6c** (20m) Climb the bulge to a rest. Thin crux moves lead to the right end of a small overlap and tree LO of **20**

**22** **Black for Good** 6b+ (20m) Start left of the pillar, through a bulge and small overlap. Trend leftward to the tree LO

**23** **Black in the Day** 6b* (18m) Climb the pillar and groove to a blank wall. Keep left of the bolts to finish. Going right of the bolts is the reachier **Black Magic** 6c*

**24** **Black Power** 6c* (18m) Start in the groove right of the pillar, pull through the roof and follow the lip to the chain

**25** **Black Velvet** 7a (15m) Climb the corner under the roof. Pull through this on slopers to finish directly up the wall

**26** **Black in Time** 6c (15m) Start as for **25** to under the roofs. Pull right with a pocket, crank through the roof into a steep groove and eventually a good hold

**WESTERN GLENS**

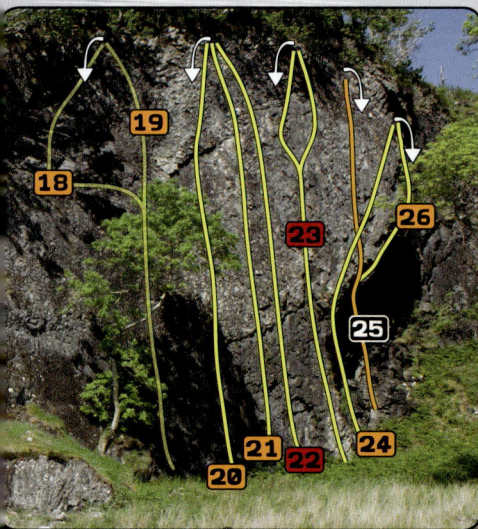

## ATONEMENT WALL
Approach description on p78

**27** **Bend it Like Beckham** 6a+* (8m) Climb the R/L slanting crack and go rightwards to the LO

**28** **The Hole** 7a+* (8m) Start at a low triangular niche. Go up to a L/R slanting flake and straight up the slab above with a tricky move to finish

The direct line from the lowest point to finish at the tree is **Atonement** 7b+*

**29** **The Duchess** 6a+* (7m) Climb up the slab to gain a shallow groove and crack to the finish at a tree

# Ranochan

56.88093 -5.577506

56.88043 -5.579592

The schist crags of Ranochan lie on the northern hillside overlooking the beautiful Loch Eilt. These south facing crags offer year round climbing, dry quickly, and are exposed to any winds that may blow to keep midges away. Ranochan Wall is steep, offering good exposure, whilst Ranochan West is slabby.

The crags lie on the A830 between Glenfinnan and Lochailort behind Ranochan house; the only property by Loch Eilt. About 150m west of the bridge at Ranochan is a small place to park on the loch side of the road, the crags are visible from here. Alternatively, a layby can be found round the corner 250m away.

From the small parking walk uphill on the path beside the deer fence that encircles the property. After 25m a corner of the fence is reached, Ranochan Wall is visible to the right and the triangular shaped Ranochan West Crag by the trees to the left.

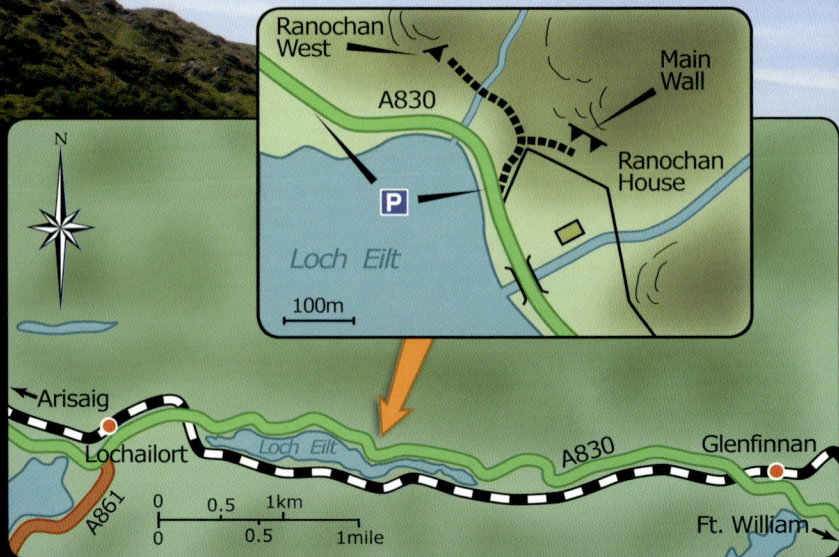

Ranochan
West

A830

Main
Wall

Ranochan
House

P

Loch Eilt

100m

N

Arisaig

Lochailort

Loch Eilt

A830

Glenfinnan

A861

Ft. William

0     0.5     1km

0           0.5         1mile

10 mins

# Ranochan

## MAIN WALL

The main wall behind the house.

⚠ At time of writing the anchors only comprise of a chain unsuitable for lowering-off; either abseil or leave a mallion if you're feeling charitable!

**1** **Cold Shoulder** 6c (9m) Tricky moves on a short crimpy wall gain the break. This route takes the left arête dynamically. From the break, straight up the slab gives **Way out West** 7c+* and the right arête is **Sneaker Freaks** 7b

**2** **Devil's Advocate** 6a+* (12m) The warm up route. Climb the lower wall, pass a small tree and climb up the slot

**3** **Kneed 4 Speed** 6c+* (12m) Climb to good holds at the overhang. Pull over and head up the featured wall to finish on the right

**4** **Bulldog Drummond** 7a+* (12m) Starting at a niche, climb to the break then keep left of the next 3 bolts before breaking left to finish at the chains of **3**

**5** **Lateral Thinking** 7a+** (12m) Start as for **4** but follow the bolt-line directly up the awkward crimpy wall

**6** **Esperanza** 6c+ (15m) Start just left of the wide groove. Pass the first break and niche above to gain the second break, followed by a tricky move to finish

**7** **Chip and Pin** 7a+* (15m) Bridging up the wide groove brings you to difficult moves over the roof. Further difficulty takes you to the second overlap to finish via the curving crack

**8** **Goosey Goosey Gander** 6c+ (14m) Mantel onto the break, then gain the wall above, which is followed to a crimpy bulge and an easier finish

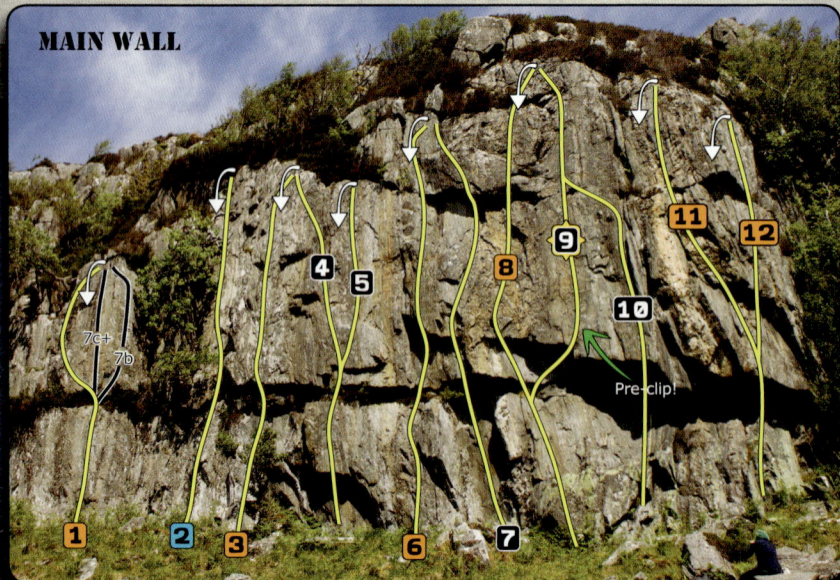

MAIN WALL

Pre-clip!

**9** **Immaculate Conception** 7a+*** (14m) Mantel into the break then pull up right to climb the crimpy wrinkled wall above to the second break. Finish up the shallow groove to the chains of the previous route. Superb

**10** **Running Blind** 7a+* (15m) Pre-clip the first two bolts of **9** and climb the overhanging crack to the right, past a spike and flakes to rejoin the previous route at the second break

**11** **When the Wind Blows** 6c** (15m) Right of the pale seam, pull through the overlap onto the slab. Continue leftwards to gain hanging flakes with good exposure

**12** **Jungle Run** 6c* (15m) Gain the slab as for the previous route, then straight through the overlap to a second slab and break. A short wall above leads to the chains

# RANOCHAN WEST

These two slabby schist outcrops each harbour one line of bolts with two route variations. The slightly lower left hand slab is hidden in the trees and the right hand slab is an obvious triangular shape when viewed on the approach.

**13** **Blue Velvet** 6c* (8m) On the left-hand slab. Climb the shallow crack on the left edge and step right to finish. Right of the bolts, via a vanishing L/R crack and straight to the chains is **Slip Sliding Away** 7b **

**14** **Lakey Hill** 6a+* (10m) On the right-hand slab, and climbing to the left of the bolts. Sticking to the right of the bolts increases the difficulty slightly and is **Niagara** 6b*. Holds reveal themselves when needed!

Seb nearing the top of **Lakey Hill** (6a+)

# Loch Lomond Crags

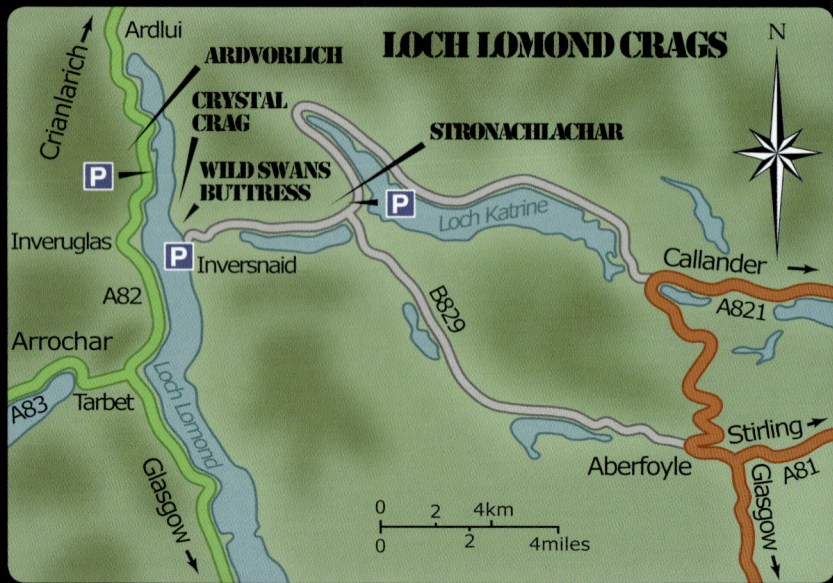

**LOCH LOMOND CRAGS**

N

Ardlui

Crianlarich →

**ARDVORLICH**

**CRYSTAL CRAG**

**STRONACHLACHAR**

P

**WILD SWANS BUTTRESS**

P

Loch Katrine

P Inversnaid

Inveruglas

Callander →

A821

A82

B829

Arrochar

A83 Tarbet

Loch Lomond

Stirling →

Glasgow →

Aberfoyle

Glasgow A81

| 0 | 2 | 4km |

0    2    4miles

The hills and bonnie banks surrounding Loch Lomond are home to a vast scattering of small schist crags and boulders, the full potential of which is far from explored. They are readily accessible from Glasgow, yet are set in a very scenic mountain environment. The crags on the east bank of the loch are also on the line of the West Highland Way, so may provide some entertainment for those embarking on the long walk. The loch itself is however a significant obstacle to navigation. The main road runs up the west side, past Ardvorlich, but for all other areas, one must make the long dogleg to Inversnaid via Aberfoyle; alternatively take the foot ferry from Tarbet: **www.cruiselochlomond.co.uk**

# Stronachlachar

**P** 56.25426 -4.589080

The wooded hillside above the hamlet of Stronachlachar contains a fallen city of giant schist boulders. The labyrinthine depths of the woods hold some short sport routes, quality bouldering, and potential for more development. Take care of hidden voids and chasms between the house-sized rocks. The upper areas, especially High Crag, afford very fine views across Lochs Katrine and Arklet.

The B829 takes you from Aberfoyle towards Inversnaid Hotel. At the obvious T-Junction turn right and park on the verge. Walk back left (west) and turn right on the newly improved path. After passing a small loch, and a large split boulder on your right, turn uphill and skirt the left (west) edge of the woods to access the sport crags.

## HIGH CRAG

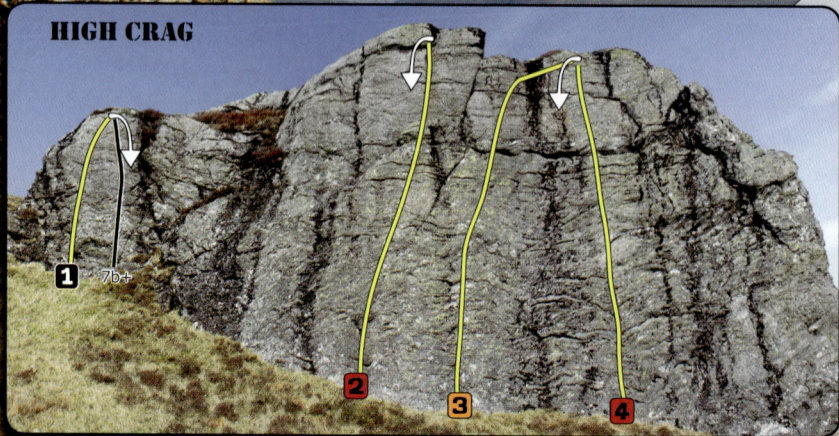

1  7b+  2  3  4

**20 mins**

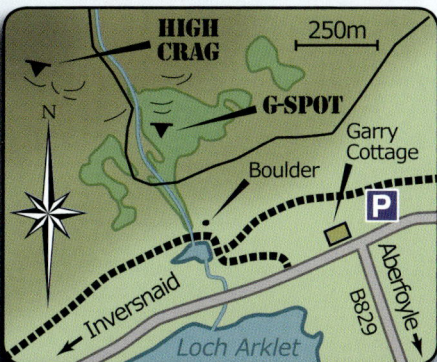

About 30m uphill from the G-Spot is the larger face of the **CHASM**. At this time it only holds a single unnamed 7b+, but has potential for several more lines.

# HIGH CRAG

56.25799 -4.604315

Follow the fenceline uphill until this face becomes clearly defined on the western skyline. Cross the fence and traverse diagonally left up the slope. The routes lie on the uppermost tier of rock.

**1** **Raksasha** *7a* (6m) A micro route up the short steep left wall. May need a clean

**2** **Lady of the Loch** *6b** (10m) A deceptive line of hidden pockets

**3** **My Own Private Scotland** *6c+** (10m) A sustained central line with a high crux

**4** **Highland Cling** *6b** (10m) A line up the right wall with a crux getting established on the break

WESTERN GLENS

# THE G-SPOT

56.25681 -4.598886

Has a reputation for being somewhat hard to find! From the path up the west border of the woods, there is a broad open area between trees and a fence where High Crag disappears from view. A faint path leads into the woods from here, which should reveal the huge boulder of the G-Spot within 50m.

**5** **Rhumba al Sol** *6a** (12m) Clip the first bolt from the ledge and follow the left arête

**6** **Hideous Kinky** *7a*** (12m) Climb the blank scoop and wall to step left into a niche and a shared lower-off

**7** **Venga Boys** *6c+** (12m) Start at the hairline crack and follow the diagonal groove past the low roof

**8** **El Mundo Fanatico** *7a+* (12m) Start as for **7**, then step right at the 3rd bolt onto the technical headwall

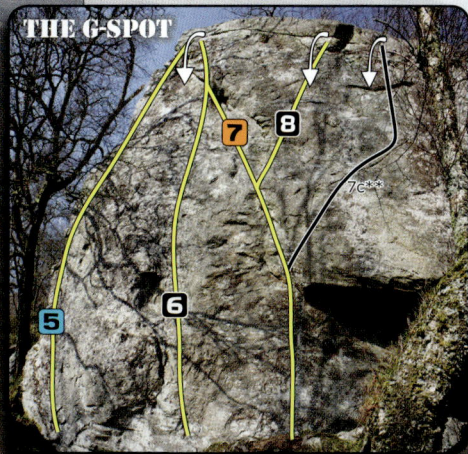

THE G-SPOT

# Inversnaid

P 56.24330 -4.685009

The eastern shoreline of Loch Lomond, north of the Inversnaid Hotel, contains a complex array of small schist crags, of which only a handful have seen any climbing development. The B829 takes you from Aberfoyle to Inversnaid, where there is extensive parking at the Hotel. From here the crags are found north up the West Highland Way, which may be walked or biked (times are given for walking).

For **WILD SWANS** follow the trail for 5 minutes, passing a boathouse, and take the second set of manufactured steps uphill. At the small bridge, cut diagonally left (north) up the slope to a terrace, and pass three impressively overhanging project crags (the first of which holds a single 7a+, **Hobble**, by a tree at its right end) before dropping down slightly to a small crag above a perched ledge and tree (15 mins total). **CRYSTAL CRAG** lies a little further north from Inversnaid. Follow the West Highland Way, passing Rob Roy's Cave. Approximately 250m after a bridge, the path squeezes between two boulders and a tree. Strike uphill here (no path) and the crag will come into view up on the left (40 mins total).

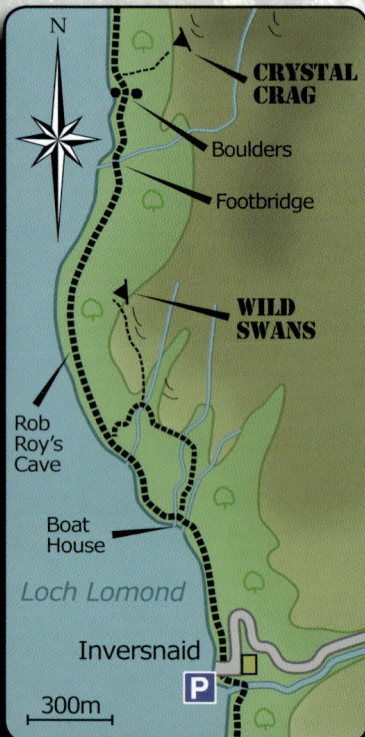

N

**CRYSTAL CRAG**

Boulders

Footbridge

**WILD SWANS**

Rob Roy's Cave

Boat House

*Loch Lomond*

Inversnaid

P

300m

# CRYSTAL CRAG

56.26185 -4.688397

This crag provides slightly longer routes on unusual quartz edges formed from a patina across the face, giving it a distinctive white appearance. The crag is a good afternoon suntrap, and is often surprisingly midge-free.

**1 Fear and Self Loathing** $7a+$** (15m) A thin traverse left from the start of **2** leads to the upper wall, when ivy allows

**2 Age of Aquarius** $7a+$*** (15m) A technical and sustained line. Crimpy holds lead to a leftward ramp, which is followed to the headwall

**3 Roadkill Recipes** $7a$** (12m) From the small tree trend right to a finishing overhang

**4 The Ruby Slippers** $7a+$* (12m) Pleasant wall climbing leads to a hard, blind crux under the overhang

**5 Far from the Malham Crowds** $7a$** (12m) Far indeed! Thin, technical and very hard to on-sight

# WILD SWANS

56.25479 -4.692149

This small crag lies perched high above the loch, affording fine views and suprising exposure. Routes are close and share a common lower-off.

**6** **The Ridge** *6c* (10m) Traverse left with difficulty to the arête, and follow this to easier ground

**7** **Dark Skies** *6b+* (10m) Crimpy moves gain the shallow groove, with better holds above

**8** **Wild Swans** *6b+\** (10m) The central line up pockets

**9** **Moonlight Sonata** *6b\** (10m) Start at the right and follow a break diagonally left to join **8** to finish

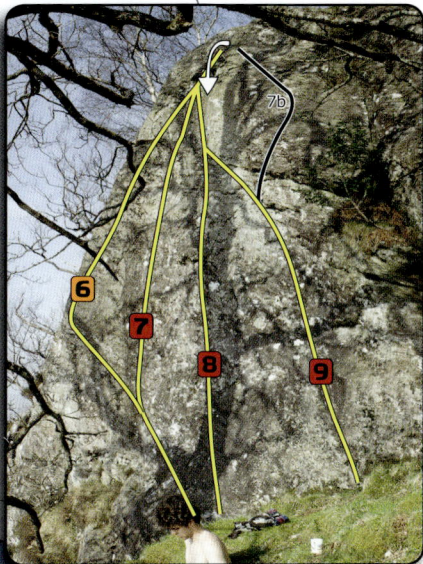

20-40 mins

# Ardvorlich

56.27266 -4.709607

56.26808 -4.703582

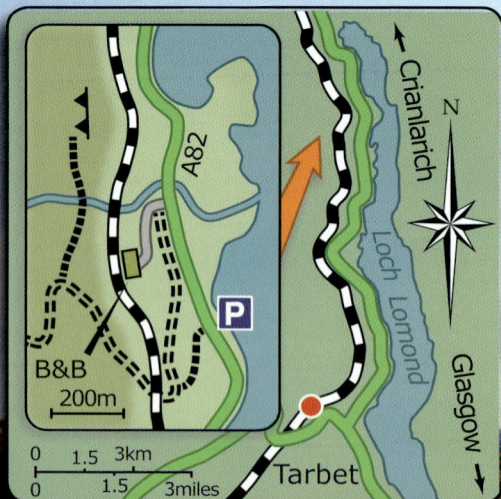

Ardvorlich is a small but delightful crag of clean pocketed schist, with fine views over Ben Lomond and the loch. While it is only a 40 minute drive from Glasgow, it feels like a different world. The routes are generally sparingly bolted and at times seem adventurously run-out. Should the last bolt feel far below you, spare a thought for those who first climbed these compact rocks as trad routes!

  15 mins | 30 mins

0 | 5 | 2 | 1 | 0

Park on the A82 in a layby 1.3 miles north of Inveruglas and 150m south of the Ardvorlich B+B (map p86). Hop the fence taking care not to cause damage, and head up a slope to the track. Follow this under the railway, and up to the right. When the track veers sharply left, cut across a slope and a stream to the crag, which will be clearly visible. There are three trains per day from Glasgow to Ardlui, from where it is 2 miles to the walk-in. Be very careful if cycling as there are many large trucks that use this narrow trunk road.

**1 Carnage** *6c* (20m) The bouldery traverse along the low roof to the left of the crag. Step onto **2** to finish if you want!

**2 That Sinking Feeling** *6a+*\* (15m) Technical climbing up the left arête with a low crux, then pass to the right of the small roof and finish up the groove

**3 The Groove** *6a*\*\*\* (15m) The central groove leads to a pocketed headwall. Finish left

**4 Drifting from Shore** *6b+*\*\* (15m) The bulge and crimpy headwall direct

**5 Lake Lomond** *6a*\*\* (15m) Up the corner to the tree, then step left onto the crimpy wall. High in the grade

**6 Dilemma** *6a+*\*\*\* (15m) Pull into a quartz pocket, and trend right on small holds, crossing **7** at half height

**7 Snake Eyes** *6a*\* (18m) Pull through the overhang onto the slab, cross **6** at the flake, then follow the scoop left to a juggy ramp

**8 Magic Carpet Ride** *6b*\*\* (15m) From behind the tree, climb to the peg at mid height, step left to the crack, and up to the small overlap, finishing direct. Due to be properly rebolted

# Other Crags

## TIGHNABRUAICH (55.94930 -5.203342)

On the Argyll peninsula, looking over the Kyles of Bute, lie several small but tranquil schist crags. The routes are few but of high quality and very scenic, so worth the bush-whacking. The midges in summer are apocalyptic, but mild winters make Sept-May the best time to visit. Either take the Gourock - Dunoon ferry or drive via Arrochar to get into Argyll. The crags are below the A8003 to Tignabruaich. 3.5 miles north of the village there is a layby viewpoint (P 55.94905 -5.204368). Park here and hop the fence to scramble down toward the water. The first crag is the aptly named **SAVAGE SLAB** (the leftmost route is **Ya Butey** *6b+*, but the rest are over 7b). The second crag that you encounter is the impressive **KRAKEN** (right). The best of the routes here are in the 7b-8a+ range, including Dave MacLeod's and Mike Tweedley's horizontal test-pieces, but the fine **Moments of Enlightenment** *7a+*\*\* skirts the Kraken roof on the left and ends rightward up its arête, while **Head of the Medusa** *6b+* goes right of the roof and finishes on the ledge. 100m right and uphill of this crag there is the **JERUSALEM** Buttress; a slab capped with a small roof. **Room With a View** *6b*\*\* takes the left edge, while the *Top30* route **Jerusalem** *6a+*\*\*\* starts from the bottom right. 50m south of the parking, the **LOST WORLD** can be glimpsed downhill from the road. Jump the barrier to access the routes from above by abseil (20m): (L-R) **Distant Cries** *7b+*\*\*; **Crouching Tiger** *6c+*\*\*; **Vanishing Point** *7a+*\*\*.

## MIRACLE WALL (56.0655 -4.986792)

This is a small crag around 9 miles north of Dunoon, on the A815, and so may be best combined with a trip to Tighnabruaich. Drive north from Dunoon, and park in a lochside layby 0.7 miles past the Coylet Inn (P 56.062991 -4.9848332). Walk north to the bend in the road and cut up the hill into the trees (3 min). One can also take the train to the Gourock ferry and then a local bus to Loch Eck. The schist crag has a steep pocketed wall and a finishing slab, which may feel a little run out! The three 10m routes are (L-R): **Angels With Dirty Faces** *7b*\*\*, **Holyman** *6c+*\*\*\* and **Bible Babble** *6c*.

## STEALL HUT CRAG (56.77106 -4.983983)

A crag famous for some big-name routes, including Hamilton's **Leopold** *8a* and MacLeod's **Fight the Feeling** *9a*, but there is also a large slab just to the left that holds some of Dave's less known routes! **Diamond Back** *6b+* (20m) starts up the left of the slab to continue through a bulge. **Diamond Groove** *6a+* (20m) starts the same but breaks right up the groove to the arête. **End of the Line** *6b+*\* (28m) takes a line up the full height of the right edge of the slabs, and *needs a 60m rope*. The left arête of the main wall is **Tipping Point** *6c* (20m). Drive north of Fort William on the A82, and from the roundabout at the Ben Nevis Highland Centre go up the Glen Nevis road 6.5 miles to its end (P 56.77755 -5.000470). Then walk 20 mins up the glen and gorge to find a cable bridge across the river at the Steall Meadow. Cross the bridge (fun!) and pass the hut to find the crag 5 min further up the hill. The scenery alone is worth the walk.

Jon Clarke finding **Moments of Enlightenment** (7a+) on the Kraken, Tignabruaich (Photo Paul Loomes)

# CENTRAL HIGHLANDS

Although at times less than an hour's drive from the populous Central Belt, the Central Highlands feel a world apart. The area holds many picturesque glens, mountains, lochs and forests, but with a more gentle climate than their northern and western counterparts. The flip side of this is a greater degree of tourist development, meaning many towns and villages can get quite busy in the summer. In the busier honey-pot areas wild camping may be somewhat more restricted. This can be a good place to bring the family, and let the non-climbing members explore lochside trails, castles and fine pubs. With the exception of Bennybeg, the sport climbing crags in the southern highlands are exclusively schist.

Loch Voil, near Strathyre, is typical of the scenic forested landscape of the central Highlands

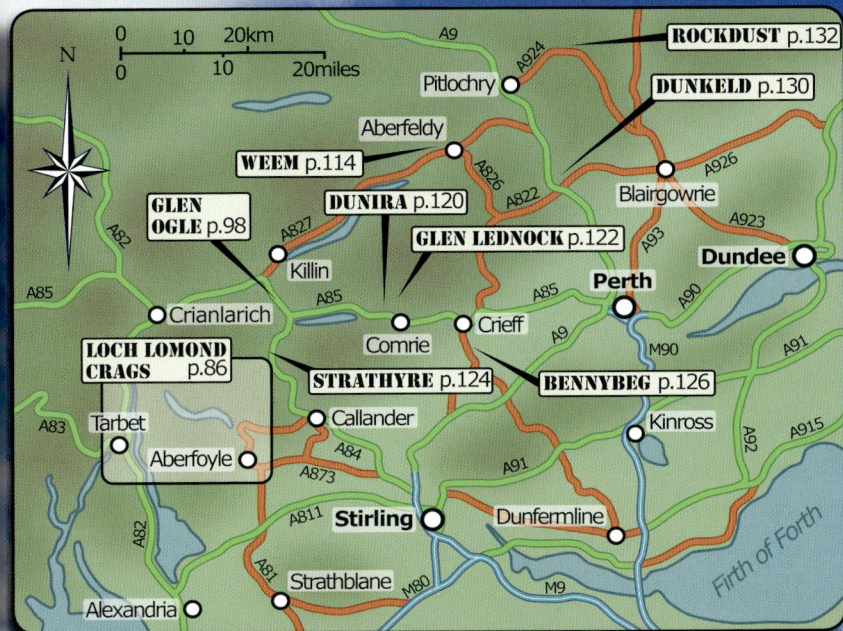

| 0 | 10 | 20km |
| 0 | 10 | 20miles |

N

**ROCKDUST** p.132

**DUNKELD** p.130

Pitlochry

Aberfeldy

**WEEM** p.114

**DUNIRA** p.120

**GLEN OGLE** p.98

Blairgowrie

**GLEN LEDNOCK** p.122

Killin

**Dundee**

Crianlarich

**Perth**

Comrie

Crieff

**LOCH LOMOND CRAGS** p.86

**STRATHYRE** p.124

**BENNYBEG** p.126

Tarbet

Callander

Kinross

Aberfoyle

**Stirling**

Dunfermline

Strathblane

Alexandria

*Firth of Forth*

A9
A924
A826
A822
A926
A923
A827
A85
A93
A85
A90
A9
A91
M90
A92
A915
M9
M80
A84
A873
A811
A81
A82
A83

# Glen Ogle

Glen Ogle, at one time the foremost Scottish sport climbing venue, has since fallen into esoteric realms due to newer, more accessible areas. On a fine day however, the crags furthest from the busy road have a picturesque outlook and a peaceful mountain feel. The schist outcrops, each typically holding a handful of routes, are scattered on both hillsides. Few paths exist, and in summer deep bracken grows on the Sunny Side, so bring your hiking boots. Some routes have antiquated bolts and single point lower-offs, so use caution. Birds of prey nest on some of the crags... do not disturb if present.

The crags of the aptly named Sunny Side (p100) generally offer mid-grade routes, although the shallow pockets may feel surprisingly hard. Park either in the large rough area **P**2 or the layby **P**1 just uphill of the small bridge.

The Dark Side crags (p108) only hold sun until mid-morning, so are slower to dry and have a sombre appearance. However, fortitude will be rewarded with some of the better hard lines in the area. To access, park at **P**2 and follow the path toward and under the viaduct (part of National Cycle Network).

The Warmup Wall (p106) is isolated from the rest of the Sunny Side and accessed from parking **P**3 - cut steeply leftwards up the slope.

**P** 1 (56.41574 -4.326798)
2 (56.41127 -4.317683)
3 (56.40200 -4.303139)

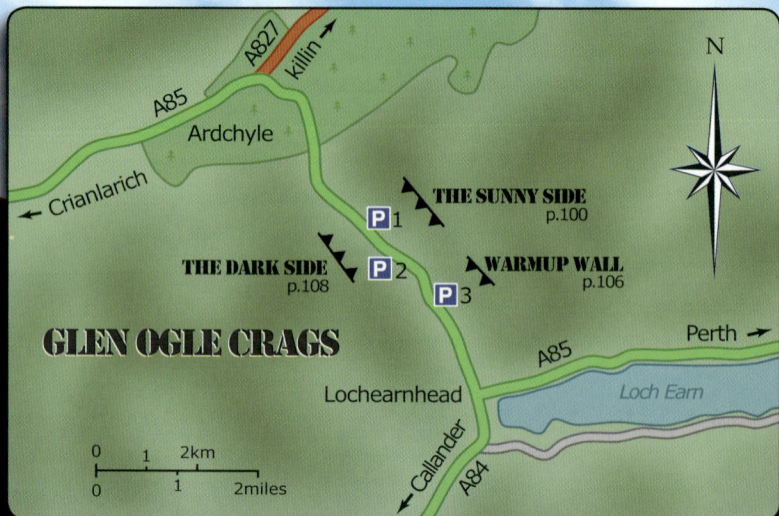

10-30 mins

Will Roper enjoying some **Loose Living** (6a)
Creag nan Cuileann - p101

# Glen Ogle (Sunny Side)

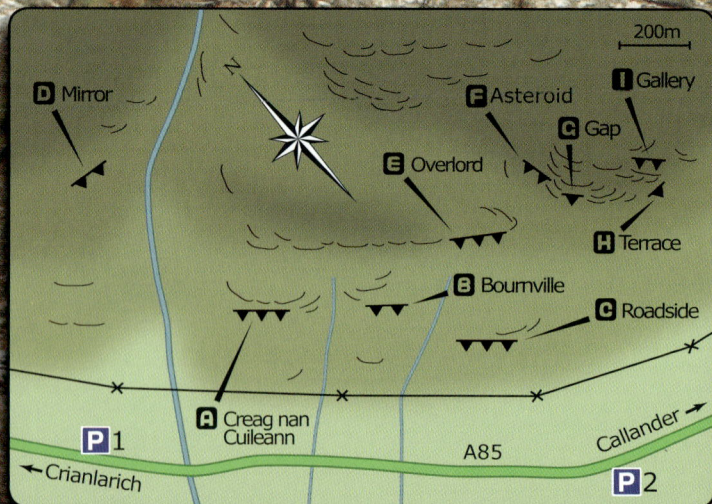

## A. CREAG NAN CUILEANN
(56.41557 -4.321975)

From the layby (P1), head up to the pylon then diagonally right over a stream. The left side of the crag holds six trad routes (E2-E5), and a 7b at its far left.

**1 Fight or Flight** 6c+ (15m) The roof and hanging wall on the right of the main trad face

**2 Slaphead** 6b+ (10m) The roof and bulge to the right of the blocky groove

**3 Fat Chance** 6c* (10m) The thin crack through the roof

**4 Fight the Flab** 6c+* (12m) The roof and blunt nose. Approach from the right taking care to avoid the loose block ⚠

**5 Let it All Hang Out** 6c+* (12m) Pull through the widest point in the roof and tiptoe up the slab to the trees

**6 Happy Campus** 6c* (12m) Through the roof just right of **5**, and re-joining that line to finish

**7 Hang On!** 6c** (12m) Pull through the smaller roof on the right and climb the wall and slab above

**8 Step on It** 6a (12m) After the roof ends, climb the wall and step left into **7** at the ledge to finish

**9 Life in the Fat Lane** 6b+* (12m) The short steep crack leads to a heathery ledge

Around the corner lies a short arête which holds the next three routes.

**10 Chasing the Bandwagon** 6a+* (10m) The wall to the left of the arête

**11 Reaching the Limit** 6b+**(10m) Follow the left side of the arête. Balancy

**12 Clutching at Straws** 7a* (10m) Climb the overhanging wall and slap up the right side of the arête

The crag then steps back uphill and presents a clean slab containing...

**0** | **20** | **29** | **12** | **7**

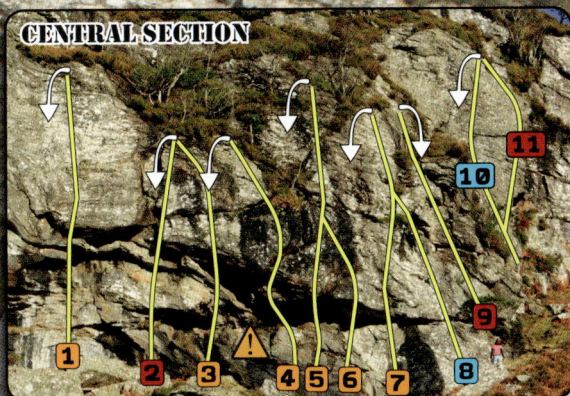

CENTRAL SECTION

1   2   3   4   5   6   7   8   9   10   11

RIGHT SIDE

10   11   12   13   14   15   16   17   18   19

CENTRAL HIGHLANDS

**13** **Dazed and Confused** *6a* (15m) The left face, using the tree to gain the ledge at half-height

**14** **Having a Little Flutter** *6c+*** (12m) The lower wall, pass through the groove, and stay left of the crack in the headwall

**15** **Ceuse Jimmy** *6c*** (12m) Climb directly up to and follow the thin crack

**16** **Kinmont Times** *6a+** (15m) The diagonal crack, finishing as for **13**

**17** **Lichen Virgin** *6a+* (12m) Start up the flake then follow the groove right

**18** **Loose Living** *6a* (12m) The crack/groove in the right wall, using the arête to finish at the ledge

**19** **Ghost Trail** *6b+*** (12m) The pale streak in the right wall. Finish as for **18**

# Glen Ogle (Sunny Side)

## B. BOURNVILLE
(56.41485 -4.319838)

From the right end of Creag nan Cuile-ann, hop diagonally up to a slightly higher terrace. This clean vertical face holds a high concentration of routes, but mostly of a similar grade.

**1** **The Dirty Dozen** 6a (6m) A scrappy route up the far left of the crag

**2** **It Ain't Over till its Over** 6a+ (7m) Face climbing passing a vegetated ledge

**3** **Coward of the County** 6a+ (7m) Similar to and finishing as for **2**

**4** **Half Covered** 6b* (8m) Pleasant climbing marred by a vegetated ledge

**5** **High and Dry** 6b (8m) A clean wall below leads up to and through the small overlap

**6** **Chocoholics** 6a+ (8m) Climb up to and through the small triangular recess

**7** **Fingers of Fudge** 6b+ (8m) Takes the left-hand line to the highest point of the crag. Can be lichenous

**8** **Sudden Alchemy** 6b+* (8m) Right of the seepage line, sharp pockets provide the right hand line to the high point of the crag

**9** **Hot Chocolate** 6b** (8m) Follow the right of the dark streak to a single bolt and shackle

**10** **Sorry Tess** 6b (8m) Thin face climbing, especially between the first and second bolts, easing thereafter

**11** **The Greenhouse Defect** 6b** (8m) Start at the left edge of a small cave, and climb pockets and edges to a high crux

**12** **Voodoo Ray** 6b (8m) Start on the face just right of the cave and step onto the arête of the main face

# C. ROADSIDE
(56.41383 -4.319329)

A short walk-in but marred by the traffic noise. Often seeps. Either drop down and east from Bournville, or head directly uphill from **P**2 parking past a pylon and a large boulder.

**13** **Don't Fight the Feeling**
$6b$* (10m) Directly up the 'barrel shaped' wall on good edges and an easy finish

**14** **Rock is Dead** $6b$ (10m) Start right of the wide crack, and follow this through the bulge on large flat holds. Rock delicately left onto the face before finishing up an easy slab

**15** **Dark Skies** $6b$* (10m) Thrutch onto the shelf, pull through the bulge and continue delicately on pockets to the top

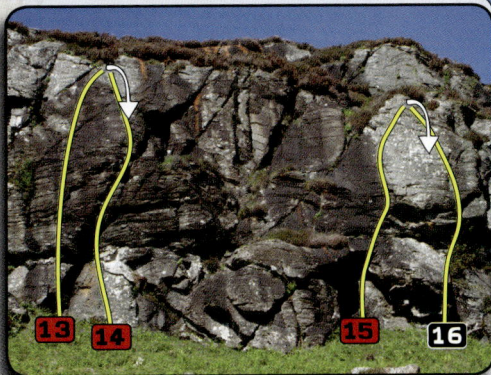

**16** **Hold the Press** $7a$* (10m) Boulder up to the ledge, then move right to pull with difficulty through the roof onto the hanging face and a shared lower-off

# D. THE MIRROR
(56.41850 -4.321396)

Follow a stream uphill from the left of Creag nan Cuileann to reach this fine pocketed slab. Far enough from the road to provide mountain tranquillity!

**17** **Munro Bagger** $6b$+** (12m)
The curving crack/groove on the left

**18** **Take a Hike** $7a$** (12m) Follow staples along a thin crack

**19** **Cony the Calvanist** $6c$+** (12m) Start on the small ledge and climb the face on illusive pockets

**20** **Fat Eagles Fly Low** $6a$+** (12m) Follow staples up a thin crack from the heathery step

**21** **Retribution** $6c$+* (12m) Painful pockets up the smooth face

**22** **Bad Religion** $6c$ (12m) Start in the scoop and improvise up the thin wall

**23** **Carry on Up the Corbetts** $6a$+ (10m) The rightmost line, finishing leftward along the break

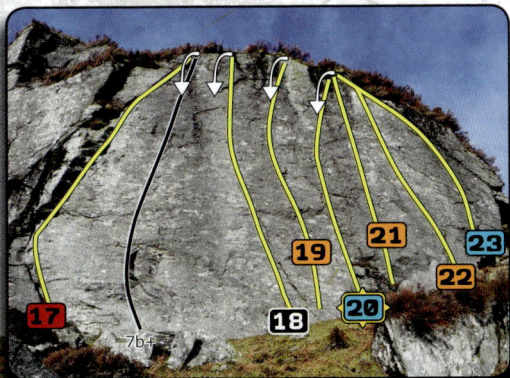

CENTRAL HIGHLANDS

# Glen Ogle (Sunny Side)

## E. OVERLORD BUTTRESS (56.41466 -4.317677)

An impressively steep outcrop in a fine position. Walk east over a small gully and slightly uphill from Bourneville, or traverse up the glen from the Asteroid. The crag is split into two sections, a steep left hand prow and a short streaked wall on the right leading to a slab.

LEFT

RIGHT

**1** **Restless Souls** *7a*** (10m) A steep, reachy line up the left side of the prow

**2** **Overkill** *7a+*** (10m) The line up the right side of the steep wall has good but elusive holds

The rest of the routes lie on the right-hand face which eases into a broken slab at 6m.

**3** **Over the Top** *6b+*** (12m) The left line starts steeply, with difficult moves to gain the slab

**4** **Pushover** *6b+* (10m) The steep start to the break is best approached dynamically

**5** **Pullover** *6b+* (10m) Start just left of the bolts, pull awkwardly onto the slab, and move left under the heathery ledge

## F. THE ASTEROID
(56.41395 -4.314919)

Short, off-vertical wall hidden from the road up the wide gully right of the Roadside Wall. Approach from **P** 2. Slow to dry and have run-out finishes to old single-bolt lower-offs. All *5+* (10m) L/R: **Mars**, **Trojan**, **Jupiter** & **Starboard**.

# G. THE GAP
(56.41378 -4.314423)

This diminutive crag is nestled into a gully, just right of the Asteroid. The routes are short but harder than they appear.

**10** **Beggar's Banquet** *6c+* (9m)
Start up the left side to a large quartz hold, make hard moves to gain the ledge, and teeter up thin pockets to the shared lower-off

**11** **Chimera** *6b+* (9m) Start up to the quartz hold, then head right up the slab to the ledge and a technical top groove

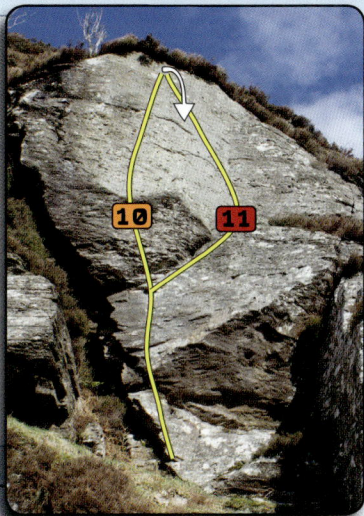

Topher pulling through the tricky crux of **Beggar's Banquet** (6c+)

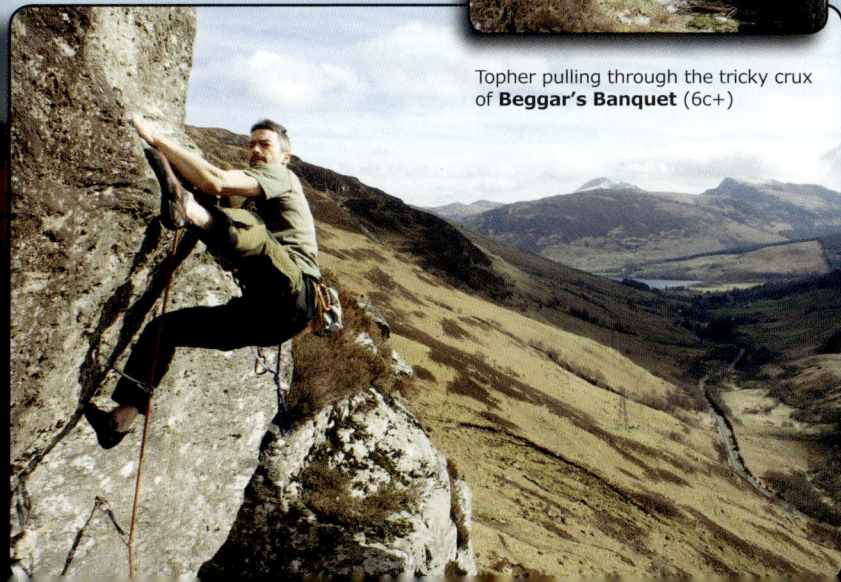

# Glen Ogle (Sunny Side)

## H. THE TERRACE
(56.41384 -4.313130)

This small crag lies 100m right, and slightly up from the Gap - on a terrace.

**1** **Saturation Point** 6b+* (12m) The highest point of the face, moving left at the break

**2** **Saturation Right Hand** 6a+ (10m) Starting as for **1**, but pull direct through the overlap

Further right, after a section of broken rock, the terrace ends with a striking arête:

**3** **Northern Exposure** 6b+ (8m) Follow the obvious arête on its left side

## THE WARMUP WALL
(56.40631 -4.301025)

This long outcrop, isolated from the rest of the Sunny Side crags, lies further down the northern slopes of the glen. It is approached by a steep pull up from parking area **P**3, a large layby about 1.2 miles from Lochearnhead. Map p98

**7** **Tam the Bam Fae Carn Bhan** 5+** (10m) Climb the slabby lower wall to a ledge and right facing wall. Lower-off under the tree

**8** **Ultraviolet** 6b+* (10m) The bulging wall, trending right at the top to a shared lower-off. The first clip may feel a little spicy, so some cads have taken to extending it

**9** **Outshined** 6a+* (10m) Climb the scooped groove right of **8** to the same lower-off

There is then a section of broken ground before a clean triangular face, which holds:

**10** **Burnt Offerings** 6b+** (10m) Up the middle of the face, via a diagonal crackline

**11** **Face the Heat** 7a** (10m) From the toe of the face take the wall direct on small pockets

WARMUP LEFT

## I. THE GALLERY
(56.41398 -4.312845)

A gently overhanging wall. From **Northern Exposure** go up the gully exiting left.

**4** **Mona Sleeza** 6a+* (10m) The leftmost line follows a diagonal crack

**5** **Modern Tart** 6b+* (10m) Through the overlap and follow the thin crack

**6** **Art Attack** 7a+* (10m) The pocketed wall

**12** **Infrarête** 6b+* (10m) Start and finish as **11**, but follow the leaning arête

**13** **Under the Same Sun** 6b+ (10m) Pull up from the rock scar and make thin moves up the slab to a roof

**14** **Burn Baby Burn** 6b (10m) The shallow hanging groove leads to overhangs

**15** **Burn it Up** 6b+ (10m) The rightmost line takes you through a low overlap with an obligatory mono

CENTRAL HIGHLANDS

WARMUP RIGHT

# Glen Ogle (Dark Side)

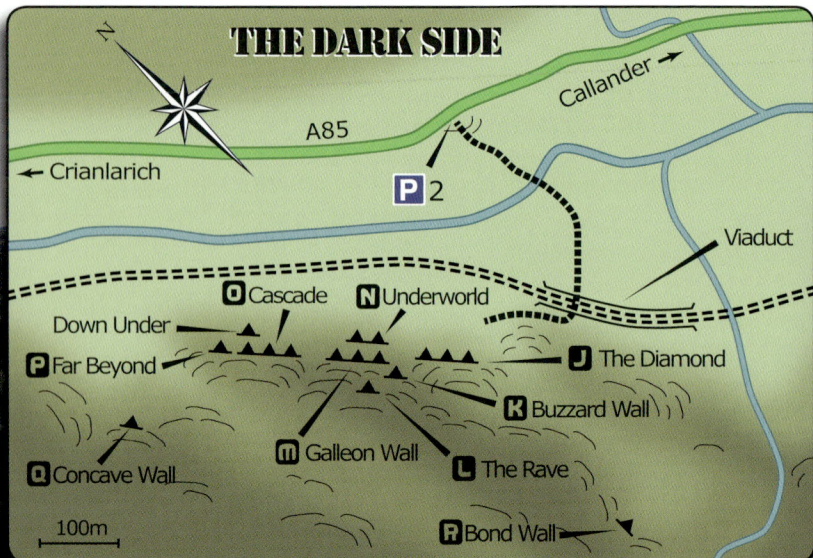

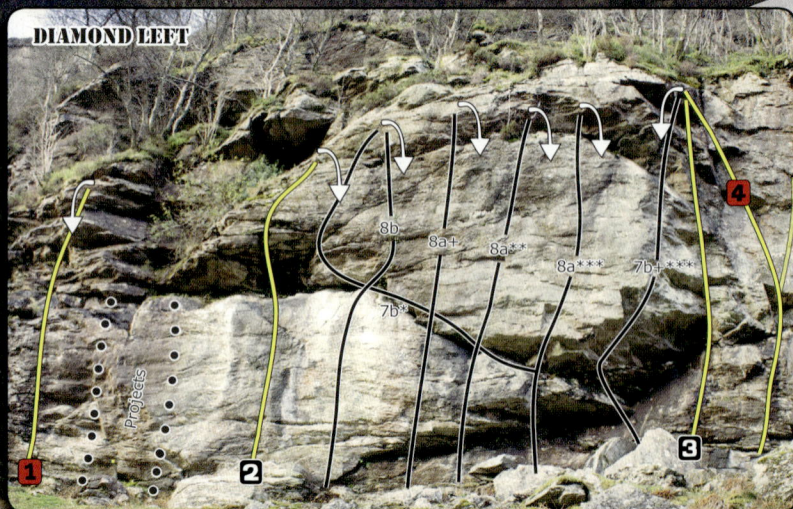

## THE DARK SIDE

A85

Callander →

← Crianlarich

P 2

Viaduct

**O** Cascade

**N** Underworld

Down Under

**P** Far Beyond

**J** The Diamond

**K** Buzzard Wall

**M** Galleon Wall

**L** The Rave

**Q** Concave Wall

**R** Bond Wall

100m

**DIAMOND LEFT**

8b

8a+

8a+**

8a***

7b+***

7b**

Projects

1

2

3

4

# J. THE DIAMOND
(56.40950 -4.321397)

One of the more popular crags in the area containing a good spread of routes. Although it can suffer from seepage, it can also be climbed during rain. From the uphill end of the viaduct, cut up the slope to reach the crag.

**1 Midge Patrol** *6b* (12m) Just to the left of the main steep wall. Often seeps

**2 Easy Over** *7a*** (12m) A varied route just right of the black streak. Steep pockets lead to the ledge, followed by a juggy roof and easy slab

The next section of the crag contains six quality routes for the hard-core, from 7b-8b

**3 One in the Eye for Stickmen** *7a+*** (15m) A line of resin bolts, following steep slopers

**4 Old Wives' Tale** *6b** (15m) A good warm-up, starting just right of the groove/ramp, and finishing just on its left

**5 Metal Guru** *6c+*** (15m) Start as **4** for two bolts, then follow the thin crack in the vertical wall

**6 After the Flood** *6c** (12m) Resin bolts follow a left facing groove, with a steep start and an awkward clip for the lower-off

**7 Arc of a Diver** *6c*** (12m) A steep start leads to the ledge, but the crux is yet to come!

**8 Wristy Business** *6c+** (10m) Climb the groove to the ledge and tricky head-wall

**9 Raspberry Beret** *6b+** (10m) The overhung wall, starting from the ledge

**10 Ship Ahoy** 6b (8m) A short scrappy route at the extreme right of the crag

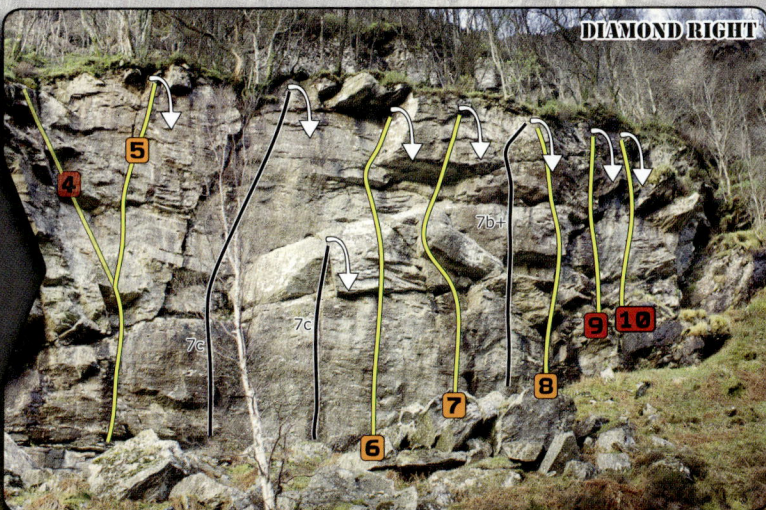

DIAMOND RIGHT

CENTRAL HIGHLANDS

# Glen Ogle (Dark Side)

## K. BUZZARD WALL
(56.40960 -4.321788)

A small roofed crag 50m right and uphill of the Diamond. Please check for and avoid nesting buzzards.

**1 Cut Loose** *7a+* (8m) Swing through the widest section of roof via the flake and head up left to chains in the heather

**2 Hang Free** *7a+* (8m) Through the triangular roof on the right to a single bolt LO in the groove

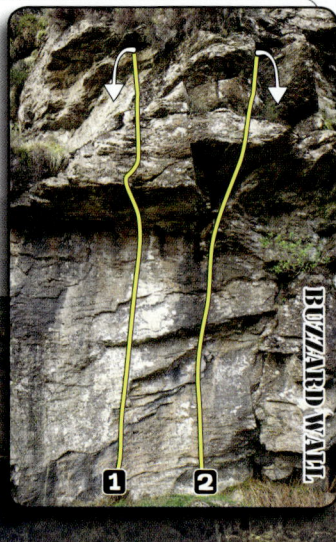

BUZZARD WALL

## M. GALLEON WALL
(56.41031 -4.322482)

On the same level as the Diamond, traverse 80m right along the grassy slope to the right. Can be slow to dry but has a good selection of short routes.

**6 Weigh Anchor** *6b+* (8m) The wall left of the corner, finishing with difficulty through the roof

**7 Frigging in the Rigging** *6c** (8m) Climb up the hanging corner to the roof, then prepare to thrutch!

**8 Slave to the Rhythm** *7a+*** (8m) Right of the corner, climb through two bulges with increasing difficulty

**9 Rum Ration** *7a+** (8m) Climb to the roof left of the hanging groove, step right into the groove then back left to reach the lower-off

**10 Blithe Spirit** *7a*** (8m) Follow the right side of the hanging groove. Slow to dry

**11 Eat Y'self Fitter** *6c*** (8m) An enjoyable juggy line through the low bulge and finishing at a big staple lower-off

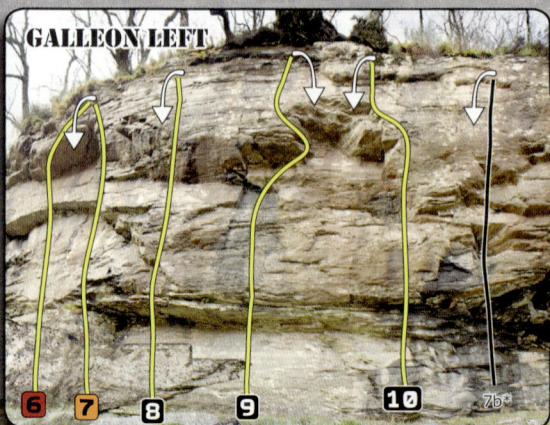

GALLEON LEFT

7b+

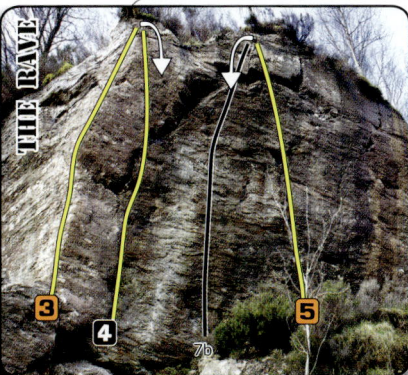

## L. THE RAVE

(56.40960 -4.321884)

A short steep face. Found by ascending the gully to the left of Buzzard Wall for 20m and then traversing right along the grassy slopes/terrace for ~50m.

**3** **The Edge of Ecstasy** $6c^*$ (8m)
The slabby left side of the arête

**4** **Rush** $7a^{**}$ (8m) The right side of the arête, following a crack before heading straight to a lower-off shared with **3**

**5** **Recreational Chemistry** $6c+$ (8m) A short powerful route up the right wall, to a shared lower-off

**12** **Infinite Gravity** $7a+^*$ (8m)
A bouldery start through the roof leads to easier ground

**13** **Waiting for a Train** $6c^*$ (8m)
Good holds follow the left slanting crack

**14** **The Pack Horse** $6c^{***}$ Thuggy, juggy climbing on pockets

**15** **Horrid** $6c$ (8m) The scoop at the right end is aptly named

Just further right, the crag provides two slabby lines with a shared finish.

**16** **Don't Pass Me By** $6a+$ (10m)
Climb the bulge to easier ground

**17** **The Guilt Trip** $6c^{**}$ (10m) A desperately crimpy bulge leads to the slab

CENTRAL HIGHLANDS

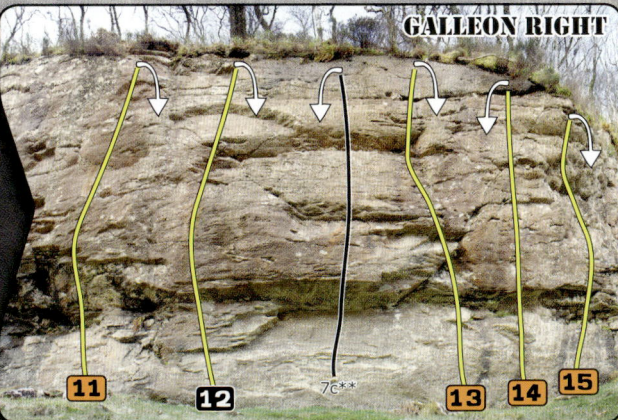

GALLEON RIGHT

# Glen Ogle (Dark Side)

The small wall directly below Cascade Wall is **DOWN UNDER** and holds (L-R):

**1** **The Bends** 7a+** (8m) Climb the slightly overhanging wall

**2** **Nitrogen** 6b+ (8m) Climb directly to the upper roof, then leftward

## N. UNDERWORLD
(56.41013 -4.322144)

A micro-crag directly below the Galleon, best accessed by traversing 80m right from the Diamond.

**3** **Carsonagenic** 6a (6m) The leftmost line, avoiding the choss low down

**4** **Hanging out on the Smalls** 7a** (6m) Nice crimping but short

**5** **Under Where?** 6b (6m) A problem of hidden holds, to the top of the groove

**6** **XX** 6c (6m) Poor rock improves with height, in time for a tricky finish

**7** **Satan's Slaves** 6a (6m) Left of the quartz band, again with some poor rock

**8** **Maniaxe** 6b (6m) A bouldery start to the first staple

**9** **Under Mind** 6b+ (6m) Starts in the cave at the right, via a large hold

## O. CASCADE WALL
(56.41073 -4.323233)

20m to the right of the Galleon on the same terrace. Can be slow to dry.

**10** **Hive of Industry** 7a+ (6m) The short steep left arête (not pictured) with one desperate move

**11** **Paradise Road** 6c* (9m) The left-slanting line

**12** **Short Sharp Shocked** 6a+*** (10m) The left edge of the wide diagonal crack is one of the most popular Dark Side routes

**13** **The Age Old Problem Rears its Ugly Head** 7a (10m) Through the overhang and headwall

**14** **Havering Skate** 6b+* (10m) The groove, arête and crack

**15** **Cauldron of Spite** 6c* (10m) From the big pocket go up right to a break, and then a quartz boss. Finish back left to a shared lower-off

**16** **Stone Junky** 6c (10m) Follow the diagonal crack to 7m then step right

**17** **Dirt Digger** 6b+ (10m) Pass through the next diagonal crack

**18** **That Sinking Feeling** 7a (10m) The steep left arête of the waterfall wall

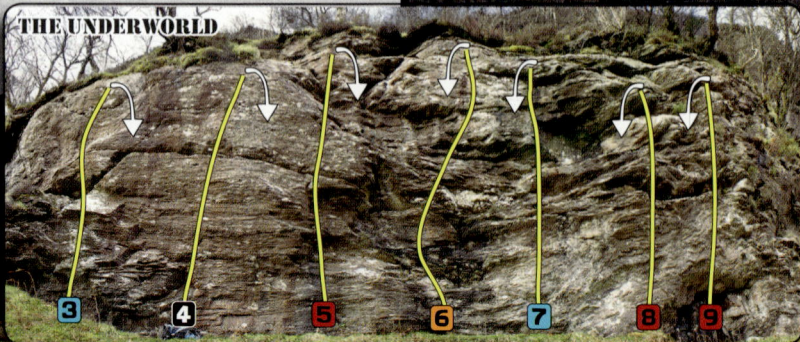

THE UNDERWORLD

CASCADE LEFT

CASCADE RIGHT

7b*

7b

**10**  **11**  **12**  **13**  **14**

**15**  **16**  **17**  **18**

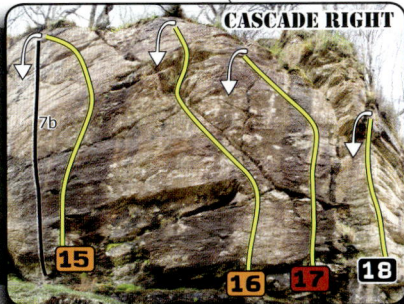

## P. FAR BEYOND (not pictured)

Further right of the Cascade waterfall, with a prominent square roof, containing (L-R):

**19** **Submersion** 7a+ (6m)

Then four open projects, followed by:

**20** **Far Beyond Driven** 6b+** (6m)

**21** **Driven to Distraction** 6b+* (6m)

**22** **Hyper Hyper** 6b (6m)

## Q. CONCAVE WALL

(Not Pictured : 56.41031 -4.323706)

A steep pale prow visible from the road. 250m right and uphill from Down Under. It catches the wind well and can be free of midges when the lower areas are swarmed. It holds (L-R): **Embrace my Weakness** (7c+); **Snipe Shadow** (8b**); **Arms Limitation** (7b+***); **Northern Exposure** 7a+*(12m)

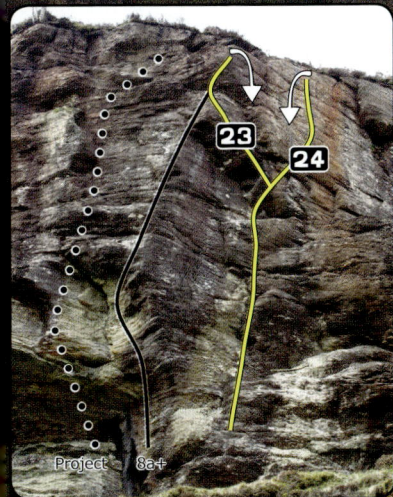

## R. BOND WALL

(56.40671 -4.320601)

Featuring longer routes than elsewhere in the glen, this crag takes a little longer to get to, but catches the best of the morning sun. From the Diamond, follow sheep trails up left to open hillside, then strike directly uphill.

**23** **Scaramanga** 7a+*** (20m) Follow the groove to a resting ledge beneath the roofs. Move left with difficulty to get established on the arête

**24** **Boldfinger** 7a*** (22m) A great and varied line, following **23** to the ledge, then breaking right onto the sustained, pocketed headwall

**23**  **24**

Project    8a+

# Weem

56.62815 -3.885430

56.62584 -3.885841

Weem provides a fine and varied selection of schist sport in the picturesque woods above the river Tay. The crags face south and west and catch the sun, especially when the trees are bare. They are generally quick to dry, although some areas may seep during winter.

If driving, leave the A9 at Ballinluig and follow the A827 to Aberfeldy. For Weem Rock, park by Weem Church, walk up the lane on its left until a small path appears on your right. After 50m there is a derelict cottage on the left. Just after, head left and then right onto the winding trail (find the rock dragon!). Once the path heads back left for 200m, look for a rough path up the loose slope just before some steps (small cairn). Western crags are best approached from Castle Menzies (see text).

Aberfeldy is served by Bus #23 from Perth, from where Weem is a 1.5 mile walk. The town also has a small outdoor shop (Munro's).

Try to stick to the trails on approach as the undergrowth is dense and rife with deer ticks!

The Weem Hotel is very close to the parking areas, providing a convenient spot to 'rehydrate' after getting pumped!

Jakob approaching the crux of
**The Long Good Friday** (6c+) - p116

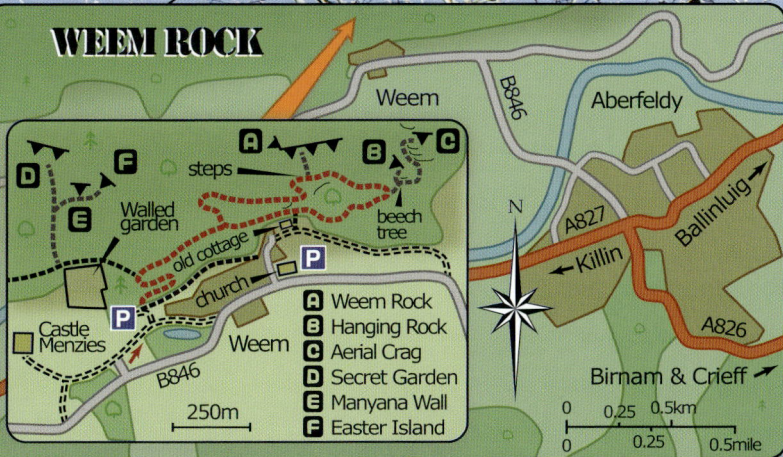

**WEEM ROCK**

| Icon | Name |
|---|---|
| A | Weem Rock |
| B | Hanging Rock |
| C | Aerial Crag |
| D | Secret Garden |
| E | Manyana Wall |
| F | Easter Island |

# A WEEM ROCK

The West face forms a steeply overhanging wall with two infamous stamina pump-fests.

**1 High Pitched Scream** 7a*** (15m) Scramble up the slab to a thin ledge from where the first bolt may be clipped at a stretch. A fingery start leads to steep but very positive climbing. Just go for it!

**2 The Screaming Weem** 7a+*** (18m) The line of resin bolts just left of the blunt arête is very sustained with two hard sections. Finish at the lower-off of **1**. Top of the grade

**3 Last Gasp** 7a+* (18m) Move out rightwards from the 5th bolt of Screaming Weem to gain the arête proper, finishing on the right

**4 The Real McKay** 6a* (20m) Finely positioned climbing initially up the right side of the arête, then more easily following a groove system to the lower-off

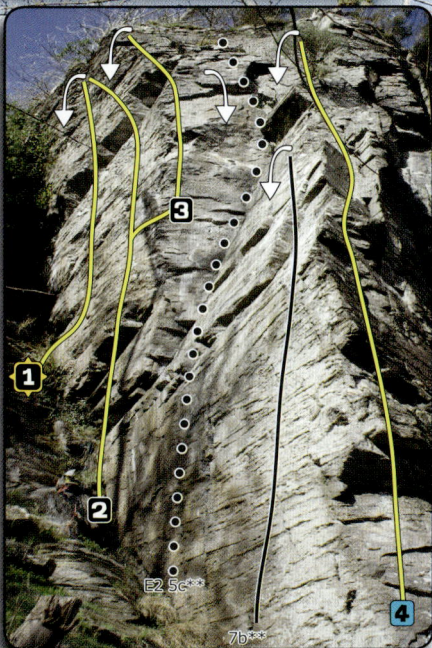

## WEEM ROCK cont.

In sharp contrast to the west side, the front face of the main crag is slabby but is less generous in its provision of holds. Small flat edges and balancy technical climbing is the theme here.

**5** **The Long Good Friday** 6c+*** (20m) Delicate moves up the left of the slab lead to a surprisingly strenuous crux at the small triangular niche

**6** **Confession of Faith** 6c*** (20m) A distinctly easier companion to **5** but still requiring precise footwork, and a tricky sequence at half height

**7** **Mannpower** 6b** (20m) The thin crackline up the right of the slab, with hard moves through a roof

**8** **Boomhead** 6b (20m) Start just left of the prominent corner. Take the first bulge direct then skip round the right side of the upper roof

**9** **Staring at the Sun** 5+* (18m) The arête right of the obvious corner

**10** **The Soup Dragon** 5+* (15m) The wall to the right of the arête is a little shorter. This line starts up a concave slab on its left side

**11** **Scooby Snacks** 6a+** (15m) Start up the centre of the broken slab, then trend right at the overhangs, to lower-offs shared with **12**

**12** **One Step Beyond** 6a** (15m) Start up to a ledge at 3m, then directly up the slab, which steepens at the finish

**13** **Down to the Last Heartbreak** 6a** (15m) From the base of the stepped ramp, climb the streaked wall direct

**14** **The Trial of Brother Number One** 6a+* (15m) Climb the pale scooped wall to a lower-off under a curving overhang

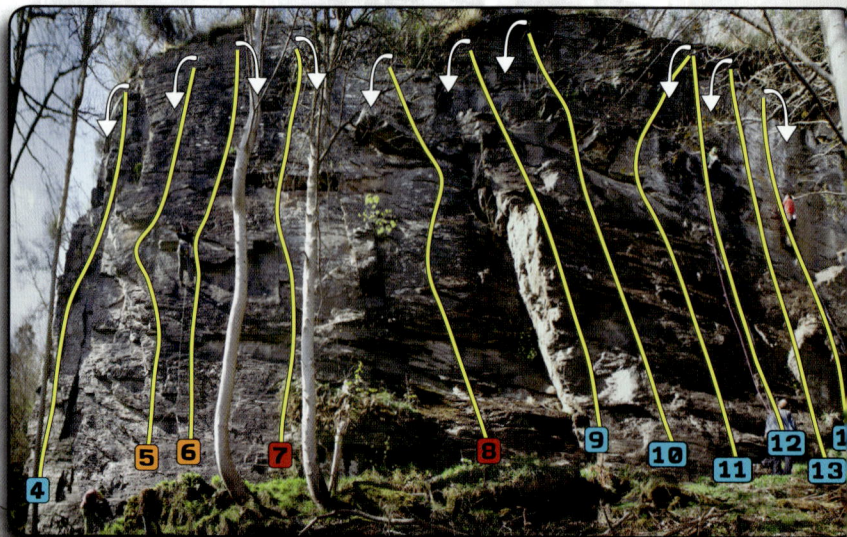

**15 Lap Dancing** *6b+*** (15m)
Start up the wall, pass a sloping ramp and finish by pulling through the capping roof

**16 The Llama Parlour** *6c*** (10m) A savagely crimpy line up the smooth face left of the corner

**17 The Protection Racket** *6a*** (10m) The obvious curving corner eases towards the top, but you have to get there first!

**18 Lighten Up** *6a** (12m) Right of the arête there is a wide shallow groove. This follows its left side, close to the arête

**19 Crowing at the Enemy** *6b+** (10m) The right side of the groove provides interesting moves

**20 Bark Barcherache** *6b* (10m) The wall on the far right of the face

From the trail hairpin, turning back left to Weem Rock (post with red band), two crags may be found by the adventurous. First, go 35m NW to a big beech tree. From there...

# B HANGING ROCK
(56.62857 -3.882817) Go 30m up and left to 3 large beeches, pass a 2m outcrop on the right, contour 25m, then head up through pines - crag behind boulders (5 min from hairpin). (L/R):

**Remanufacture** *7c+*; **Crushed by the Wheels of Industry** *7a+*; **The Chemical Generation** *7b*; **Alien Artefact** *7b*; **The Glass Ceiling** *6c**

# C AERIAL CRAG (56.62949 -3.882570)
Hard to find. Contour right past a 4m outcrop and pine trees on left for 100m. Cut uphill over mossy rocks to broken outcrops. Follow their left side uphill around 50m. Traverse right (4m 'gully') to the crag (still hidden) before a rhododendron patch (15min from hairpin).

**Kissing the Witch** *6b+** (16m)
On the left, just right of the arête

**Static in the Air** *6b+** (15m)
The thin crack line to the same lower-off

CENTRAL HIGHLANDS

# Weem

56.62701 -3.895257

P 56.62476 -3.892602

## D SECRET GARDEN

A nice steep slab with an obvious deep roof on its right edge. From the car park near the Castle, follow the smaller path uphill into the woods. At the second zigzag, cut left, eventually skirting behind a walled garden. Just after this a faint path cuts uphill towards the crag.

**1** **100 Ways To Be A Good Girl** 6b+* (8m) The grey streaked line on the left, passing through three small overlaps

**2** **Batweeman** 6b* (10m) The left-facing corner and technical wall above is a good warm up

**3** **Forbidden Fruit** 6b+* (12m) Start just right of the arête, climb slopers to a ledge, and finish up the crux headwall

**4** **The Missing Link** 6c+* (20m) A worthwhile and sustained linkup of the first half of **5**, traversing diagonally left after the roof, to finish on the headwall of **3**

**5** **Faithless** 6c+** (15m) Starting at the toe of the crag, head leftwards to pull through the left end of the roof

**6** **The Watchtower** 6c+** (15m) Start as for **5**, then head slightly right to take the centre of the roof

**7** **Caledonia Dreaming** 6c* (15m) Follow a crack just left of the arête and swing spectacularly through the widest part of the roof

**8** **Don't Knock the Block** 6a+ (15m) Starting up the first bolt of **9**, step left onto the arête and follow it to a ledge. Step left above the roof to finish as for **7**

**9** **Brass Monkeys** 6b* (6m) A micro-route up the right wall of the crag - hard start

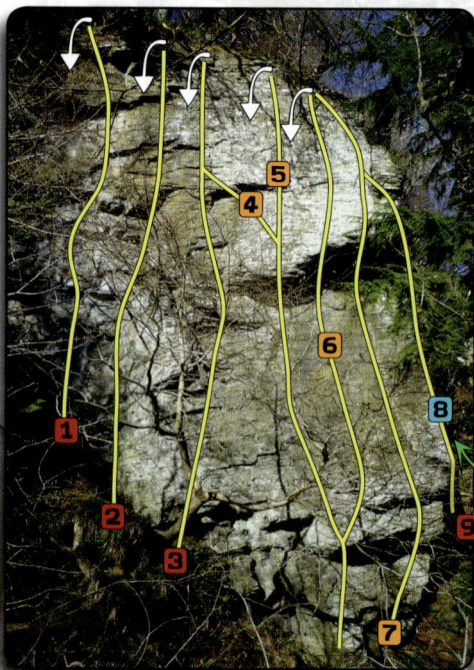

About 50m left of the Secret Garden, by small stream, lies **STREAM WALL** which contains one bolted line:

**Justice** 7a* (10m) Climb steeply to gain the hanging crack

## E MANYANA WALL

About 50m down and right from Secret Garden lies a small slabby buttress.

**10 Tomorrow Never Comes** 6b*
(12m) The right side of the arête, via a small overlap

**11 Sometime Soon** 6a* (12m)
Follow cracks to the V-notch and slab. Shares a lower-off with **10**

**12 Don't Do Today What You Can Do Tomorrow** 5+ (10m)
A slightly steeper line on the right

## F EASTER ISLAND

Slightly up and right (~20m) from Manyana Wall lies a small fin of rock with an abundance of bolts!

**13 Motion Sickness** 6c+*
(12m) Follow the left wall breaching the roof on its left to climb the steep wall above

**14 Left on the Shelf** 6c+*
(12m) Follow **13** but head to the ledge, then climb the steep wall above to the shared lower-off

**15 President Shhean Connery**
7a* (8m) Close to **14**, take a direct line past many bolts to the lower-off on **16**

**16 The Republic of Scotland**
7a+** (10m) Start close to the arête, pull onto the face and crimp up the centre of the wall

**17 Right in the Face** 6b**
(10m) A line up the right arête, stepping left to the lower-off of **16**

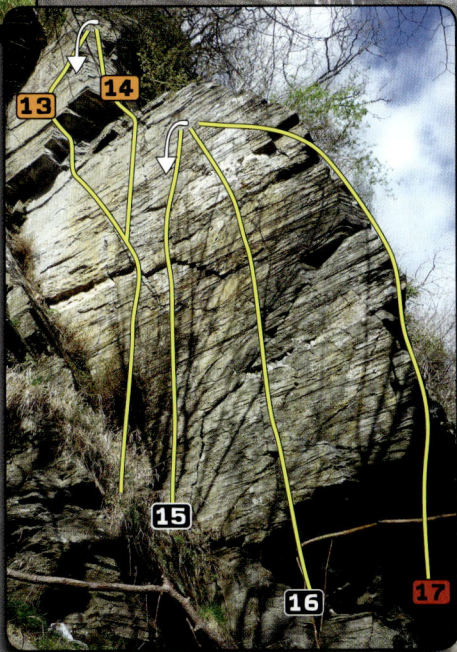

CENTRAL HIGHLANDS

# Dunira

56.39748 -4.038383

56.38846 -4.058114

A small but enjoyable schist crag overlooking Strath Earn. Worth the walk-in. Routes vary from cracklines to thin face climbing, often with a sting in the tail. Approach 2.6 miles from Comrie along the A85 (Bus #15a) and turn off at the road marked 'Dunira - Private'. Park considerately at the triangle by the cottages. Walk east towards Whitehouse but take the left 'Y' branch passing behind the houses. Shortly after this, cut up across a field. Back on the track continue for ~100m taking another track right over a bridge then immediately left steeply uphill into the forest. At its end, cross the stream leftward passing boulders to the crag.

⚠ There have been issues with parking on the estate so please follow instructions and be discreet!

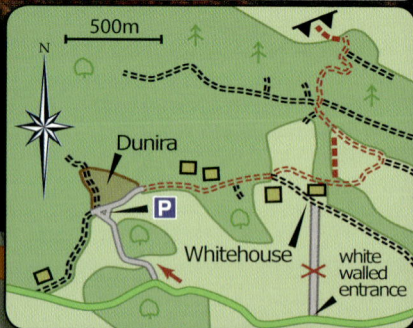

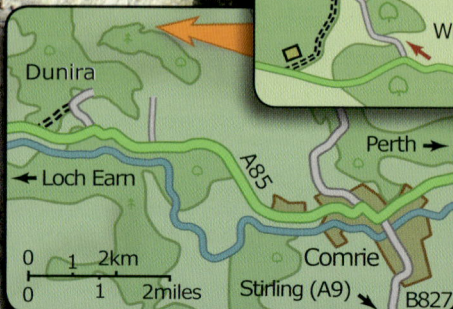

500m

N

Dunira

P

Whitehouse

white walled entrance

Dunira

← Loch Earn

A85

Perth →

Comrie

Stirling (A9)

B827

0    1    2km
0    1    2miles

**2  3  2  2  1**

30 mins  |  35 mins

1 **The Whitehouse** 6a+* (16m)
Gain the flake then traverse left to gain the right-slanting break

2 **Whitewash** 6b* (16m) A direct eliminate on tiny holds to reach the break of 1

3 **Twenty Shilling Woodworm** 6a* (16m) Start as for the previous routes and follow the large fault to the top

4 **George's Bush** 6a** (16m) Follow the fine flake-crack into the fault at half-height and finish as for 3

5 **Glen Bolt'achan Big Guns** 6c*** (16m) A fingery start and entertaining finish through the overlap

6 **The Fort Dundurn Gurner** 6c+** (16m) Crimp up to the flake and breach the roof rightwards at the crack

7 **Dunira or Die** 7a+** (16m) The right end of the face, with a crimpy start and a desperate crux at the roof. A hold may have been lost there since it was first etablished

8 **Dun Moanin'** 6b* (16m) Start in the crack then trend right to roofs

9 **Tullybanocher Tearoom** 5** (14m) The leftwards groove

10 **Strath Earn Shangri-La** 4+* (14m) Follow the right edge

CENTRAL HIGHLANDS

# Glen Lednock

56.39235 -4.008328

P 56.39367 -4.006140

The serene Glen Lednock is home to traditional climbing, bouldering and sport climbing. The crag was originally home to trad routes which were later retrobolted. The bolts were removed in 2007 but the trad climbs were largely ignored, so after consultation, the lines were rebolted by the SMC in 2012.

The cliff catches the morning sun, dries quickly, and offers great views with interesting and exposed climbing. Despite being well cleaned, care should be taken on some sections of rock, notably below the roof. Some routes need a 60m rope. Stay clear of any birds that nest on these crags.

On the A85 at the west end of Comrie is a junction on a sharp bend (phone box). Follow the sign for 'Glenlednock' through Monument Rd. Drive up the glen 1.9 miles where a footpath branching right is passed. Soon after this, park on a small area opposite the sign for the third passing place. (If you pass the 'Kindrochet Maam Road' sign you have gone too far). From here go up the short path to the bench, left up the track for 100m, and the crag is just up on the right.

**1 Zombie Nation** *5+*** (28m) Climb the arête of the left hand side of the crag. Mantel awkwardly and climb the wall above on the left

**2 Quidditch** *6a** (25m) Climb the wall and crack to the ramp. Pull through the steep wall to the right by a L/R handrail then pass the roof on the left. Bailing left via the ramp to finish up **1** gives **Clairvoyant** *5+* (28m)

**3 The Deil** *6b**** (25m) From the slanting groove, climb to the undercut flake above the ledge. Above this go up the steep groove to the capping triangular roof, which is climbed directly

**4 The Road to Hell** *5+*** (30m) Better than it sounds! Follow the groove to a slabby block. Pass this and follow the ramp to finish on **1**

**5 Cauldron of Fire** *6a+*** (25m) A nice route. Climb the lower section of wall which steepens to mantel onto the ledge under the overhang. Pull over the left edge of the overhang and slab above

**6 Black Magic** *6b+**** (25m) Climb the lower wall of **5** and the steep broken wall above on the right. The committing overhang is easier than first appears once the right holds are found! Climb the satisfying slab direct to the lower–off.

**7 Harry Snotter** *6c+** (25m) Follow the left hand bolts up the broken groove, and climb the black blocks rightwards to the niche in the overhang. Climb through this (a much harder crux since the 'Snotter' fell off) to the exposed slab above.

**8 Witch Hazel** *6a** (25m) Climb the right hand bolts up the broken groove and trend rightwards to the recess right of the overhang. Go leftward back onto the slab to the lower-off of **7**

**9 Resident Evil** *6a/b** is a half-girdle, starting up **Witch Hazel**, crawling along the hanging ramp, and finishing up either **Quiddich** (6a) or **The Deil** (6b)

5 mins

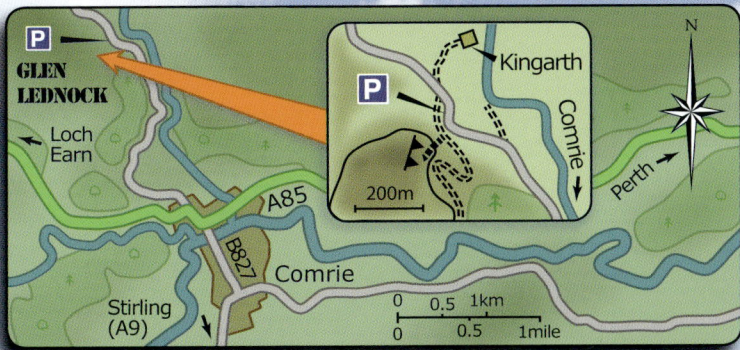

P

**GLEN LEDNOCK**

Loch Earn

Kingarth

P

Comrie

N

Perth

200m

A85

B827

Comrie

Stirling (A9)

| 0 | 0.5 | 1km |
| 0 | 0.5 | 1mile |

CENTRAL HIGHLANDS

# Strathyre

56.34348 -4.339452

**P** 56.34602 -4.336965

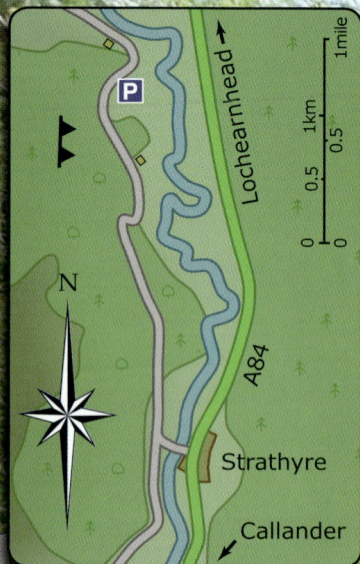

**1** **Electrodynamics** $7a$*** (10m)
The steeply overhanging prow is thankfully juggy

**2** **Bridging the Gap** $6c+$** (10m)
Strathyre's 'Quarryman'? The prominent groove requires a full set of technical contortions

**3** **Short Circuit** $6b$* (10m) The smaller right hand groove may be dirty

**4** **Clam Chowder** $7a$* (10m) The line of staples up a groove and via a small ledge at half-height

**5** **Crossed Wires** $6a+$ (12m) Start at the base of the grooves as for **3**, then follow the line of flakes right

The next section of wall holds six routes at 7b to 7c, including the local classic -
**6** **Static Discharge** 7b***, which climbs past the shield before finishing as for **5**.

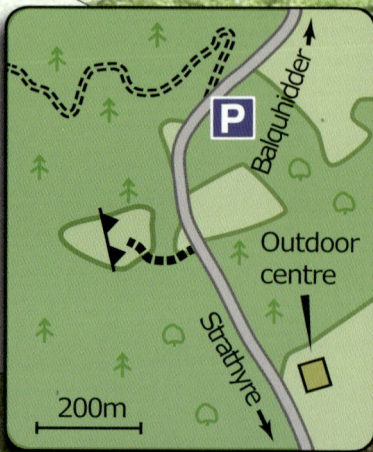

This short, steep crag of good quality mica schist lies on the wooded hillside above the village of Strathyre.

If driving take the A84 to Strathyre village and turn off opposite a hotel onto a single track road (signed NCN7 Balquhidder). This is part of the National Cycle Network. Cross the bridge and take the right hand fork. 0.4 miles past the outdoor centre, park opposite a forestry access road. Walk back down the road for 200m, cut uphill at a clearing and then bear right past a boulder to find the crag.

**LEFT WALL**

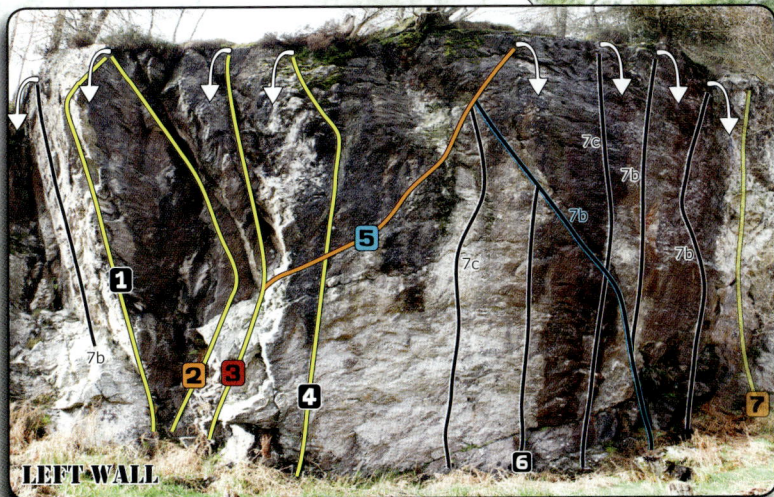

The next two routes start on a small pedestal under a short corner.

**7** **Power Surge** *6c** (10m) Starting at a pale streak, climb to a scoop and groove

**8** **Spark Thug** *6b** (10m) From the platform, climb the corner to the slab

To the right of the main crag there is a smaller wall containing two routes.

**9** **Circuit Bored** *6c* (7m) Start on wavy holds and head up rightwards to a shared lower-off

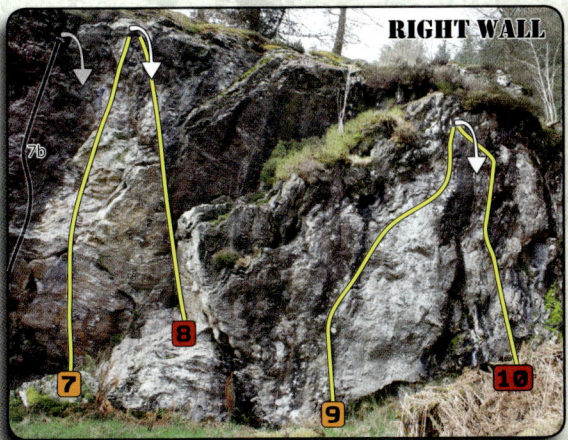

**10** **Bloody Shocking** *6b* (6m) Start at a broken flake and climb the shallow groove

**RIGHT WALL**

# Bennybeg

56.34868 -3.841155
56.34838 -3.843762

A sunny, accessible area, popular with beginners and groups. Bennybeg provides a good selection of short, vertical routes on amenable, blocky dolerite. Beginners may find some of the holds disconcertingly slopey, but it's good for your footwork! All routes may be topped out and top-ropes can be easily set up from above.

Approach from either Stirling or Perth along the A9 and follow signs for Crieff (A822). One mile after Muthill, the Benny Beg Smithy and Ceramic Experience (has a cafe) are found on the right. Turn off about 50m further towards Crieff to park in a small rough area immediately at the end of the crag. Bus #47 runs between Crieff and Stirling, and stops by the ceramic centre.

19 9 0 0 0

2 mins | 2 mins

# LEFT SIDE

The first face encountered from the approach. The short wall to the far left may provide some warm-up bouldering. There is one route which stands alone, to the left of the tree.

**1** **Route Minus One,** $3+$ (6m)
Climb the wide stepped crack

The rest of the routes lie in the cleaner central section, starting about 5m right of the tree.

**2** **Route Zero** $4+$ (10m) A meandering crack leads to a ledge and a hanging V-notch

**3** **Bill and Benny the Flower Pot Men** $3$ (10m) A blocky crackline, prone to seepage

**4** **Benydorm** $5*$ (10m) The crackline holds plentiful good jugs and sidepulls. Worthwhile, although obvious climbing

**5** **Driven Round the Benny'd** $5+*$ (10m) A pleasantly technical and sometimes crimpy excursion up the clean face

**6** **Benny and the Banshees** $4*$ (10m) The cracked groove is more interesting than it looks - the holds may not face the way you want them to!

**7** **Benny Hill** $5+*$ (10m) Climb the wall on rounded holds. The crux is passing through the small overhang, without a jug to spoil the fun!

**8** **United Colours of Bennyton** $3*$ (10m) The deep chimney provides good large holds, entertaining thrutching, and even a fist jam

**9** **Scorchio!** $5*$ (10m) The faint crack leads with interest through a deep niche to a lower-off or belay on the ledge

**10** **Route Eight** $4*$ (8m) Follow the crack to the break, then trend left onto the face to avoid the vegetated groove

**11** **Benny Goodman - King of Swing** $5**$ (20m) Pick a quiet day to crown yourself on this fun traverse. Start up **8** to the upper break and follow it up left to finish up **3**

CENTRAL HIGHLANDS

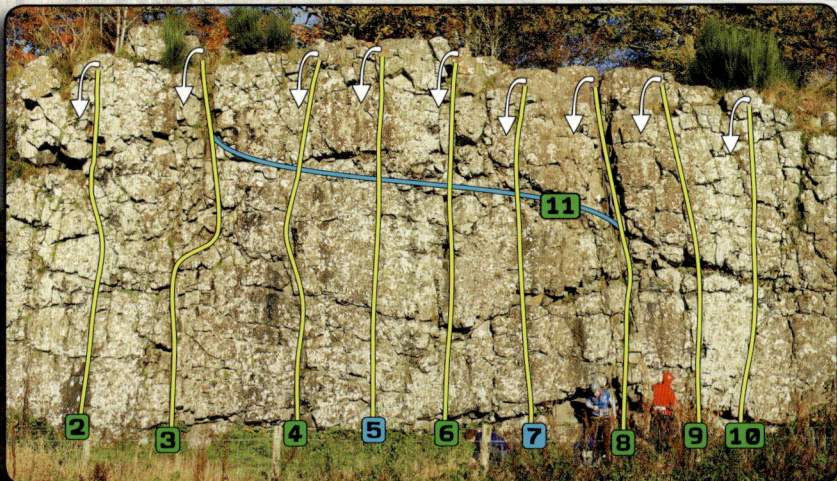

# Bennybeg

## RIGHT SIDE

At the left end of this face there is a stepped groove, left of the arête: **Benny's Groove** (2). Right of this is the first route proper.

**1** **Beggars Belief** $4$* (10m)
Broken green cracks right of the arête

**2** **New Beginning** $5$ (12m) 10m right of the previous route. Easily to the first break, some trickier moves to reach the second, then romp to the finish

**3** **Beguile** $5$* (12m) Climb the crack to the ledge and finish up the short face (crux), swerving briefly left

**4** **The Spanner** $5$* (12m) Start just to the left of the dark streak, and join the next line at the mid-height break

**5** **Benny's Black Streak** $5$+** (12m) A fine climb up the dark face, keeping to the right of a small tree and a vegetated crack

**6** **Lady Willoughby** $4$** (12m) Start at the curving break and climb to a left facing corner. Prone to seepage

**7** **Beg to Differ** $5$+* (12m) Follow the faint S-crack through the dark plaque to the twin cracks, and directly up these to the dead tree

**8** **Beg'tastic** $5$* (12m) Climb to a small point, then follow the zigzag crack on hidden jugs to finish right of the tree

**9** **Benny Lane** $6a$* (10m) Left of the wide crack, climb the face on small flat, spaced holds. When the crack leads left, continue straight up on smaller holds

**10** **Ally's in Wonderland** 3+** (10m) The obvious wide crack to a tree

**11** **The Beg Issue** 4+* (10m) Start right of the wide crack, pass the scoop, and then follow the cracks rightward on the upper face to the boulder

**12** **The Beggar** 6a* (10m) Start at a low protruding block, and climb on small flat holds and occasional jugs, to the boulder

**13** **Beggar's Banquet** 6a* (10m) Follow the faint crack through the bulge to the left hand lower-off. The climbing is steady, and easy for the grade once you find the hidden jugs

**14** **The Smiddy** 6a* (8m) The blocky crack leads to an interesting, thin finish

**15** **Begone** 5* (8m) The meandering cracks lead left to the shared lower-off

**16** **Beg Pardon** 5+** (30m) A bit anti-social, but a good outing. Start up **2** to its second bolt, traverse right via a lone bolt in the central area and continue to the last bolt and finish of **14**

Liza getting her teeth into
**Benny and the Banshees** (4)
photo: Lasma Sietinsone

# Dunkeld

56.57633 -3.599274

56.57519 -3.591448

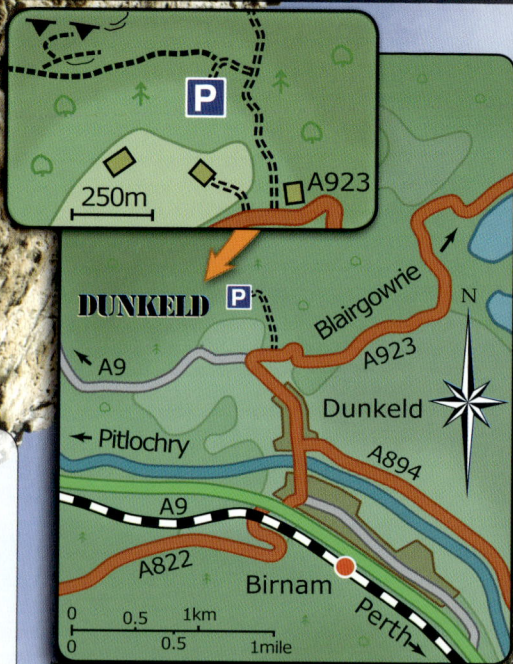

250m

A923

DUNKELD

Blairgowrie

A9

A923

Dunkeld

← Pitlochry

A894

N

A9

A822

Birnam

Perth

0    0.5    1km

0         0.5         1mile

Whilst all the routes on the main section of Upper Cave Crag are outwith the stated grade range of this guide, they are included due to their popularity and significance within Scottish sport climbing. All are steep endurance test-pieces on high quality sculpted schist.

Approach from Dunkeld (off the A9 or from the train station 1.7 miles away), passing directly through the town and taking the first turning on the right, then second left up a dirt road. Park and follow the trail up left through the forest. After a fallen tree look for a path that doubles back rightward. A few meters along this a faint track heads steeply uphill, across a small stream, to the crags.

6   7        8        9

10 mins    20 mins

# UPPER CAVE CRAG

The main crag holds a selection of high quality hard trad routes, but in the middle of the face is a steep prow that sports several bolted lines. The rock overhangs steadily such that it is generally climbable even in heavy rain, although your belayer may suffer from drainage off the top!

**1** **Marlina** 7c*** (20m) The most popular sport route in Scotland? After a difficult start (often stick-clipped) head up rightwards to a diagonal crack. Follow this leftwards (crux) to the lower-off shared with **2**

**2** **Ultima Necat** 7b** (20m) Start up **1** to the 4th bolt then step left and strike directly up for the shared lower-off. **Ultima Direct** (7b+) adds an independant start to the left on the lower wall

**3** **Hamish Teddy's Excellent Adventure** 7b+*** (25m) Start as **1** as far as the crack, then continue rightwards on slopers to finish up the arête

**4** **Silk Purse** 7c+*** (25m) Start up the right bolt line on small edges, to reach the base of the Marlina crack. Follow this for a few metres before heading directly up a scoop on sloping sidepulls to a lower-off under the roof

**5** **Silk Teddies** 7c** (25m) Start as for **4** but climb directly to the arête avoiding the crack, and finish as for Hamish Ted's

# SINNER'S WALL

This small face can be found up left of the approach path. The rock and climbing don't nearly match the main crag but can be a useful warm-up area.

**6** **Sinner's Paradise** 7a* (8m) Directly up the steep left prow

**7** **Six Fours les-Plage** 6b Start up the groove then left on sharp flakes to pull through the overlap

**8** **Fear of the Dark** 6b (8m) Just right of the groove. Make bouldery moves into the brief right facing corner and easier climbing above

**9** **Father Figure** 6b+ (8m) Boulder through the initial overhang then up the face

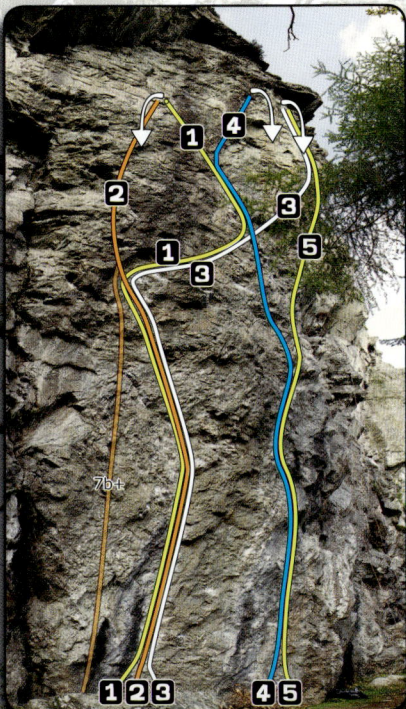

CENTRAL HIGHLANDS

# Rockdust

56.75877 -3.587118

56.75528 -3.595991

On the slopes of Creag an t-Sithein in Glen Brerachan, Rockdust, with both trad and sport routes, has a somewhat 'mountain crag' feel. The cliff is made of compact schist, lending itself to slopers and tiny edges. There is unstable rock, particularly at the top, so helmets are advised.

From Pitlochry, take the A924 (Blairgowrie) for 8 miles. A ½ mile after a small bridge over the river Tarvie, a layby below the SEER centre is found; park at the bottom of this, clear of the entrance. Go through the gate and traverse up slopes toward the telephone mast, crossing walls and fences with care. The lower tier is found first, from where a steep path leads rightwards to the upper tier, which is often nicely sheltered from the wind!

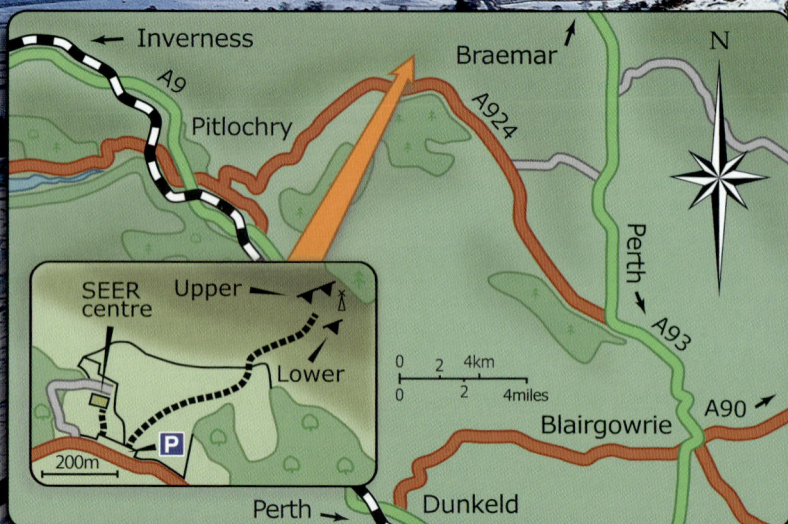

Inverness ←
A9
Pitlochry
Braemar
A924
Perth
A93
N
A90 ↗
Blairgowrie
Dunkeld
Perth →

SEER centre
Upper
Lower
P
200m

0   2   4km
0       2       4miles

20 mins

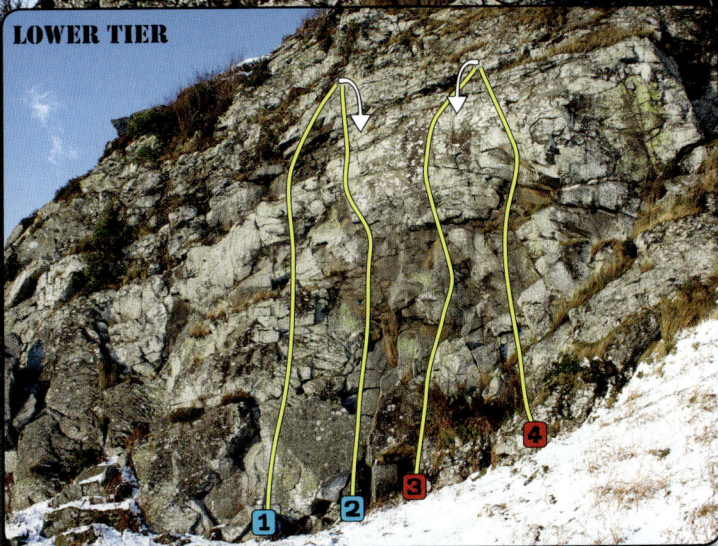

LOWER TIER

Falcons sometimes nest on these crags and should not be disturbed. Please check the situation in spring-summer with the MCofS (p15)

The crag is named after the main product of the **SEER** (Sustainable Ecological Earth Regeneration) Centre, located close to the parking area. Rockdust is finely ground, untreated volcanic rock, that provides multiple mineral supplements to soil. It provides a promising alternative to nitrogenous fertiliser, as well as accelerating composting. The centre can be visited during April - October.

## LOWER TIER

The first part of the crag to become visible. Also contains 7 trad routes from HVS to E4. Routes tend to start easily and have a short technical crux on the upper slab.

**1** **Millennium Madness** *5+*** (16m)
A pleasant route on surprisingly positive holds

**2** **Virtual Life** *6a+** (16m) Another fun line that is steeper than you might expect

**3** **Sending the Wrong Signal** *6b*** (12m) The crux gaining the slab is short-lived

**4** **Cat Scratch Fever** *6b** (12m)
An abrasive journey! Try to avoid the 'cheat' step off to the right at the crux

# Rockdust

Chad enjoying the sun on
**Gimme Shelter** (6a)

# UPPER TIER

**1 Downshifting** $6c$ (12m) A viciously crimpy number up the left side of the low overhang with hidden edges, finishing up an easier slab

**2 Twilight Shift** $6c$ (12m) The right side of the low overhang has more obvious holds. Finish up the slab to the same lower-off as **1**

**3 Rubrique** $5+$ (18m) Climb the obvious central arête, and break right at the top to cross the groove and finish up a short headwall

**4 Cabaret** $6b+$ (18m) A slightly eliminate route immediately right of the dirty groove, starting up the blunt arête. Finish as for **3**

**5 21st Century Citizen** $6b+$** (20m) Follow the groove through the triangular overhang just right of **4**. At the ledge find the juggy handrail that leads up right to the lower-off

**6 Moulin Rouge** $6c$* (20m) Start up the corner then make powerful moves on the steep wall, to finish up the arête on sloping holds

**7 Quiet Revolution** $6a+$* (20m) Follow the faint ramp to the v-notch in the small roof. Pull through this on good holds and finish up left

**8 French Onion Soup** $6a$* (14m) Climb the slab, and pass the roof to the right on jugs to a lower-off at the rose bush

**9 Gimme Shelter** $6a$** (14m) Pull onto the face just left of the chimney. Pleasant balancy climbing up the slab

**10 Egyptiana Jones** 6a* (20m) Climb **9** until it is possible to step across the ledge to finish high on the right face

**11 Wandering Minstrel** $6c+$* (8m) A short crimpy route up the small tower right of the chimney (Only 6c if climbed on the right side)

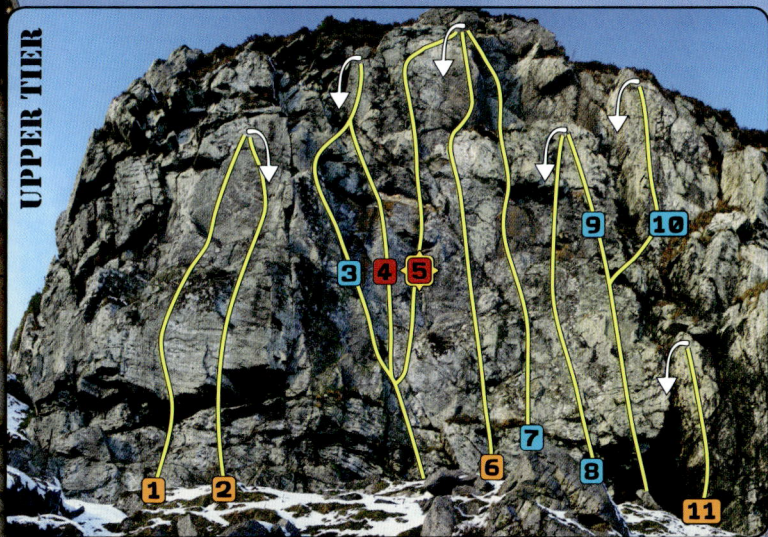

UPPER TIER

# ANGUS AND NORTHEAST

The birthplace of Scottish sport climbing was in the Angus quarries during the early 1980s. Since the arrival of the first sport routes at Legaston, developments have continued unabated and the county remains the principal Scottish sport climbing area. Lying in the rain shadow of the Caringorm Mountains to the west, the northeast coastal region is one of Scotland's driest and warmest areas, covered in rich farmland and dotted with small fishing towns.

The atmospheric Mermaid's Kirk at Arbroath, with the line of **Diagon Alley** rising out of the cave on the left wall, and Warship Wall on the far right (p167)

The sport climbing crags in Angus are largely sandstone or conglomerate, although further north in Aberdeenshire schist and granite climbing can be found. The region's venues provide something for all, with crags ranging from friendly and easily accessible quarries, to more adventurous and exposed sea-cliffs. Many venues can be climbed year round making some crags quite popular. The infamous sea fog, locally known as the 'haar', can affect coastal areas after a period of warm weather. In such conditions the sea-cliffs can become greasy and unpleasant to climb, while sunnier skies may often be found just a little way further inland.

Cruden Bay

Huntly

**LONGHAVEN** p.140

A95

A97

A9

Grantown-on-Spey

A96

A90

A939

A944

**Aberdeen**

**CAMBUS O' MAY** p.138

Banchory

N

A93

Ballater

Braemar

The Cairngorms

Stonehaven

A957

**ABERDEEN CRAGS** p.142

**KIRRIEMUIR** p.176

**ROB'S REED** p.186

Montrose

A90

A92

**ELEPHANT ROCK** p.154

A9

A924

**LEY** p.200

Pitlochry

A926

Forfar

**LEGASTON** p.194

Blairgowrie

A94

**RED HEAD** p.208

Dunkeld

A93

A933

**ARBROATH** p.158

C. Angus

A923

Arbroath

**Perth**

A90

**Dundee**

**BALMASHANNER** p.200

A85

A9

M90

A92

A91

St. Andrews

0   10   20km
0        10        20miles

**ANGUS & NORTHEAST**

# Cambus O' May

57.07500 -2.996087
57.07000 -2.985262

The left-hand quarry at Cambus O' May offers some enjoyable, slabby climbing on clean granite. The quarry has routes on three sides, but only the east face is described. The short routes on the west face are (L/R): 4+ (**Scuffer**), 7b, 7c*,7b*, 7b+*** (**Idiot Savant**) and 7a+ (**Sticks 'n' Stones**). The scrappy vegetated climbs on the north face are (L/R): 5, 5+, 6a, 6b+, 5+, 5+.

2.4 miles on the Aberdeen side of Ballater (A93) park as for the Cambus O' May forest walks near the Crannach Cafe. Bus 201 (Banchory-Ballater) stops just opposite. Follow the path past two gates, passing under powerlines before trending right at the split to find the quarry.

Please respect a climbing ban at the right-hand quarry due to protected birds.

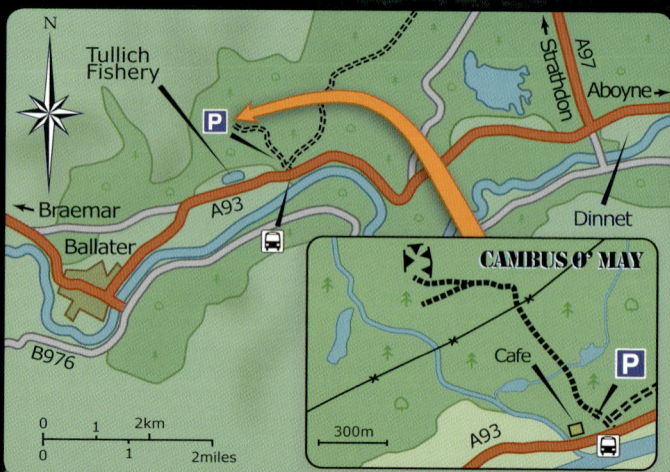

7b**
7b+*
1
2

**10 mins**  **15 mins**

**3 10 2 2 3**

**1** **Sun City** 7a+** (22m) Directly up the main wall on incut edges and drilled pockets

**2** **Welcome to the Working Weak** 7a (22m) The sustained crack and flakes right of the corner. Check the condition of the bolts

**3** **Indian Summer** 6c+ (15m) Start up the thin crack then head to the left of the large flake, and finish up the face

**4** **Sharp Practice** 6a*** (15m) Climb the enjoyable flake, stand on top, then finish delicately right up the face - a good route

**5** **Technical Merit** 6c+* (15m) Make a long reach up the face to gain the arête. Follow this before stepping left to the shared lower-off

Photo - Stuart Stronach

Further right a large ledge with an *in-situ* tree splits the face. The first three routes lie below the ledge, and can be linked with routes on the upper tier at no grade change.

**6** **Bonsai** 6a (6m) A small route leading directly up to the tree

**7** **Wimpy Construction** 6a+ (6m) The central line on the lower tier

**8** **Wind in The Willows** 6b* (6m) The rightmost line on the lower face to a shared lower-off

**9** **Viral Infection** 5+ (6m) The left route on the upper tier, start just left of the tree

**10** **Stump** 5+ (6m) Start at the tree and trend rightward

The last two routes lie right of a small step-down in the ledge.

**11** **Quality Street** 6a+** (10m) Start directly then trend left, with a high crux and spaced bolts

**12** **Roses** 5* (8m) The rightmost route on the face contains pleasant climbing to a single-bolt lower-off

**ANGUS & NORTHEAST**

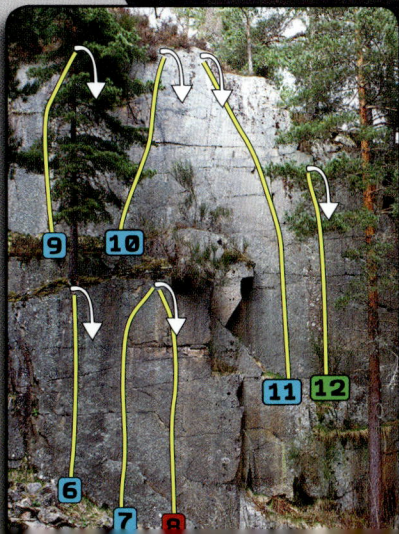

# Longhaven

57.44698 -1.799183

57.44495 -1.810390

A good addition of mid-grade routes in two quarries on the coast just south of Peterhead at the Longhaven nature reserve. **NORTH GLASH** comprises of two opposing slabby walls of clean red granite. It is quite sheltered and the upper portion of Revision Slab gets the evening sun. Route names are indicated with painted pebbles, how continental!

Nearby is **RED WALL QUARRY**, known for its hard lines. There are however a few easier routes there worth visiting in combination with North Glash, or the nearby trad areas. The routes tend to be technical and sustained and the crag gets the morning sun.

250m north of Longhaven (Bus stop by post office) on the A90 there is large slipway onto a wide track towards the coast. 400m down this is a Scottish Wildlife Trust car park near a ruined cottage, and the start of the coastal path. For **North Glash**, walk north along the scenic cliff tops to the obvious deep inlet of South Glash about 750m from the car park. The rim of the quarry is just round the end of this. Walk along the inland side of the quarry and a cairn or bit of old fence mark the scramble down into the quarry.

## NORTH GLASH
## BROKE BACK WALL

**1** **Brace Yersel** *6c+** (10m) Start in the shallow groove, make thin moves by the 2nd bolt to continue more easily via an undercling to the rail. Finish right

**2** **Up 'n' Aboot** *6b*** (10m) A sustained route straight up the middle of the wall. A mantel is followed by the thin wall above with a spicy finish to the lower-off

**3** **Crack 'n' Up** *5+** (10m) On the right, climb following the crack to the LO on the left. (Staying well to the left of the bolts, particularly the 3rd, gives **Roon the Bend**, an eliminate 6a+)

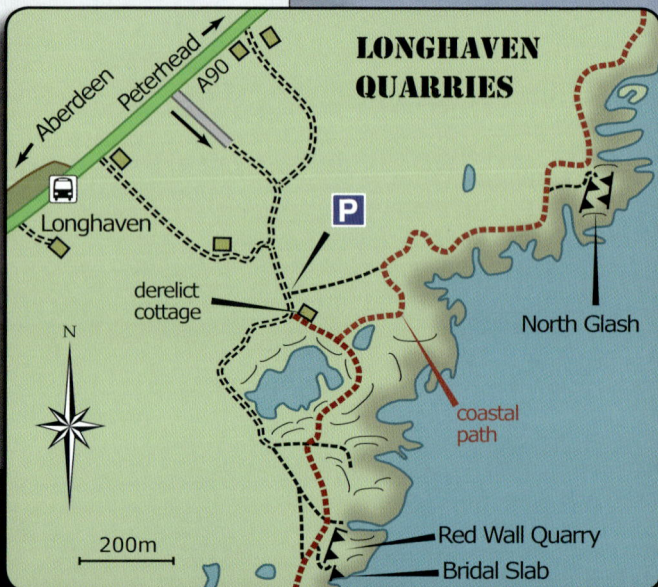

**LONGHAVEN QUARRIES**

Aberdeen

Peterhead

A90

Longhaven

P

derelict cottage

North Glash

coastal path

N

Red Wall Quarry

Bridal Slab

200m

6a+

6a+

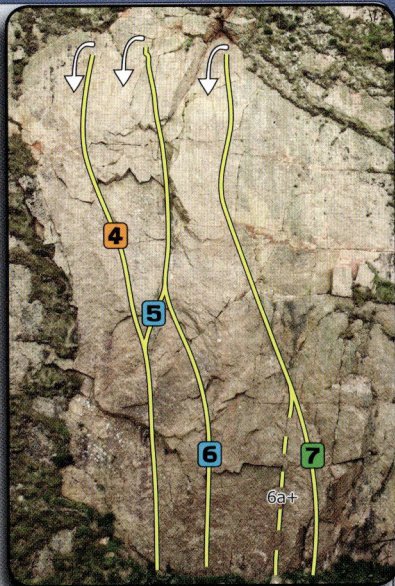

# REVISION SLAB

**4** **AWOL** *6c** (16m) The far left route, avoid going into **5** near a crux between 3rd and 4th bolt. Low in the grade

**5** **A Little Bit Irish** *6a** (16m) Climb AWOL past the overlap and go right after the 3rd bolt to the corner of **6**

**6** **Resit** *6a+*** (16m) Start just left of the first bolt, pass a tricky move at the second, trending left to gain a shallow corner

**7** **In the Army Now** *5** (16m) A thin start leads to a juggy continuation. A direct start to the left is 6a+

# RED WALL QUARRY

Park as for North Glash. Follow the main track as it twists down into a large gravel expanse. At the far side of this, cross the fence and take the right hand of two less distinct tracks. Follow this for a couple of minutes until a post becomes visible over on the cliff edge to the left (shortly before the track merges with another coming from the left). This post marks the start of an exposed scramble down a ramp into the quarry (10min).

The left most Back Wall routes are:

**8** **Joker** *6c** (12m) On the right of a thin crack to an undercut flake at the 2nd bolt, continue up the thin crack above to the LO

**9** **Harley Quinn** *7a** (12m ) Start as for Joker but move right just before the undercut flake (avoided), then join the upper crack of **Jester** (7b*) - clipstick useful

Just right of the Back Wall and corner:

**10** **Diamond in the Rough** *6c** (9m) The small right-facing corner pulling into a left facing niche, then exit rightwards onto the slab and lower-off above

To the south and at a lower level, but facing the same way as Back Wall is the triangular **Bridal Slab**.

**11** **Kingdom of Granite** *7a+* * (22m) Start up the V-groove, bridge to gain the slab. Follow flakes to the overlap and a ledge. Climb the tricky wall above

ANGUS & NORTHEAST

# Aberdeen Sea Cliffs

Along the coast south of Aberdeen, by the villages of Newtonhill and Portlethen, is a complex cluster of deep coves and bays concealing old fishing communities, deep geos and cave-riddled crags. There is a good mix of trad, sport and bouldering to be found here. Fun for all!

Sea birds can affect some of these crags in the spring and summer.

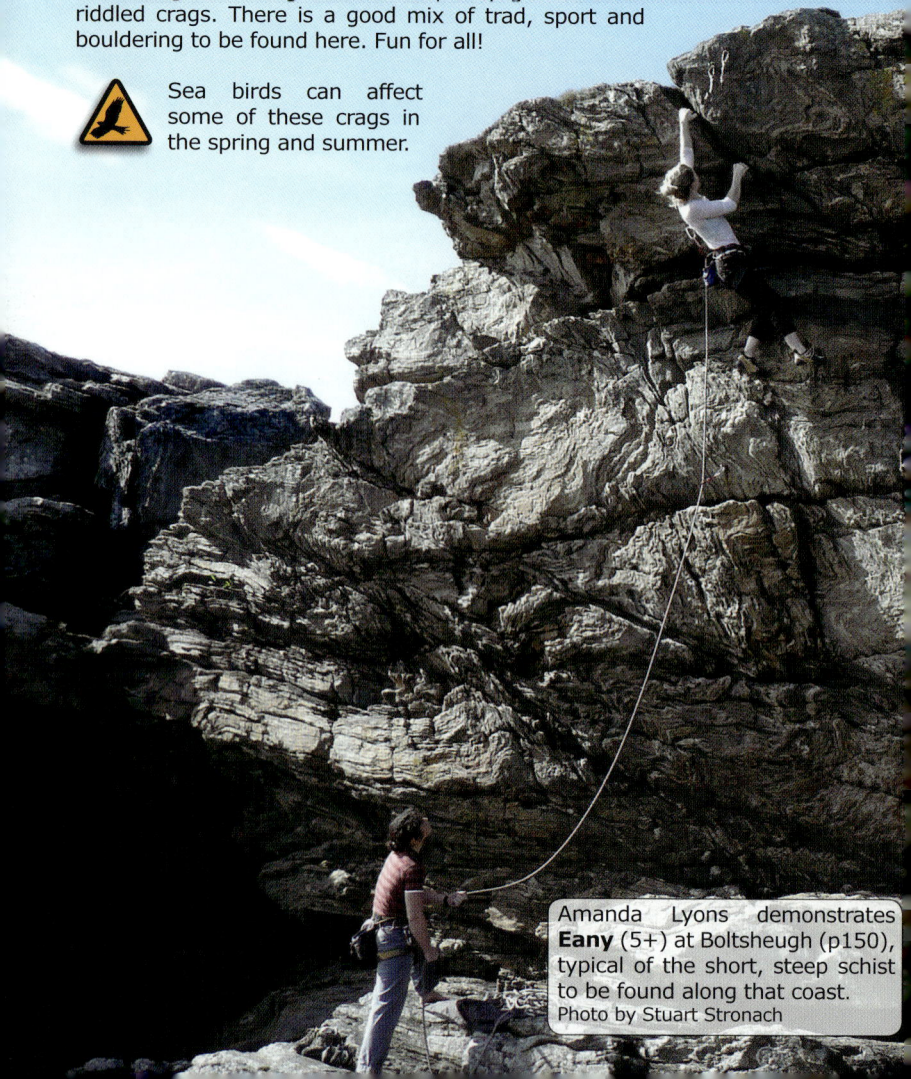

Amanda Lyons demonstrates **Eany** (5+) at Boltsheugh (p150), typical of the short, steep schist to be found along that coast.
Photo by Stuart Stronach

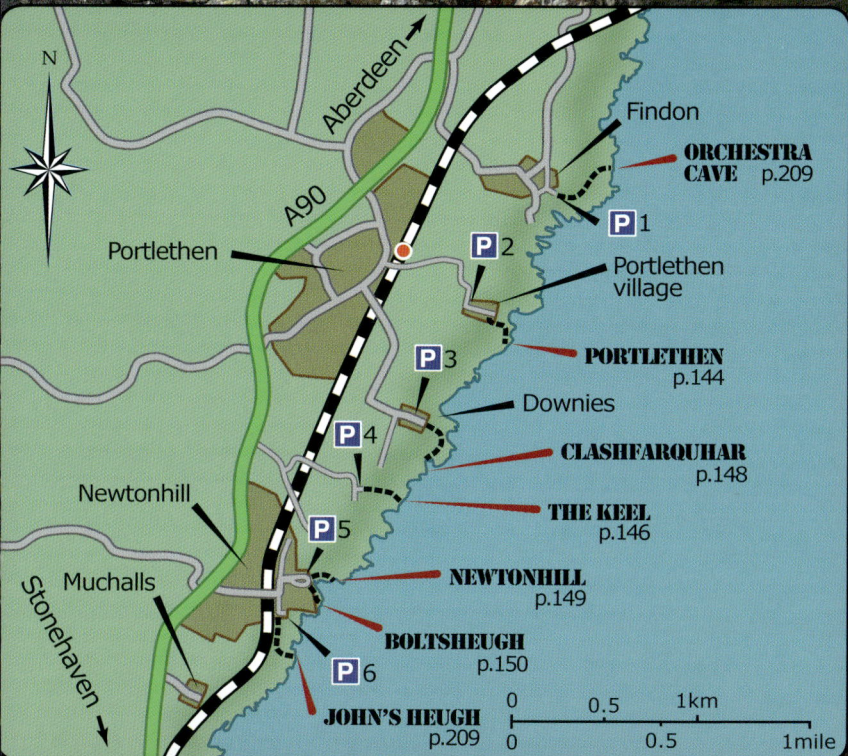

N

Aberdeen

A90

Portlethen

Newtonhill

Muchalls

Stonehaven

Findon

**ORCHESTRA
CAVE** p.209

P 1

P 2

Portlethen
village

**PORTLETHEN**
p.144

P 3

Downies

P 4

**CLASHFARQUHAR**
p.148

**THE KEEL**
p.146

P 5

**NEWTONHILL**
p.149

**BOLTSHEUGH**
p.150

P 6

**JOHN'S HEUGH**
p.209

ANGUS & NORTHEAST

| 0 | 0.5 | 1km |
| 0 | 0.5 | 1mile |

# Portlethen

57.05495 -2.111363

57.05700 -2.116331

Also called Sportlethen, the crag is only a little higher than its popular neighbouring boulders. However, what it lacks in height it more than makes up for in gradient. The routes here are short and sharp (literally!) and some my even be soloed with bouldering mats. The outlook by the sea is pleasant and you may be lucky to see pods of porpoises swim by.

From the A90 turn into Portlethen. From the centre follow signs for Portlethen village and park at the top near the Neuk Bar (P2). Do not park at the bottom as it is easy to block entrances in the small streets. Walk a short way down the village road. The last possible right turn goes into a small cul-de-sac. At the back of this, take an alley way bounded by concrete brick walls left round a house and to the coast. Cross the stile and after 50m trend left and follow a faint path down a south-facing ramp to the crag.

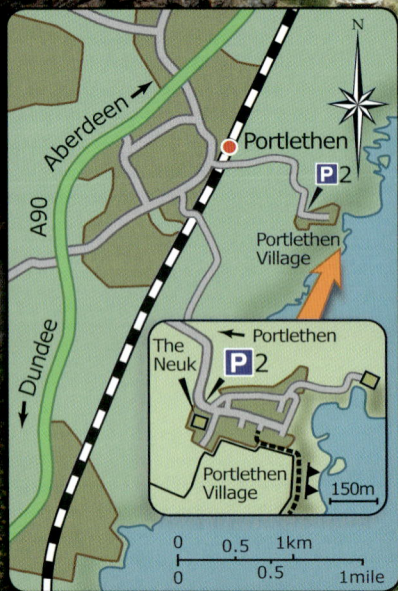

Aberdeen

A90

Dundee

N

Portlethen

P2

Portlethen
Village

Portlethen

The
Neuk

P2

Portlethen
Village

150m

| 0 | 0.5 | 1km |
| 0 | 0.5 | 1mile |

10 mins · 15 mins

**1 1 0 1 3**

The stand-alone route climbing through the lichenous roof to the left of the main wall is **The Incredible Sulk** 7b.

**1 Bosch** 7a (8m) Pre-clip the first bolt of **2**, traverse along the sloping rail, pull up to the second bolt then trend right to finish as for **The Portlethen Terrier**

**2 Hilti** 6c+ (6m) Clip-stick the first bolt. Climb the left/right crack using bolts of **1** to easier wall above and an extra bolt

The left side of the overhang, sharing a start with **3** is **Stigmata** 7b*

**3 Dogs Abuse** 7a+ (9m) Weaves diagonally left to right, starting up **Stigmata** to the ledge, then hand traversing right and finishing up **4**

The central, steepest line is **The Portlethen Terrier** 7c+** or start as for **The Lurcher** to hand-traverse the stamina-fest of **Dogs of War** 7c*

**4 The Lurcher** 7a* (7m) Climb the arête via a steep start to its end then trend back right to the lower-off of **5**

**5 Long Dogs** 6a+ (7m) Climb the wall direct keeping the second bolt to your left and climbing the wall above to the lower-off

**6 Collie Corner** 5 (7m) Bridge up the obvious corner to the lower-off

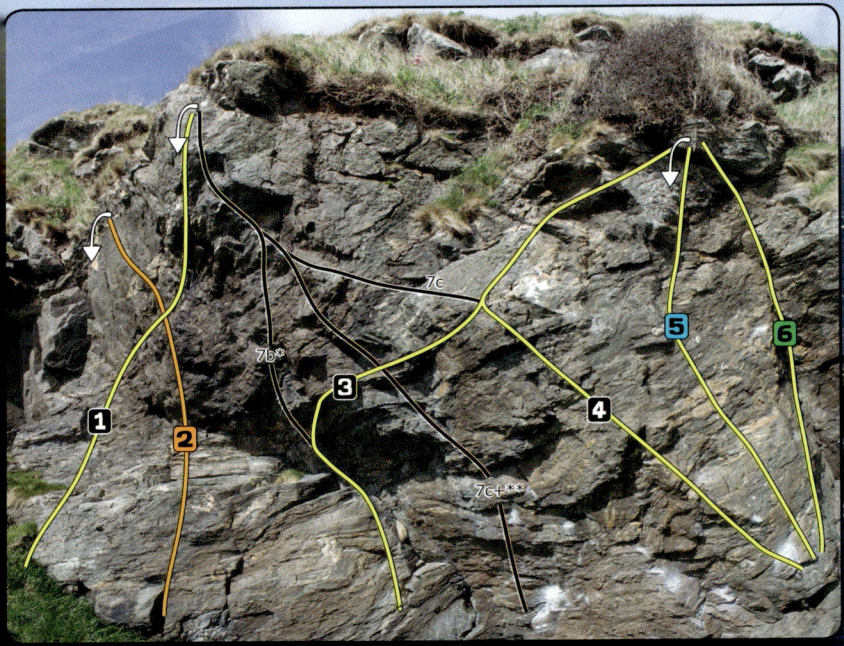

ANGUS & NORTHEAST

# The Keel

57.03924 -2.129473
57.04062 -2.13511(

A short coastal schist crag comprising of two walls, one so steep it's more akin to a ship's bow than keel! This wall's flakey jugs and crimps may not always be entirely reliable, so take care. Facing NE, the cliff is slow to dry and may not be in condition in winter.

The first routes are found on the very steep left wall of the inlet, which may often be greasy due to shade, but may equally be climbable in the rain!

**1** **Makosi** *6b+*\* (12m) The left-most line is steep but juggy. Start by a block and pull straight up to the lower off

**2** **Titanic** *6c+*\*\* (12m) So named as you could be climbing the ships bow! Follow a rightward rising traverse mostly on flakes

The blunt central arête with staples is the eponymous **Keel** *7b*\*\*, and then **The Closer** *7c* to its right.

**3** **Span-Utan** *7a*\* (8m) The line between the main wall and the backwall. Follow the 'C' shaped crack to a ledge then the overhanging wall to the lower-off. Or swing left on big holds to the finish of **The Keel** (same grade)

The next routes lie on the less steep back wall of the inlet, which receives more sun. There is often seepage between routes **4** and **5** but the climbing is not affected.

**4** **The Smile Child** *6c*\* (12m) A juggy but steep outing straight up the left side of the back wall. Often dirty

**5** **Lewbee Doobie** *7a+*\* (12m) Start on the left side of the big niche, climb through two roofs, then hand traverse right to join a crack and wall

**6** **Superlew** *7a*\*\* (10m) A nice route following the faint crack straight up the right hand side of the back wall. Sustained

Please do not disturb the raven's nest at the top of Titanic / The Keel if it is occupied!

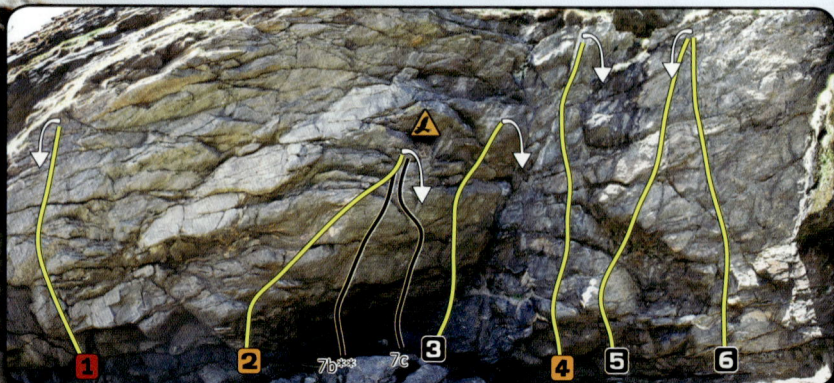

From the A90, take the single-track road signposted East Cammachmore 1 mile north of Newtonhill or 1.4 miles south of Portlethen. Follow this past houses until a hidden left turn before the railway (sign for 'Backburn'). Follow this over the railway and continue to reach the end of the road at Cobbleboards Farm (P4). **Ask for permission** to park here to maintain good relations with the farmer. From the farm head straight down the field to the coast to arrive just south of a stream. The closest train is Portlethen (1.5 miles). From Portlethen Academy, walk or cycle down Downies Road, turn left in the village and follow the single-track to the house, from where a gated track leads onward to the stream and farm. The Keel is also easily approached from **Clashfarquar**.

The climbs are non-tidal but the approach is effected. At low-mid tide descend the headland on the south of the inlet and cut back in to the the main wall. At high tide descend the north ridge and scramble down the last 10m to the beach (hidden knotted rope for safety, please tidy away carefully after use).

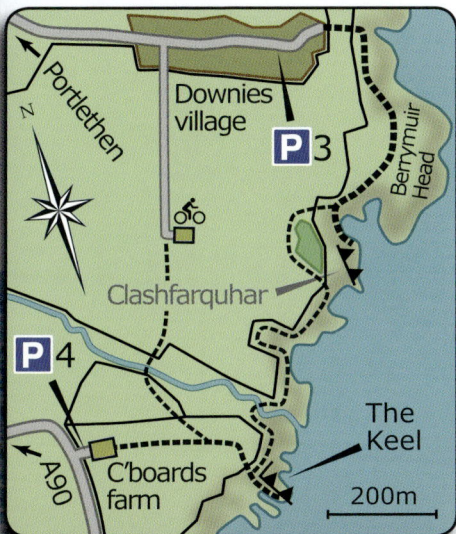

ANGUS & NORTHEAST

Rory Brown hauling on the jugs of **Makosi** (6b+). photo - Stuart Stronach

# Clashfarquhar

15 mins    25 mins

One of the tallest sport crags on the coast, but the schist only catches the sun during the morning. Although not as steep as its neighbour the Keel, it is less juggy. The surrounding rock offers bouldering and trad lines.

From the A90, turn into Portlethen via Bruntland Road. Take the turning for Downies and park considerately in the village taking care not to block any entrances (P3). It is a 10min cycle from Portlethen train station to the parking area. From the bottom of the village walk towards the coast and follow the faint path south until the cliff on the south side of Clashfarquhar bay appears (15min). It is also easily approached from the **Keel**. At the lone rock beside the path drop down the slope to the bay. The sport crag is landward of the platform. **The cliff is non-tidal but access is only possible at low to medium tide.**

Nesting sea birds can affect this crag in summer months

57.04260 -2.124951

57.04658 -2.123363

There are many sharp edges at the top of the routes. For the sake of your ropes it is advisable to thread the rings and abseil down, rather than lowering off.

**1 Toll Route** 6b+* (15m) The left-most line. Start as for **2** and go leftwards. Make a tricky move to gain the ledge and then head straight up

**2 Pay and Display** 6a* (17m) Follow the crack and groove to the top

**3 Sweet Charity** 7a* (18m) After the third bolt of **2** go right to climb the steep bulge and fine arête above

**4 Black from the Brink** 7a** (18m) Start up the niche just left of the corner to the ledge. Climb over the two steep walls pulling into the slab to finish as for **3**

The classic **Spice of Life** 7b+*** continues rightwards just before the last bolt of the previous route

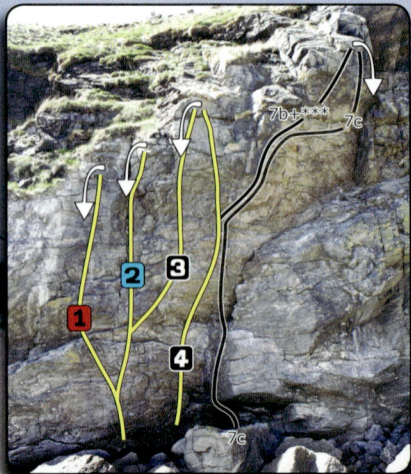

# Newtonhill

15 mins    25 mins

57.032581 -2.141012    57.03174 -2.144193

This recently developed crag (2011) lies on the northern side of Newtonhill Bay. The crag has some brittle rock, and suffers from seepage in winter, but is steep enough to avoid summer rain. Although not extensive, its worth combining with a visit to Boltsheugh.

Turn off the A90 signed for Newtonhill, cross the railway and follow the road downhill to the benches overlooking the cove (P5). Bus #7 runs from Aberdeen to Newtonhill via Portlethen, where there is also a rail station, although the cycle route requires sections of the A90. From the parking take the steps north down to the beach and the northern edge of the bay where a boulder hop leads to the crag, at the back of an inlet about 100m from the beach. The inlet can also be reached via a grassy slope from the top. The climbing and approach is non-tidal.

While the two leftmost routes are also used for drytooling, this practice should not spread onto the other lines!

**1** **Drookit** 6a (12m) The juggy left hand line, straight up from the ledge. Also used as a drytooling route, so beware potentially damaged rock

**2** **Credit Crunch** 6a+ (14m) Follow the crackline, starting below the overhang, to a sustained finish. Also used as a drytooling route

**3** **Toolbags** 6b+* (15m) Start at the flake at the bottom of the wall just left of the arête and tackle the roof direct

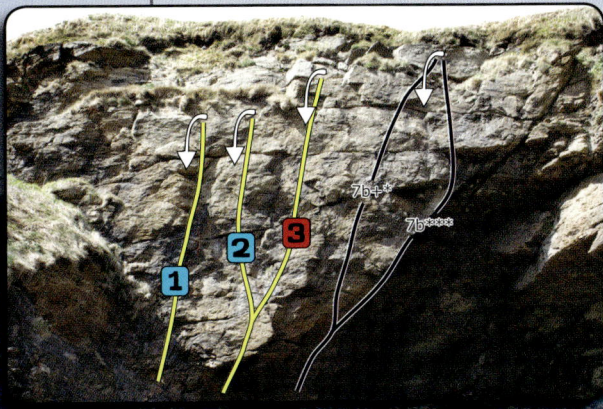

The striking arête that rises from the cave is followed by **Underbelly** 7b*** a classic test piece of the coast, bolted by Tim Rankin.

ANGUS & NORTHEAST

# Boltsheugh

57.03030 -2.142418

**P** 57.03174 -2.144193

Boltsheugh's schist holds both trad and sport lines, the latter tending to be short and steep, but on good positive holds. The area catches the morning sun, and is often sheltered. Turn off the A90 signed for Newtonhill, cross the railway and follow the road downhill to the benches overlooking the cove (**P**5). Bus #7 runs from Aberdeen to Newtonhill via Portlethen, where there is also a rail station, although the cycle route requires sections of the A90. From the parking in Newtonhill take the frequently boggy path south for 200m to reach a drier area. From here easy scrambles descend to either the upper or lower tier (map overleaf).

**BOLTSHEUGH**

## UPPER TIER

The upper tier is the first area reached on approach. It is not affected by the tide and is split into two sections. On the left, a short bulging face over a pool:

**1** **Meany** $5+$ (6m) A steep but juggy start leads to a diagonal crack

**2** **Eany** $5+$ (6m) The wall immediately left of the wide crack

**3** **Mo** $6a*$ (6m) Pull through the lower bulge at a small corner to follow a ramp more easily

**4** **The Dark Side** $6c*$ (7m) This tackles the double bulge directly, both parts of which are challenging

**5** **Automatic** $6c$ (8m) A steep start then pull up and left around the bulge with difficulty. Resist pulling into....

**6** **The Dregs** $6a$ (8m) Poor rock up the vague corner earns this route its name

On the right of the tier is a short but steeply overhanging prow:

**7** **Little Creatures** $6c*$ (6m) A short but brutal route up the wall immediately right of the obvious crack

**8** **Crossroads** $6a+$ (6m) Start at a flake and climb the short wall

**9** **Aches In Provence** $6b+*$ (6m) The steeply overhanging arête. So short that a sitting start (6c) is recommended!

**10** **Traverse of the Cods** $7a**$ (12m) Start up **7** then traverse entertainingly rightwards to finish up **9**. Just remember how close to the ground you are whilst clipping!

5 mins
30 mins

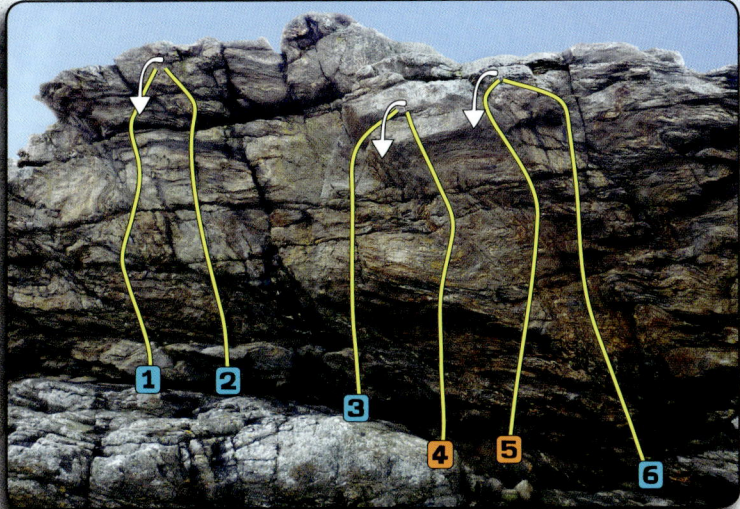

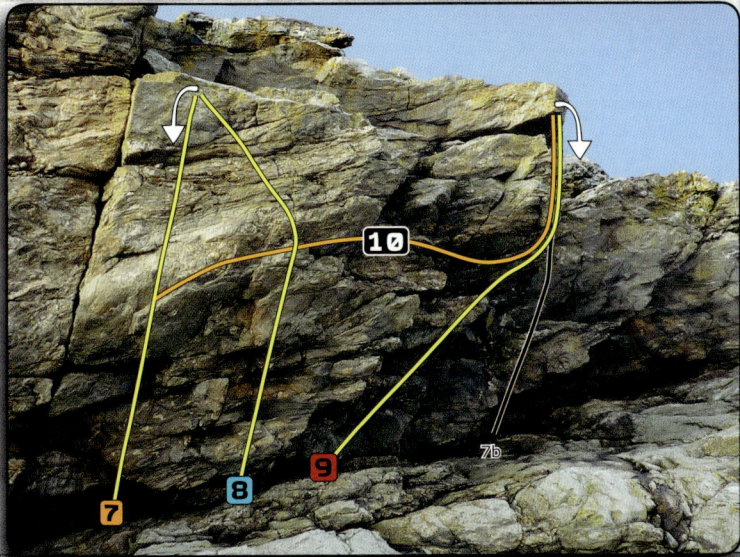

# Boltsheugh

## LOWER TIER

The routes on the lower tier are longer and offer a pleasing outlook by the sea. From the open grassy area an easy seaward scramble can be found south of the upper tier. This leads down and rightwards to a pleasant rocky platform just above sea level where the cave will be first encountered. A short walk south along the platform leads past a small inlet to another smaller platform in front of the Down Under area - **this is only possible at lower tides.**

**1** **Go West** 6b+* (10m) Technical and tricky for the grade

**2** **Down Under** 6c** (10m) The most direct line to the chains is steep but affords generous holds

**3** **Out Back** 6b (10m) The diagonal line is somewhat contrived and escapable onto the ramp

The next area is characterised by a large square roof at half height, to the left of a corner.

**4** **Morrison's Missed Adventure** 7a** (15m) Climb up into the roofed hanging corner, then swing excitingly leftward through the roof. Steep, but with big holds

**5** **Rankin's Rain Games** 6b** (15m) Start as for **4** until the base of the corner then traverse right to the spike on the hanging arête, and finish up the headwall to a lower-off shared with the previous route

**6** **The League of Whingers** 6b+* (15m) Pulls impressively through the widest part of the roof before following a crack up then left to the lower-off

**7** **Hardy** 6a+** (15m) Where the roof lessens to the right, pass the ledge at the crack and head left up the face

**8** **Laurel** 6a* (15m) Start as for **7** but follow the crack into the corner before heading left for a steep finish

The last three lines centre around the obvious cave on the right of the tier:

**9** **Cheeky Madam** 6b* (15m) Low in the grade, but steep. Start up the left arête of the cave before jugs lead the way to the lower-off on the nose

**10** **Trouble Monkey** 7a+** (12m) A bouldery start up the right side of the cave leads to sharp holds across the roof. Keep to the left of the bolts. Finish easily as for **9**

**11** **Trouble Monkey Variation** 6b+** (12m) Start as for **10** but skirt up the right side of the roof then traverse left to meet the original line

> ⚠️ Due to saltwater erosion, there has been bolt failures on **Laurel** and **Hardy**. Please check all bolts in this area before committing to them!

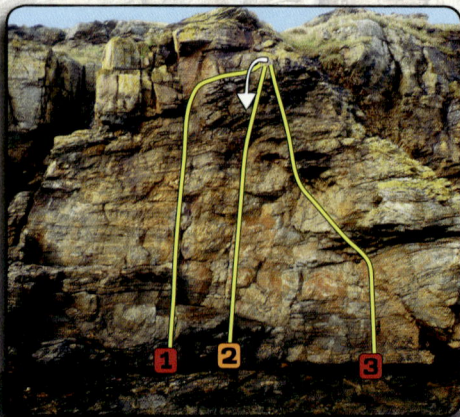

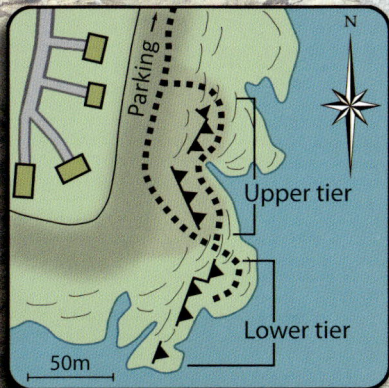

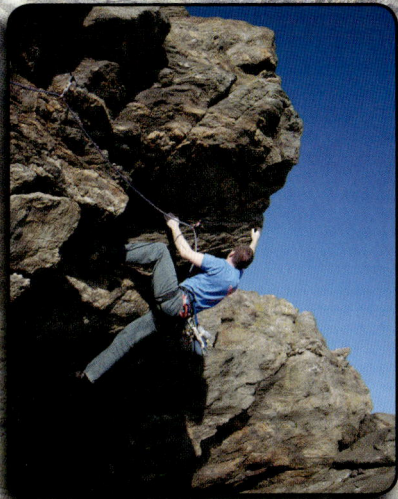

Stuart Stronach on **Traverse of the Cods** (7a) - p150 (Photo M.Bernstein)

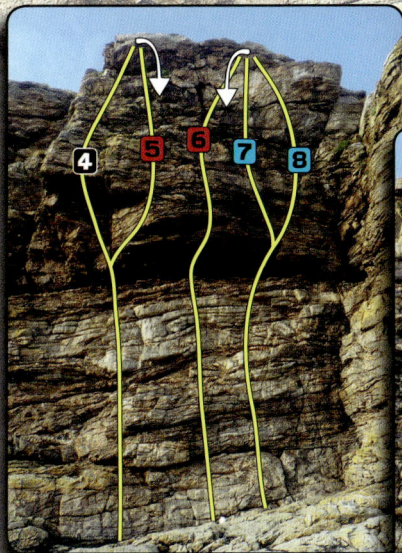

# Elephant Rock

56.67591 -2.466137
56.67870 -2.469881

The Elephant is a bizarre volcanic intrusion, emerging like a 150m tooth from the Angus coastline, just south of Montrose. The rock, a volcanic felstone, has eroded to produce a highly sculpted and varied surface, as if limestone was crossed with gabbro. It provides steep juggy hauls, hanging grooves and thin technical slabs from 6a upwards. Some of the rock looks and feels like it should just fall to bits, but somehow it doesn't! The lower sea washed rock is generally better.

There is little seepage, but as the rock faces east it loses the sun around 1pm and can feel greasy later in the afternoon. House martin nests dot the overhangs, and care should be taken not to damage these. Thankfully the fulmar's nests are confined largely to the loose upper ledges above the lower-offs.

Routes #1-16 are increasingly affected by the tide, so be sure to check the Montrose tide tables: **tidetimes.org.uk**

10 mins

25 mins

0 3 5 8 5

As with many coastal sport venues, the bolts take a pounding from the corrosive conditions, especially the expansion bolts with hangers. Please use good judgement as to their safety. Thankfully, some of the routes are equipped with resined staples, as are all the lower-offs.

Approach along the A92 from Montrose or Arbroath, and take the turn signed "Usan 2.5 miles". Follow this over a crossroads, through some tight bends, and another sign for "Usan 1.25 miles". A 1/2 mile later the road bends left by a white gate. Park here and walk down under the railway, and past an old graveyard. At low tide it is possible to descend to the south of the ridge and reach the climbing area via a cave. At higher tides, follow the field edge north until a small track leads down into the bay. The closest train link is Montrose, a 20 min cycle.

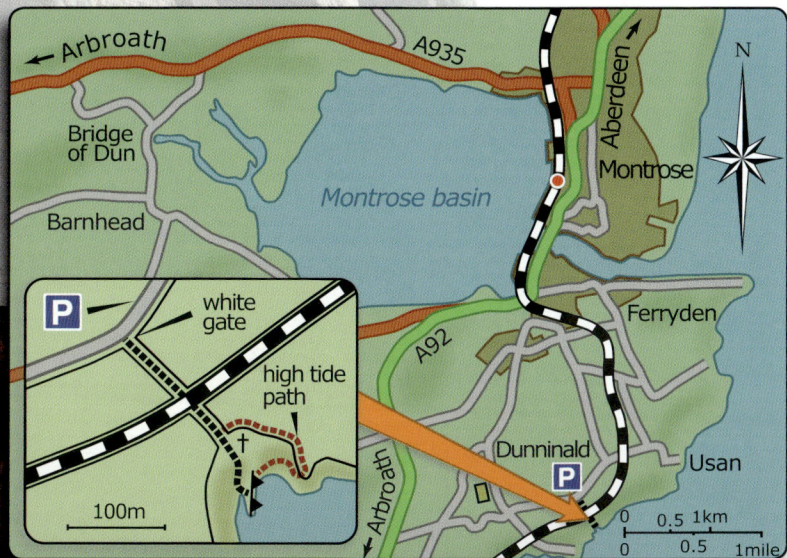

# Elephant Rock

**1** **Can't See the F in Elephant**
**Anywhere** 7a* (14m) Start up the crack in the seaward wall of the cave

**2** **Pas de Charge** 6b** (16m) A bit bold into the cave and high in the grade

**3** **Seeing is Not Believing** 6c* (15m) Start and finish as for **2** but break out through the bulge onto the headwall

**4** **Tale of the Tape** 6a+*** (15m) Excellent climbing in a fine position. Follows the narrow pillar just left of the deep fault-line - sustained

**5** **Big Lug** 6b+* (16m) Necky climbing up the left side of the slab

**6** **Viagra Falls** 6c+** (18m) Start up a tricky hanging groove (crux), then follow the right edge of the slab to a niche

**7** **The X-philes** 6c* (20m)

**8** **Hanger 18** 7a*** (21m) The monstrous overhanging groove

**Bodysnatcher**, the rightward variation, is now 7b after the loss of a hold

**9** **Shapeshifter** 7a** (14m) From the corner, step L onto arête and span R to pass the roof to the upper corner

**10** **The Ex-Pert Route** 6c (22m) Start as for **9** but skip right under the roof to the arête. The direct start up the nose is **Pert's Buttock** 7a

There are five routes that tackle the deep wave-cut cave. They generally involve hard bouldery starts and easier continuations. L-R: 7b+**, 7b*, 7b, 7c, 7b**

Low-Tide Access

**11** **Big Girl's Blouse** $7a+$** (14m)
The savagely steep roof crack. Start by
bridging up the huge fault then break
right

**12** **Mahoots Mon** $6c+$ (13m) Start
direct to the jug on **13**, before climbing
the red plaque and slab

**13** **Beware of the Wellyfish** $6b$** 
(13m) A popular warm-up route, starting
at the right end of the undercut

**14** **Don't Blame Me!** $6a+$ (20m)
Start up the slab right of the undercut,
and pull the bulge to reach the left side
of a hanging slab

**15** **It's Not My Fault!** $6a$ (20m) Start
up the fault 5m right of **14**, up an easy
groove, and the right side of the slab

The rest of the climbs are above the tide line,
on rock that is more solid than it looks.

**16** **Right Wing Extremist** $6c$*
(14m) A pumpy line directly up from the
fallen block

**17** **Pig on the Rig** $6c+$* (14m)
Another steep and sustained line, following the ring-staples from the block

**18** **The Beggars are Coming to
Town** $6b$ (14m) Good warmup for the
harder outings. Lower-off as for **17**

**19** **Hornblower** $6c$ (14m)

**20** **Whistleblower** $6b$ (14m) Start as
for **19** then break out right to improving
rock and a separate lower-off

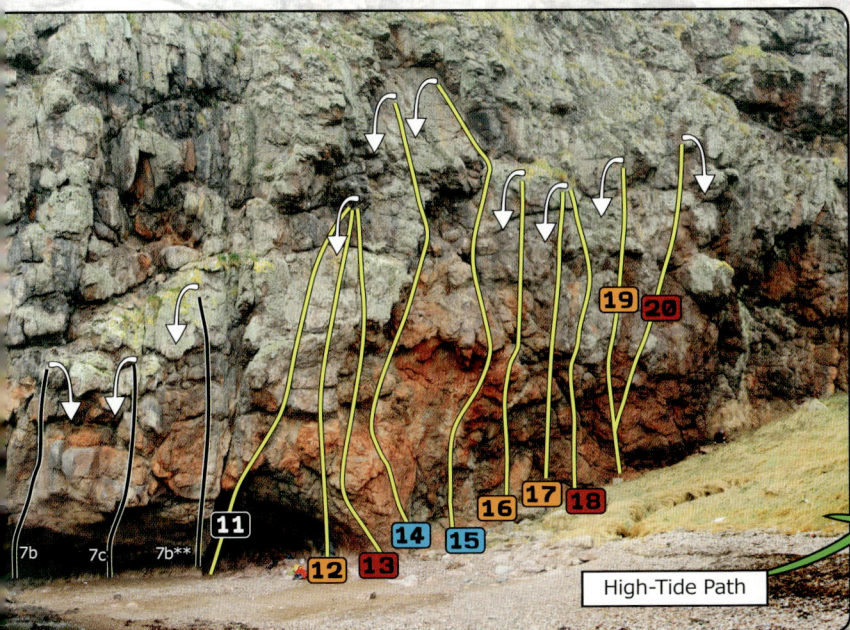

ANGUS & NORTHEAST

7b    7c    7b**    **11**    **14**   **15**
**12**  **13**    **16**  **17** **18**   **19** **20**

High-Tide Path

# Arbroath

56.56196 -2.550283

56.56089 -2.557557

A distinctively adventurous sport climbing experience, the many sandstone coves and caves of Arbroath are well worth exploration. The coastline is complex and consequently there are nearly always crags that favourably face the sun. In contrast, north facing routes can be greasy and need extended dry spells to come into condition.These unique crags are not for fragile egos, the routes require good technique and resilient skin. Some routes may not be tidal but may still not be accessible during rough seas. Many areas lack lower-offs requiring the leader to top-out and the second to climb the route to remove the quick-draws - how traditional!

The authors explore the atmospheric delights of the **Deil's Heid** (p175)

29 35 35 23 21

5-15 mins   5-10 mins

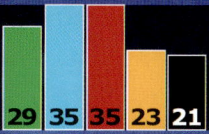

If driving, the A92 approaches Arbroath from the south via Dundee or the north from Aberdeen. There is a rail station in the town. Once in the centre follow signs for 'Victoria Park and Cliffs'. Park at the end of the promenade, by the toilets and *in-situ* ice cream van. The path then leads along the cliff tops; the first climbing area is reached within five minutes. Numbers indicate the *new* white-topped 'AS' rescue marker posts.

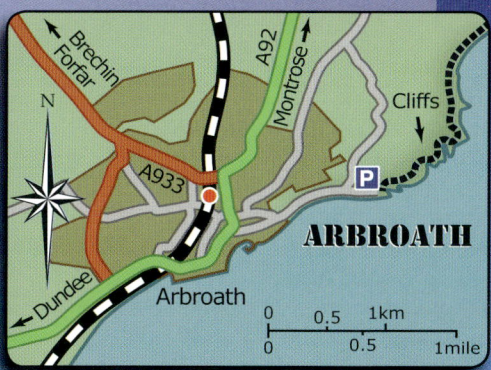

Brechin
Forfar

A92

Montrose

Cliffs

N

A933

P

Dundee

ARBROATH

Arbroath

0   0.5   1km
0        0.5     1mile

Dickmont Den

**A** The Rut
**B** The Platform and Tower
**C** Non Tidal Wave
**D** The Promontory
**E** Sector Cartoon
**F** Sector Parental Guidance
**G** The Steppes
**H** Sector Mini

Mermaid's Kirk
Needle's E'e

Parking

100m

13   16
15
12   14
11   N
10   M
9    L
K
J
I   **I** Conning Tower Inlet
8   H   **J** The Haven
7   G   **K** Battery Inlet
6   F   **L** Doom Hole
5   E   **M** Grannie's Garret
D   **N** The Deil's Heid
A B C

ANGUS & NORTHEAST

# Arbroath

## A THE RUT

Faces SW, Semi-Tidal, Topout

The first area encountered about 400m from the ice cream van. Walk down from the coastal path at AS Post 5. Short bouldery routes top-out to resin anchors 5m back.

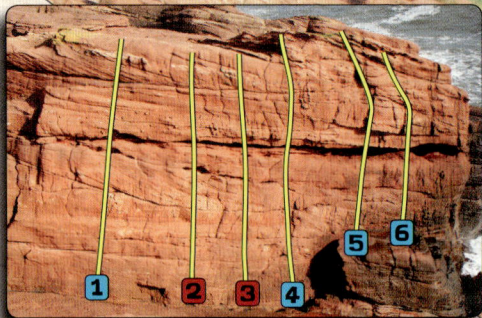

**1 Stag Night** 5+ (5m)

**2 Strut Yer Stuff** 6b (5m)

**3 Burning with Anxiety** 6b+ (6m) An easy start but a tough finish

**4 Road Rage** 6a+* (6m)

**5 Flaked Out** 5+** (7m)

**6 Stuck in a Rut** 6a+* (7m)

An abseil over the back of the Rut leads to the steep, north-facing and often damp **DIVING BOARD**, offering L-R:

**7 In at the Deep End** 7a* (12m)

**8 Take the Plunge** 6b+* (11m)

**PLATFORM LEFT**

To North Side

# 8 THE PLATFORM

Faces SW, Semi-Tidal, Topout/lower-off
A popular area. The lower routes are more tidal. 50m north of AS Post 6, descend a grassy path with great care to a flat area and abseil bolts.

**9** **Smokies** $6b+$* (10m)

**10** **Ride 'em Cowboy** $6b+$** (10m)

**11** **Waves of Emotion** $6b+$* (11m)

**12** **Parson's Nose** $6b+$* (12m)

**13** **Caught Red Handed** $6c$** (13m) Start directly up the nose

**14** **Impaled on the Horns of Indecision** $6c+$* (15m) From the 2nd bolt on **13** traverse right into a hanging corner

**15** **Cast Adrift on the Ocean of Uncertainty** $7a+$* (16m) Hand traverse to breach the left end of the roof

**16** **At the Crossroads of Destiny and Desire** $7a$** (14m) Start up a roofed corner, then traverse left to a hanging groove

**17** **Foundering on the Rocks of Obsession** $7a$* (12m) Start up the rib to a flake and small roof

**18** **Seaside Special** $5$ (12m) Starts up Original Route and breaks left

**19** **Original Route** $3$* (16m) The stepped flake line. Direct start $5+$*

**20** **Climbers Wear Platforms** $6b$* (15m)

**21** **Towing the Line** $6a$ (16m)

**22** **Rubbin' Salt into the Wound** $6b+$** (16m) Takes the nose direct

There are two routes on the north side of the Platform, accessed via the cave. (R-L): **Swimming Against the Tide of Tradition** ($6c+$**) and **Out of the Red and Into the Black** ($7a$*). They are good but rarely dry.

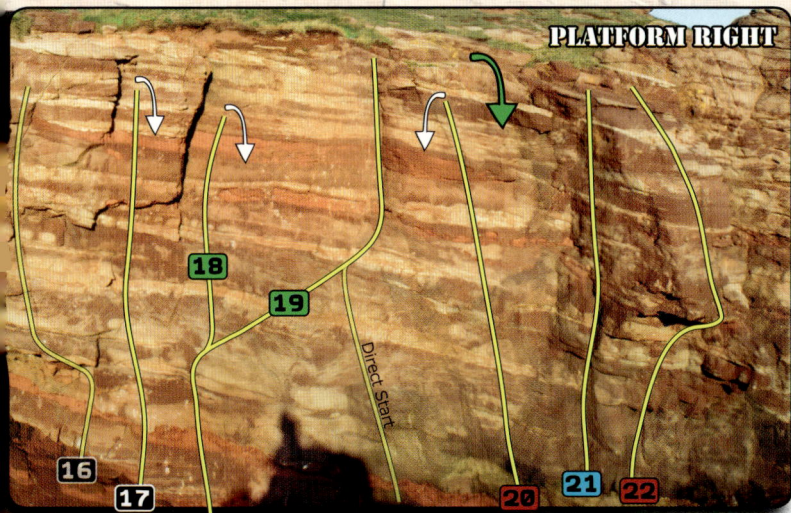

PLATFORM RIGHT

Direct Start

**18** **19** **16** **17** **20** **21** **22**

ANGUS & NORTHEAST

# Arbroath

## 8 THE TOWER

Faces N, Semi-Tidal, Topouts

While containing good quality mid-grade routes, this cliff needs a good east wind to dry out the greasiness. Topouts require care and lead to bolts on the summit.

Approach from the top of the Platform area, and descend a gully before stepping right onto the triangular ledge below route 7. Routes 1-4 use semi-hanging belays accessible by traverse from the ledge.

**1 Screamin' Demon** *6a* (10m) Start from the left-most hanging stance and take care of friable rock at the top

**2 Ukrainian Mermaid** *6a* (12m) Easy climbing until a steep finish

**3 The Selfish Shellfish** *6a* (12m) From the right-hand stance, climb the wall direct to the small groove

**4 The Krab** *6b** (12m) From the right-hand stance. Good but often greasy

**5 Declaration of Intent** *6a** (12m) Step left off the ledge to start

**6 Meaty Hefts** *4*** (10m) The crack, clipping the bolts of **7** on the right

**7 Wall of Hate** *5* (8m) The wall directly above the ledge

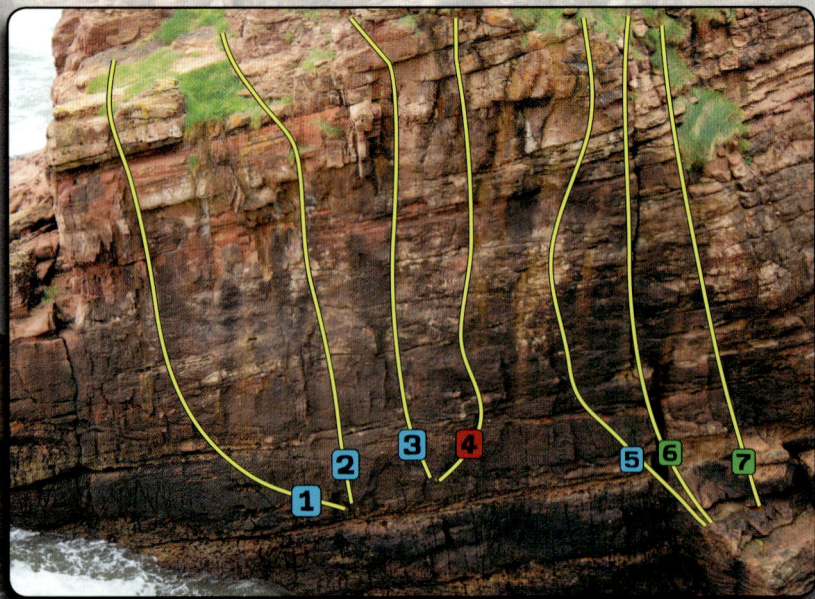

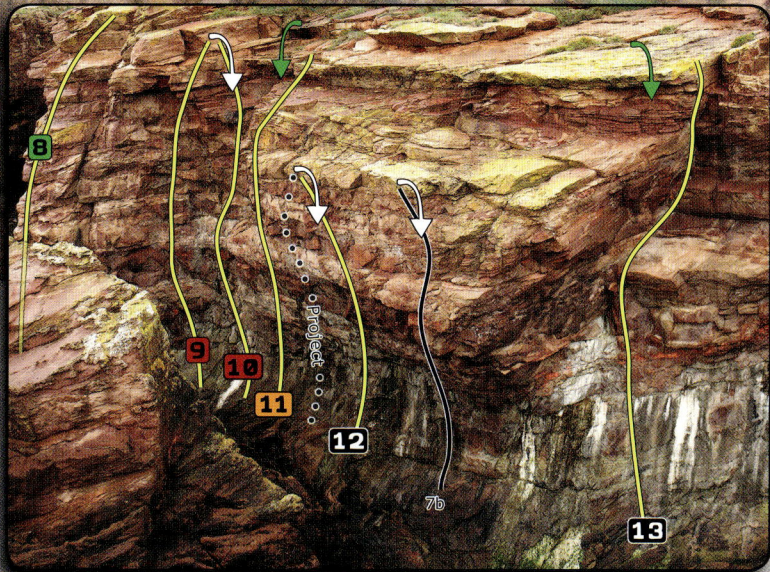

# C NON-TIDAL WAVE

Faces E, Non-Tidal, Lower-offs / Topouts

This short steep face is clearly visible from south of the Needle's E'e rock, but approach from here is treacherous. Instead follow a faint path across the slope from near the Needles E'e turn-off. Abseil down Brain Wave or 7th Wave. The face is steep enough to stay dry in rain, but often suffers from seepage.

**8** **Wave Escape** 3 (14m) May be a useful escape if things get too tough. Belay staples 10m back left

**9** **Say Hello but Wave Goodbye** 6b+* (10m) Sustained climbing on flat holds to the highest point of the crag

**10** **Brain Wave** 6b* (10m) Climb the crack and groove to the top, trending slightly leftwards to a lower-off. Harder than it appears

**11** **On a Different Wavelength** 6c (9m) A short sharp start leads to an easier finish

There is a closed project left of Shockwave with its first hangers removed.

**12** **Shockwave** 7a+ (9m) Shallow flakes lead directly up the centre of the wall to a lower-off

**13** **7th Wave** 7a* (11m) Climb the pale wall to the big ledge, an awkward mantel and the steep corner to finish

# Arbroath

## D THE PROMONTORY

Faces SE, Non-Tidal, Topouts

This small but dramatic pinnacle points south from the Needle's E'e viewing area, with a slabby landward face and a serious overhang to seaward. The first line, on the landward side, can often remain greasy while the remainder faces SE and gets good sun. Abseil decent from belay staples at the top of **The Buoys of Summer** to small non-tidal belay ledges.

Two routes on the landward face left of **1** are rarely climbed due to persistent damp and poor rock. L-R: **Barging into the Presence of God** (6b+) and **The Red Litchie** (6a+)

**1 Pilgrims Progress** 7a* (10m) Tricky sustained climbing on the wall left of the arête. Has its own starting ledge

**2 The Abbey Habit** 6a (10m) The left arête from a small belay ledge at the toe of the buttress

**3 Stitch in Time** 6b* (9m) Step left from the belay ledge and climb the face directly on pleasing features

**4 Buoys of Summer** 6b+** (9m) Straight up the shallow groove. High in the grade, especially for the short

**5 The E'Evil Dead** 6c*** (13m) A local classic. Break right from the 3rd bolt of **4** to the wild arête and a tricky, sloping finish

**6 Flesh E'eter** 7a+ ** (16m) Continue traversing around the wild overhang to finish up the east face

# E SECTOR CARTOON

Faces SE, Non-Tidal, Topout

This is a popular children's or beginner's area with very short routes and low grades. It provides a gentle introduction to the art of pebble-pulling. From the Needle's E'e, scramble across the 'bad step' by the Promontory and round left towards the sea to first reach the south face with the distinctive nose. The rest of the routes start just round the corner to seaward. Belay anchors 6m up from topouts.

Amanda Lyons on **Disney Look Too Bad** (6a) - photo Stuart Stronach

## SOUTH FACE

The small scoop encountered while scrambling round to the main face

**7 Loony Tunes** 5+ (6m) The short arête, keeping right. Tricky for the grade

**8 Fred Flintstone** 3+ (6m) The groove with the big cobblestone

**9 Disney Look Too Bad** 6a* (6m) (But harder than it looks!) The right hand groove, passing the huge nose

## EAST FACE

**10 Cow and Chicken** 3+* (7m) The diagonal crack

**11 Top Cat** 4 (7m)

**12 A Grand Day Out** 4+* (7m)

**13 The Wrong Trousers** 4* (7m)

**14 Pinky and the Brain** 4* (6m)

**15 62 West Wallaby Street** 3+* (5m) The central crack is tricky for the short

**16 The Pearls of Penelope Pitstop** 6a+* (5m) Feels easy, until the finish!

**17 Rugrat's Revenge** 5* (5m) Saves the best for a tricky topout

**18 Fantastic Four** 3 (6m) The easy crack is reached by stepping out over the drop

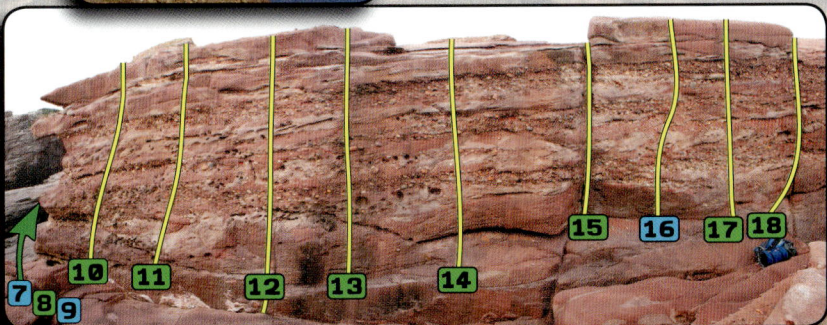

ANGUS & NORTHEAST

# Arbroath

## F SECTOR PARENTAL GUIDANCE Faces East, Non-Tidal, Topouts

Definitely a certificate above the adjacent area, routes here centre around a huge sea cave, giving some very memorable exposure over water.
The first routes are found a 2m step down rightward from Sector Cartoon.

**1 Silver Surfer** *4* (8m) An amenable short route on good holds

**2 Be Calmed** *5\** (9m)
Starting one step further down

**3 Parental Guidance** *6b\** (10m)
...and now try without the positive holds

**4 Layin' Down the Law** *6b+* \*\*\*
(15m) Traverse along the sloping ledge over the cave to finish up **6**. Fun!

**5 'O' Zone Slayer** *6c\*\** (11m) Start down left of the cave and gain the groove

The audacious line breaking through the apex of the arch is **Pushing the Limpets** 7b\*\*

The next two routes are accessed via the Needle's E'e arch, then turn R to find two staples on a small ledge.

**6 Grounded** *7a+\** (12m) Traverse 2m left from the belay (crux) to make hard moves on sloping ledges

**7 Not for Childrens E'en** *6c\** (9m) Climb up then step left at the first bolt into a fine position, to finish up the arête

Finally, on the wall to the right of the Needle's E'e there are two routes accessed by abseil to finely positioned hanging stances (not pictured).

**8 Do as I Say not as I Do** *6a+\**
(15m) The leftmost line

**9 Loose Lips Sink Ships** *6a+\**
(15m) An easier start leads to a roof and hard headwall

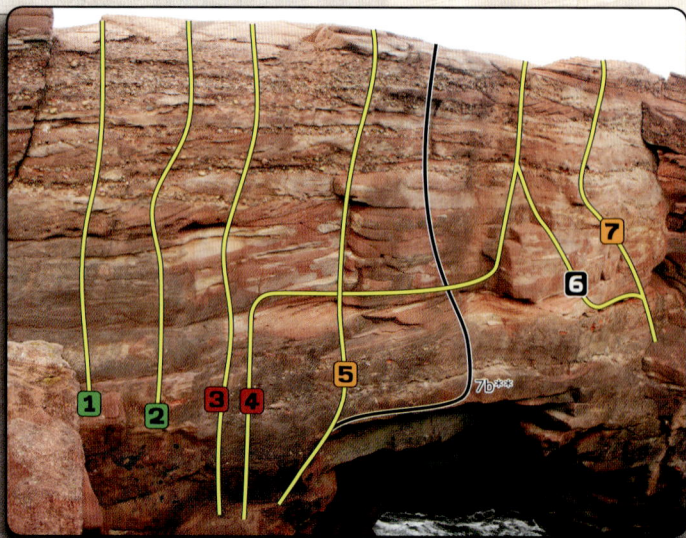

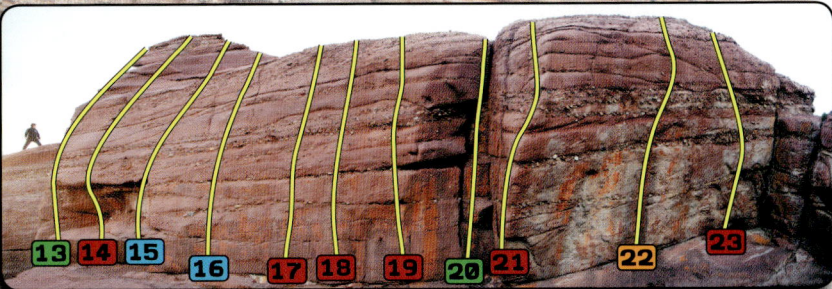

# THE MERMAID'S KIRK

From the Needle's E'e, scramble NE past the huge cove (photo p136). This contains a few tidal routes including:

**10** **Diagon Alley** 6a+* (20m)
Right-slanting crack on the NW wall. The lower-off is more tidal than the start!

On the slabby SE 'Warship' wall are:

**11** **Dread Knot** 6b (12m)
The smooth black face on the left

**12** **Broad Side** 6b+ (12m)

Sophie discovering classic Arbroath slopers on **Silence of the Clams** (5+) - p170

# C THE STEPPES

Faces East, Non-Tidal, Topouts

Continue down seawards to emerge by **23**. Both the steep right and slabby left walls provide short hard routes with belay staples 8m back up the slope.

**13** **Steppin' Out** 5* (9m)

**14** **High Stepper** 6b (9m) Pull through the roof at the crackline

**15** **Put out to Grass** 6a* (9m) A line of ring bolts at the right end of the shelf

**16** **Two Steppes Back** 6a+** (8m) Some larger cobbles provide relief

**17** **One Steppe Forward** 6b* (8m)

**18** **Kazakhstani Castaway** 6b+ (8m) Don't let the easier angle fool you

**19** **Steppes Back in Amazement** 6b (7m) Has a hard start

**20** **Steppeladder** 4 (7m) The corner

**21** **Steppe in the Right Direction** 6b (7m) The delicate slabby arête

**22** **Wicked Steppe Mother** 6c+ (6m) Gets increasingly hard!

**23** **Welcome to the Steeeppes!** 6b+ (6m) Despite the temptation, bridging is definitely not on!

ANGUS & NORTHEAST

# Arbroath

## H SECTOR MINI
Faces South, Partlly tidal, Topouts

This more recently developed wall is, like Sector Cartoon, a good place for beginners. The routes are very short but host a good range of features and holds on clean wave-washed sandstone, making for nice climbs. There are belay bolts at the top of each line but if top-roping be sure to extend the anchors over the edge to avoid rope drag.

Immediately north of the Mermaid's Kirk, just past AS post 8, follow a prickly path down to the sloping platform from where the routes start.

**1** **Minital** 4* (5m)
Climb the slab and crack directly

**2** **Minitiation** 4 (5m) Start up the small black corner to climb the featured wall. Nice climbing after a somewhat bold start

**3** **Minimal** 4+ (6m) Follow the arête left of the niche to easy pockets and a nice top-out

**4** **Minimical** 6a+ (6m) Surmount the pedestal in the niche to take on the tricky overhang. Thuggy, but good holds where you need them

**5** **Miniquity** 5 (6m) Start in a small notch on the nose and make a nice mantel to a top out reminiscent of a boulder

**6** **Minitiative** 5 (6m) Just round to seaward from the main face. Climb up to a tricky slopey mantel and an easier finish. May be affected by high tide

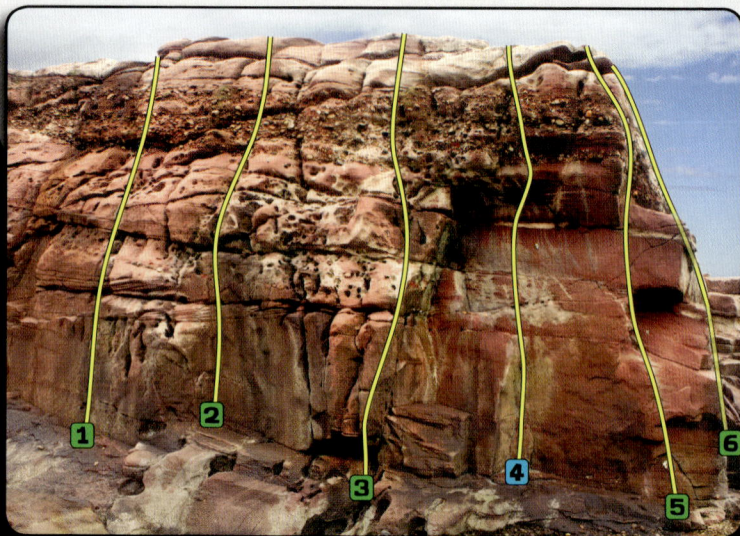

Topher reaching for the sun on the spectacular prow of **The Siren** (6c), the Doom Arch - p172
Photo - Sophie Buckingham

# Arbroath

## ① CONNING TOWER INLET

Follow the coastal path northwards past a large inlet with a 'tombstone' until you reach AS post 10. From here narrow paths lead down to the north and south sides of the inlet. The southern ridge is very narrow and may be loose. **Belay ledges are dangerous in high seas.**

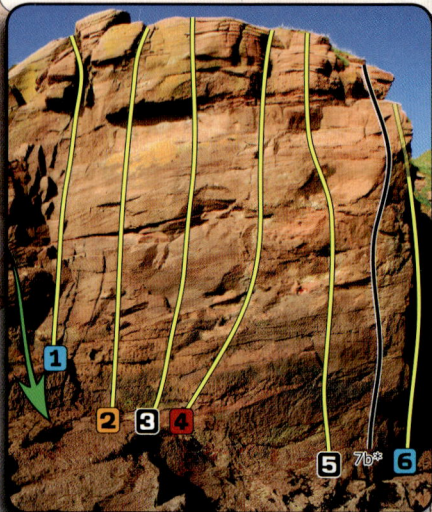

## THE CLAMS LEDGE

The large corner at the back of the inlet. Abseil in to the non-tidal ledge.

**⑦ The Codfather** $7a$ (12m) Head left from the ledge. Poor rock but a fine position

**⑧ Vast Mango in Tardis** $6c+$** (14m) The intimidating flake line

**⑨ Mutton Dressed as Clam** $7a+$* (14m) Directly up the wall left of ⑩

**⑩ Silence of the Clams** $5+$*** (14m) Directly up the huge corner. One of the best easy routes in the area

**⑪ Galley Slave** $6c$* (12m) The right wall of the corner

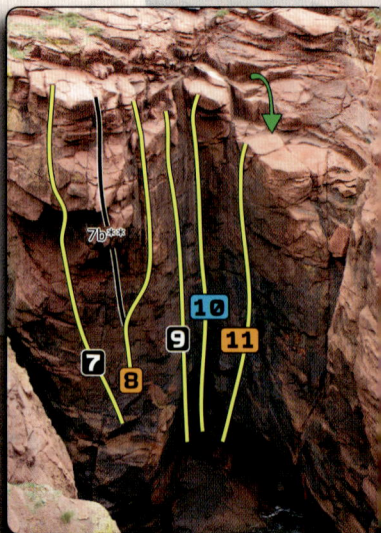

## LOST (SOUTH) WALL

Abseil from the south ridge to a wide, partly tidal, ledge.

**① Lost in Line** $5+$ (12m) Finish through a slot in the overhangs

**② Lost but not Least** $6c$** (12m) A delicate slab leads to a blocky roof

**③ Lost the Plot** $7a+$* (12m) The slab leads to a hard move through the roof

**④ Hanau's Quint** $6b$* (14m) Steep but mostly positive holds

**⑤ Lost at Sea** $7a$** (15m) Start where the ledge narrows. Steep moves through the scoops to a ledge

**⑥ Pringles Wave** $6a$ (16m) Just round the corner and often greasy

## THE CONNING TOWER

The tower is clearly visible on approach. Abseil down the gully behind the tower to a spacious ledge.

**12** **Pulling Muscles from a Shell**
$6c$* (15m) Traverse left from the ledge to a delicate slabby face

**13** **Swindlers List** $6a$+*** (12m)
The arête - lovely

**14** **Concentration Camp** $6c$* (12m)
The steep wall to the right of the arête - sustained

**15** **Short Arms, Deep Pockets** $6b$*
(14m) Starts just right of the descent gully on the main wall

**16** **The Peem Machine** $6c$+**
(15m) The steep pocketed wall leads to a rounded crux

## THE HARPOON STANCE

Small non-tidal ledge with staples.

**17** **Whale of a Time** $7a$* (15m)
May also be started from the Conning Tower. Rounded wall climbing!

**18** **Curse of the Pharoes** $6b$+*
(12m) The featured open groove with a reachy move higher up

**19** **Neptune's Kiss** $7a$** (16m) Start up the arête, then rightwards to gain a black streak. Often greasy

## THE LIFE RAFT

Small triangular ledge. Tidal

**20** **The Mystic** $6c$+*** (16m) Breach the overhang via the hanging crack, gain a ledge and finish left up the wall. Class

**21** **Haarbinger** $6b$+** (17m) Climb the arête and crack right of the stance, step left to a ledge, and right to a slab

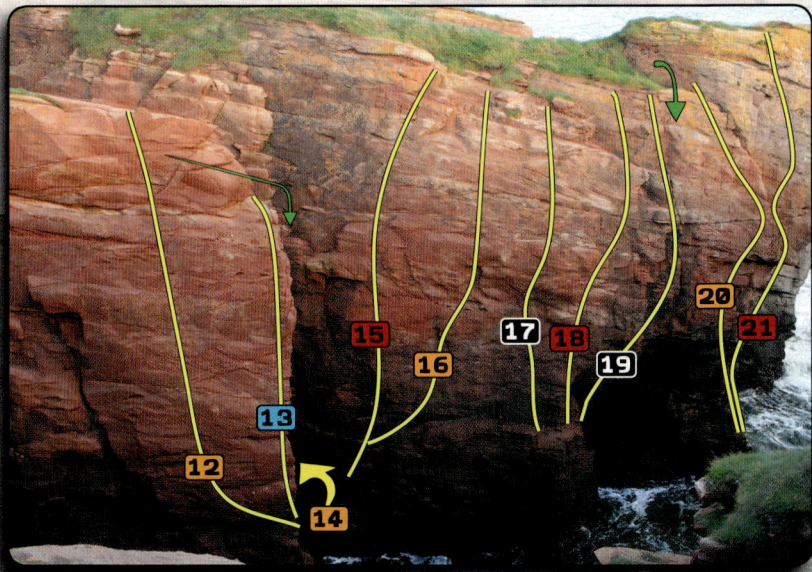

# Arbroath

## J THE HAVEN
Faces NE, Semi-Tidal, Topouts

The next inlet north of the Conning Tower contains a distinctive roofed nose. Access is via the path from post AS10, and abseil down a gully below a rock bollard. Most of the routes have good dry ledges even at high tide.

The headland of the peninsula holds two routes (inaccessible at high tide).

**1 Killer Wail** *6c+*** (16m) The crack-line leads onto a hanging slab. Tricky!

**2 Eight Year Itch** *6b+*** (14m) Climbs the nose directly on good rock

The wall then turns to enter the inlet:

**3 Haven Fun** *6b** (14m) A gentle start leads to a trickier, steeper finish

**4 A Close Shave** *6c* (14m) In contrast, a hard crimpy start soon eases

**5 Shaven Haven** *5** (14m) Much more amenable, with good holds

The abseil gully can be climbed as **Haven Escape Route** *3** (14m)

**6 Haven Can Wait** *6a+* (14m) Just right of the abseil. Deceptively steep and pumpy!

**7 Don't Bridget Neilson** *6b* (14m) The name contains crucial instructions for a valid tick

**8 Dark Sar-Chasm** *5+*** (14m) An entertaining journey into the chasm before chimneying upwards

The nose holds two desperate routes. **Vulgar Display of Power** (7b+**) and **Knockin' on Haven's Door** (7b**)

**9 David's Route** *5** (13m) The slabby wall right of the nose, on good holds

The slabby frontal face further right is known as **BOLLARD BUTTRESS** (not pictured). Belay at staples on the large bollard itself:

**10 The Grade Escape** *5+** (12m) The left groove, exiting left of bollard

**11 Sun Seeker** *6a+** (12m) The delicate and deceptive right-hand groove, exiting right

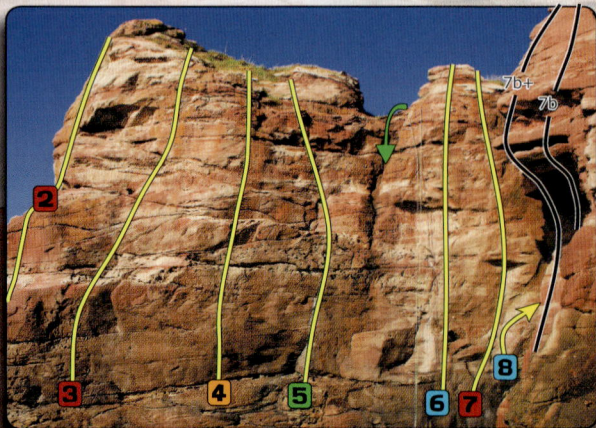

# K THE BATTERY INLET

The next inlet can be approached as for the Haven, and then descend a wide gully from the north edge of the grassy area.

## THE GARGOYLE

Faces NE, Non-Tidal, Topouts
There are three staples on top to belay from. The holds are generally slopey and may feel sandy. Character building but ego bruising!

**12 Gruesome** 6c+* (13m)
  Slopey, pumpy and well named

**13 Medusa** 6c* (12m)
  The crux is to gain the 'antler'. Deceptively hard

**14 Gorgon** 6a+ (12m) Up the thin groove to easier ground

## THE BATTERY

Faces E and NE, Non-Tidal
The buttress facing the Gargoyle - may be accessed by a tricky traverse from there, or by abseil.

**15 Artillery Arête** 5+** (14m)
  The superb slabby arête - tricky start

**16 Bringing out the Big Guns**
  6b** (14m) Traverse right from the start of 15 to a hidden bolt, then up a layback crack and slab, finishing as for previous route

**17 Ever Ready Arête** 7a** (12m)
  The arête opposite the pinnacle. The top-out is the crux!

**18 Fully Charged** 6c (12m) A good route but rarely in condition, on the wall right from the arête

# Arbroath

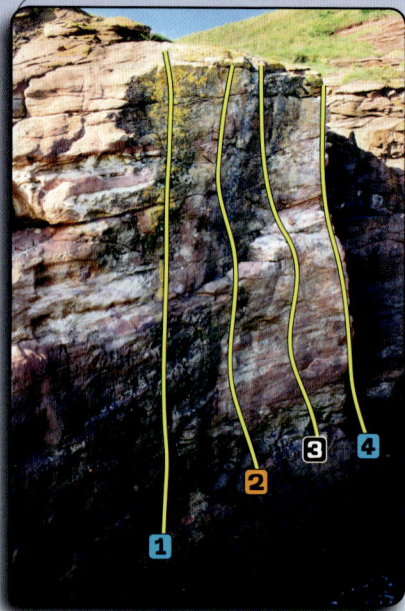

## 🇯 THE DOOM HOLE

Just south of the large inlet of Dickmont Den, scramble down past the south side of the giant blow-hole.

### THE HAUL WALL

Faces NE, Non-Tidal, Topouts
Can be greasy. Abseil to belay bolts.

**1** **In Too Deep** $6a+$ ** (10m)
Excellent featured holds

**2** **The Jug of Jug Haul** $6c$** (10m)
Similar to **1** but steeper

**3** **Haul Anchor** $7a+$* (10m) The steep wall left of the arête. Reachy

**4** **Heave Ho!** $5+$* (12m)
The rounded right arête

### THE DOOM ARCH

Faces S and E, Non-Tidal, Topouts
The spectacular entrance to the Doom Hole. Abseil in down the lower slabby wall on the right side of the cave entrance.

**5** **Kiss of Doom** $4$ (13m) Directly up the slab from the belay

**6** **Black and Decker** $5$ (17m) The ramp and corner crack

**7** **The Siren** $6c$*** (20m) A stunning line out left across the arch and up the prow with a full-power finish

**8** **Air Raid** $7a$** (24m) Continue left from the arête on **7** to a difficult and wild groove. Unclip the last bolt shared with **The Siren** to avoid killer rope drag

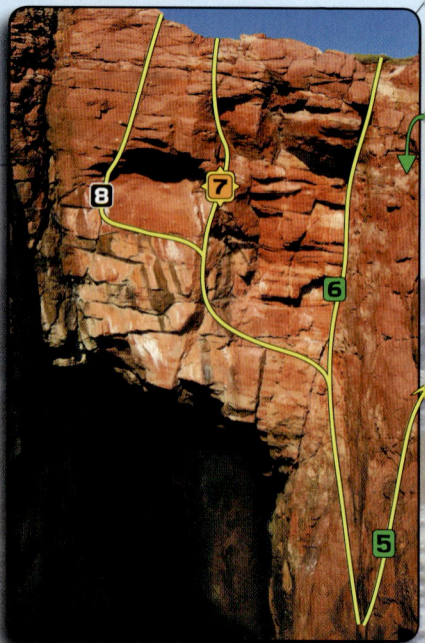

On the east face of the Doom Hole headland, facing Gull Rock island in the inlet of Dickmont's Den, lie two small faces accessed by an often slippery step down (bolt) to non-tidal ledges.

**SECTOR ACHILLES** (inland) holds (L/R): **Beware Geeks Bearing Gifts** $7a$ and **Trojan Gift Horse** $7b$. Just right of the descent is **SECTOR GULL**, with (L/R) : **Seegull** $4$; **Gullable** $5+$; **Gulliver's Travels** $5+$ and **Engulfed** $6a+$

# N THE DEIL'S HEID
Faces SE, Occasionally Tidal, Topout

The only bolted sea-stack in Scotland! This striking natural feature, although not truly separated from the land, lies at the northern end of the Arbroath seacliffs and provides memorable atmosphere (Photos page 2 and 160)

**12** **Between the Deil and the Deep Blue Sea** $6c^*$ (15m) Follow a steep line up the SW arête to lower-off rings. Long quickdraws are required due to bolt placements, which are also sometimes invisible whilst climbing!

**13** **Deil's Heid Route** $5+^{**}$ (20m) The original route on the stack was previously a piton-protected HVS. Delicately follow a rightward diagonal line up the slabby seaward face, to top out with care. There is a resined anchor in softish rock on the summit. Abseil decent to landward

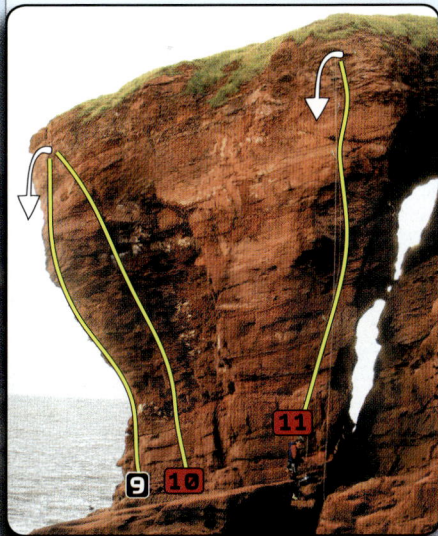

# M GRANNIE'S GARRET
Faces NE, Non-Tidal, Lower-offs

From the path towards the Deil's Heid, cut down right across rock shelves to the base of this partially detached headland. Caving/chimneying fun can be had exploring this rock, which is also known as the 'Three Storey Hoose'. Three intimidating and unlikely-looking routes are found on the north face.

**9** **Sweet Dreams are made of This** $7a+$ ** (16m) Follows the spectacularly overhanging prow. Bigger moves and fewer holds than **10**!

**10** **Satan's Serenade** $6b+^{**}$ (16m) Pull steeply out of the imposing cave on huge, but sometimes friable, holds. Enjoy the swing!

**11** **The Mushroom Treatment** $6b^{**}$ (16m) A juggy steep start leads to a trickier finish

# Kirriemuir

56.67894 -2.994006

56.67904 -2.999092

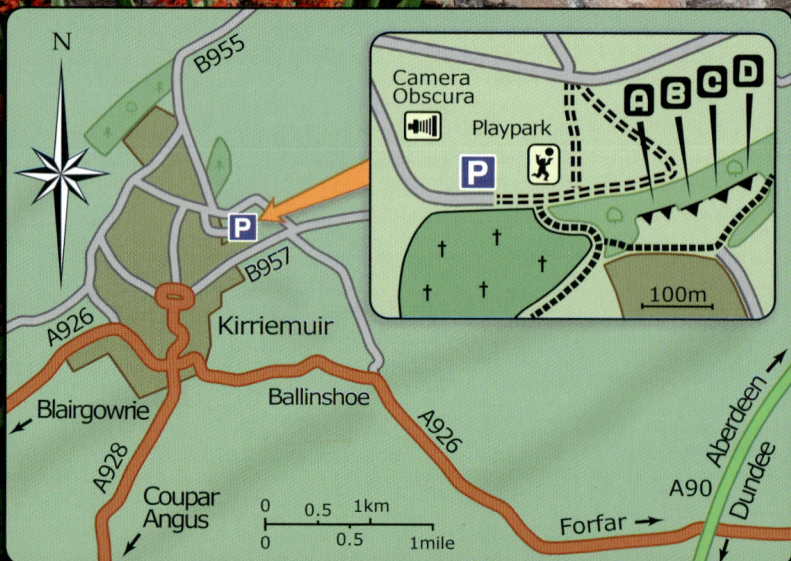

N

B955

P

B957

A926

Kirriemuir

Blairgowrie

A928

Ballinshoe

A926

Coupar
Angus

Forfar

Aberdeen

Dundee

A90

| 0 | 0.5 | 1km |
| 0 | 0.5 | 1mile |

Camera
Obscura

Playpark

P

A B C D

100m

14 33 17 6 3

5 mins    15 mins

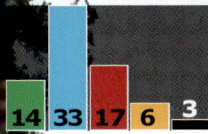

The extensive quarried escarpment of Kirrie has become one of the most popular sport climbing locations in the country, virtue of its easy access from the lowland cities and its good spread of mid-grade routes. The crag is south facing, free of seepage, and sheltered making it an enjoyable destination for a sunny day whatever the season. The rock is a mixture of pleasantly featured sandstone and conglomerate. Whilst the rock can be soft in places, it often provides some surprising pebble-pulling cruxes. Good training for the harder routes to be found nearby at Rob's Reed.

Approach via the A90 from Dundee or Aberdeen, taking the A926 to Kirriemuir (Bus #20 Dundee-Kirriemuir). From the village centre take the Roods Road and follow signs for the Camera Obscura. Park by the Neverland playpark and follow the footpath down the left side of the graveyard. At the bottom of the hill turn left and the West Bay of the quarry will be reached after 100m.

## A. THE WEST BAY

The first area encountered from the approach path, with a distinctive mound. A sheltered suntrap containing some good easier routes.

**1** **Unenforced Layoff** *5* (14m) Through the first roof then pass the second to the right

**2** **Mushroom Heads** *5+* (14m) Steady climbing and low in the grade

**3** **Another Green World** *6a\*\** (14m) Follow the groove at half height on excellent rock

**4** **Sprints Drifting** *6a+\** (14m) Pull through the roof (crux) and direct to an easier finish

**5** **Becalmed** *4+\** (13m) Steep for the grade

**6** **Sombre Reptiles** *5+\** (12m) A thin start continues on better holds

**7** **On the Up** *5+\*\** (11m) Balancy climbing on good rock

**8** **Mound Over Matter** *5+\*\** (11m) Passes the roof to the left on good holds

**9** **Grassy Knoll** *6a\** (11m) Straight through the roof

**10** **Hard Labour** *6a\*\** (13m) Follow a pillar leftward, then back right to finish. A sustained and tricky crux

**11** **Dogmatic** *6a+\** (15m) Technical right-facing groove. Finish right

**12** **Caned and Unable** *6c* (15m Eliminate, very squeezed in

**13** **Paws for Thought** *6b\** (14m) A thin start leads to a steep juggy finish

**14** **Thorny Issue** *6b+\*\** (15m) Pass the bulge to the left, onto the slab and finish through niche

**15** **All Chalk no Traction** $6c$** (15m)
Sustained moves through the bulge. Finish left

**16** **Boarding Party** $6b$* (14m) Start left of
the prow and pass the bulge to its right

**17** **Dubh be Dubh** $6a+$* (15m) Start on
the left of the dark slab, through overlaps to
finish high on the left-facing wall

**18** **The Kirrie (beach) Ball** $6b+$* (15m)
A long reach past the 'ball' leads to airy moves
on the hanging arête. Finish as for **19**

**19** **Let There be Rock** $6a+$* (15m)
The cracked groove then the thuggy chimney

**20** **Bon the Edge** $6b+$** (15m) The delightful arête leads to a crux at the roof

**21** **Whole Lotta Kirrie** $6b+$* (15m) Start
in the crack right of the arête, then up through
bulges past the roof to a slab

**22** **Black int' Back** $7a$** (15m) Use the
crack to gain the flake, turn the bulge to the
left and finish as for **21**

Malcolm Fletcher hugs **The Kirrie
(beach) Ball** (6b+). Photo Fraser Harle

ANGUS & NORTHEAST

## B. THE CUTTING

Immediately to the right of the West Bay is a small area containing six short routes.

**1** **Hanging by a Thrumhold** *6a+*\* (7m) Follows a borehole and passes to the left of the roof via the notch - high in the grade

**2** **Wisdom's Door** *6b+*\* (8m) Good holds lead to a slabby recess. Pass the roof to the right and make a surprisingly tricky mantel

**3** **The Twa Dogs** *6c*\* (8m) Reachy moves lead to a rail, where a short technical sequence leads to easy ground

**4** **Tim'rous Beastie** *5+*\* (8m) Pleasant but straightforward climbing up huge holds

**5** **Sonsie Face** *6a* (8m) Gain the hanging slab to finish as for **4**

**6** **Glaikit Folly** *5* (7m) The right hand line, needs traffic to improve the rock

Caitlin cruising **Grassy Knoll** (6a) - P178

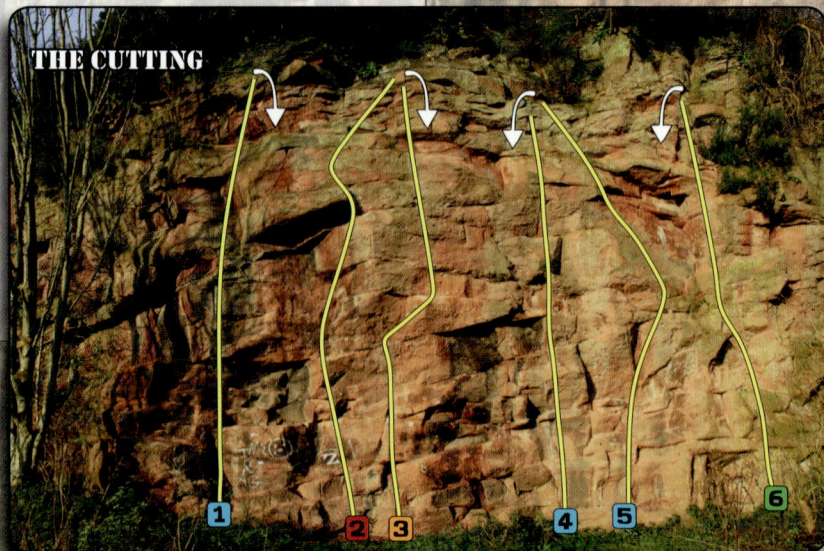

THE CUTTING

**SECTEUR D'INITIATION**

7 8 9 10 11 12 13 14 15

Seb 'enjoying' the mantel of
**Wisdom's Door** (6b+)

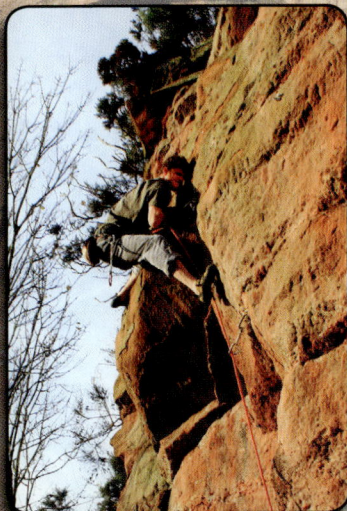

# C. SECTEUR D'INITIATION

The first section of the large central area lies around a silver birch tree and is generally more broken than the neighbouring faces. As the name suggests, it contains some easier routes.

**7** **Screwless** 3* (10m) Easy Fun!

**8** **Kirrie on Regardless** 3+* (10m)

**9** **Spent** 6a* (11m)

**10** **Badly Overdrawn Boy** 6a+* (11m)
An easy start leads to a high crux

**11** **Joining the Debt Set** 6b (11m)
The crux is at the top, harder for the short

**12** **Never Never Land** 6a+* (11m)
High in the grade

**13** **La Plage** 4* (9m)
The left-facing corner, may be sandy

**14** **Hill Billies** 4* (11m)

**15** **The Hill Has Eyes** 5+* (11m)
The rock improves with height and provides an awkward move

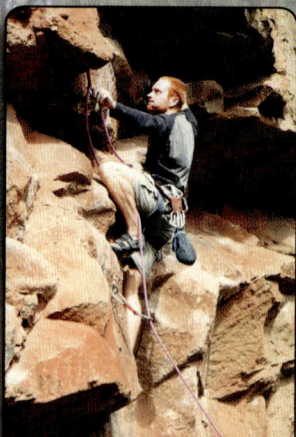

Ollie working off some
**Xmas Excess** (6a+)
Photo Lasma Sietinsone

## D. MAIN WALL LEFT

This section starts on the left with a prominent steep black wall, and contains some of the area's best harder lines.

**1** **What Every Woman Wants** 7a* (12m)
Hard moves through the top bulge, especially for shorties

**2** **Where There's Muck There's Brass**
6c+* (12m) A tricky boulder problem start and a harder crackline to finish

The central line gives **Slim Pickin's** 7b** and the quarry's hardest challenge.

**3** **Dig Deep** 6c+** (11m) Long powerful moves on good holds lead to a thin crux at the very top

SECTEUR
D'INITIATION

**4** **Ginger's Jewels** $6b$+** (12m)
Directly through two roofs just right of the faultline. Steep!

**5** **Beat the Bulge** $6b$+* (12m) Technical and fingery moves to pass the roofs on their right side

**6** **Weighty Issue** $6b$ (12m) Straightforward initially but with a tricky finish

**7** **Gut Feeling** $6b$+* (12m)
An awkward start and steep finish on good holds (once you find them)

**8** **Touch Too Much** $7a$* (12m) Low in the grade. The technical and steep moves round the nose should be taken on the right for the grade. Left is easier

**9** **Xmas Excess** $6a$+** (12m)
Pull onto the slab with difficulty, then easier ground leads to a high lower-off

**10** **Serious Beef** $6c$* (12m)
Move through the awkward niche to get established on the pleasant slab

**11** **Fat of the Land** $6b$* (12m)
A crimpy start leads to a pleasant slab

**12** **Fat Boy Slims** $5$** (12m)
The corner/ramp is a good easier route

**13** **Monkey See Monkey Do** $6b$+*
(12m) Pull through roofs and bulges to a slab

**14** **The Zoo** $6a$+* (12m) Start up a groove, pass through tricky overlaps and onto the slab

ANGUS & NORTHEAST

## D. MAIN WALL RIGHT

After a small tree, the last section to the east contains generally easier lines, but not always of equivalent quality.

**1** **Walking the Plank** *6a+** (14m) Start in the corner then break out left. The crux is short-lived but tricky

**2** **Crocodile Corner** *5+*** (14m) The obvious large corner - tricky for the grade

**3** **By Hook or by Crook** *5+*** (14m)

**4** **Smee Day** *5*** (14m) Steep but good holds. Pass just to the left of the roof, and lower off as for **3**

**5** **Wings Would Help** *6a+** (14m) Bronze hangers lead the way through the scoop and centre of the roof

**6** **Flyboy** *6b** (14m) Climb direct through the first roof, above the slab, and pass the upper one to the right

**7** **Wrong Turn** *5+* (13m) Pass the lower roof to the left to gain the arête and slab

**8** **True Path** *6a+** (14m) Start up blocks then step left onto the arête

**9** **Seeing the Light** *6a+* (14m) After a soft start the difficulty increases with height. The crux bulge is best approached from the left

**10** **Peddle Power** *6a+** (14m) Steep moves to reach the upper black roof

**11** **Done and Dusted** *6b*** (14m) Difficulty increases with height

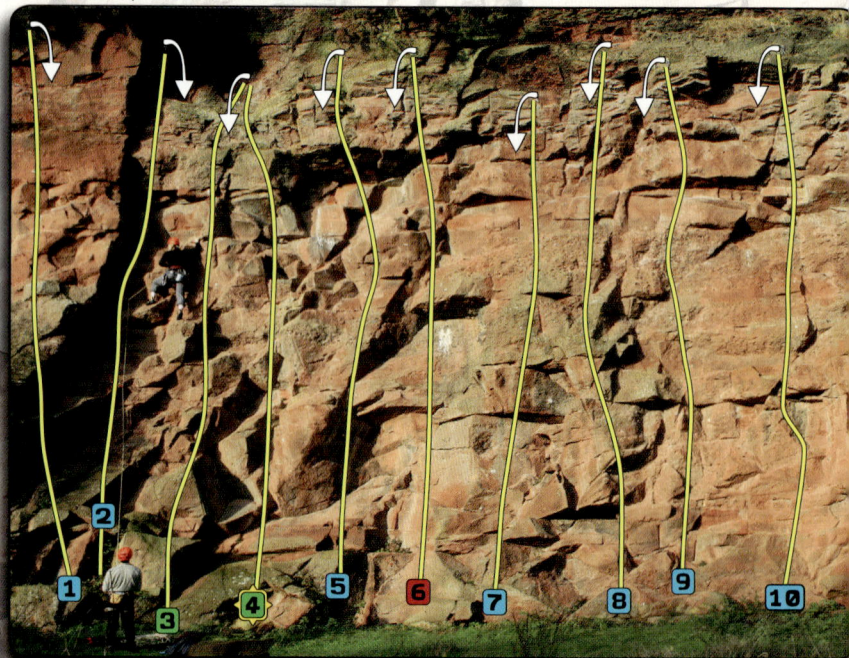

**12** **Curtain Call** $6a+$ (14m) An easy start leads to tricky moves from the 3rd bolt onward

**13** **When Annabelle Met Tinkerbelle** $6a*$ (12m) Start in a small alcove, head up past an overhanging block then step right into the large crack to finish (*may be loose*)

**14** **El Captain** $5+$ (12m) Directly up the face before crossing the large crack rightwards and up to a small roof. Lower-off to right or left

**15** **El Boa** $6a$ (12m) Follows the left-trending fault direct on poor rock

**16** **Kirrie Sutra** $6a**$ (12m) Start up a short arête to ledge, then follow thin crack through pebbles with care

**17** **Awe!** $6a+**$ (12m) Pull through roof with obvious borehole, and continue through two more to lower-offs on slab

**18** **Stiff Little Fingers** $6b*$ (12m) Climb a series of ledges and slabs, avoiding the corner. Low in the grade

**19** **Markerhorn** $4+$ (10m) Bridge up the obvious corner

**20** **Grand Jorassic** $5$ (10m) The wall to the right of the corner

Two lines lie on and to the right of the arête:

**21** **Ruthosaurus** $3+$ (8m) Climb just right of the arête

**22** **Stegasaurus** $4$ (9m) Follow the spikey 'dinosaur's back'

ANGUS & NORTHEAST

# Rob's Reed

56.65991 -2.834550

P 56.65964 -2.827953

Rob's Reed is a long, south-facing outcrop of hard sandstone and conglomerate. Its steepness and sheltered aspect allow year-round climbing. It provides a good selection of hard technical routes, largely on vertical walls, but with a few testing roofs. Pebbles may occasionally break from the conglomerate matrix, especially on newer routes, so care should be taken by both climber and belayer.

The crag is most commonly approached from the east, and so the routes are described in sectors starting from that end.

If driving, approach from Forfar along the B9113. After 2.5 miles, turn left at a small road signed 'Wemyss Farm'. After driving carefully through the farm, park **off the tarmac** at a switchback to avoid blocking access. Walk 50m further along a muddy track and then climb carefully over the gate and follow the path up and left to reach the east end of the crag (10mins). Buses 21A and 23B from Forfar lead to Lunanhead, from where one can walk (20mins) to the west end of the crag. Follow the green 'Forfar Path Network' signs to Myreside/Pitscandly.

⚠ There is **strictly no access between 1st Sept - 31st Oct** each year during the deer rutting season. Please respect this, both for your own safety and to ensure good relations with the landowner.

Evening light behind the steep prow of **Little Bo Peep** (6b)

0 5 8 15 16

 10 mins  20 mins

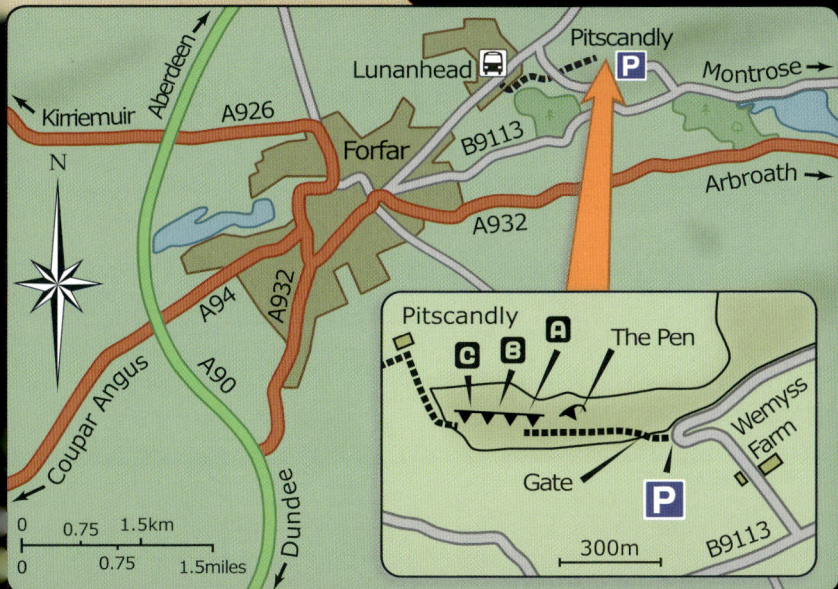

Kirriemuir

Aberdeen →

A926

Lunanhead

Forfar

B9113

A932

Pitscandly

P

Montrose →

Arbroath →

N

A94

A932

A90

Coupar Angus

Dundee

0  0.75  1.5km

0  0.75  1.5miles

Pitscandly

C  B  A  The Pen

Gate

P

Wemyss Farm

300m

B9113

# Rob's Reed

## A MAIN WALL RIGHT

The eastern section of the main wall, which is reached first from the approach path.

**1 Forfaraway** 6b* (12m)
Start up the steps to tricky pebbles

**2 Italian Stallion** 6a+* (12m)
Thin moves starting up the V-notch

**3 Horny Deer?** 5+* (12m)
A reachy start leads to good holds

**4 Squeal Like a Piggy** 6b* (16m)
A technical start and a steep finish

**5 Fire in the Hold** 6a+* (16m)
Another reachy start

**6 Burning Desire** 6c* (16m) A big move gains the ledge above the scoop

**7 High Voltage** 6b+** (13m)
A thin start, then follow the crack

**8 Power Flower** 6c* (15m)
Start up the lower cracks then move up and left with difficulty

**9 Going Through on Aggregate** 7a** (16m) Sustained climbing through the break and overhang

**10 Beyond the Call of Nature** 7a* (14m) Very thin moves lead to easier climbing in the groove

**11 Loose Cannons** 6c** (16m) Start up the roofed corner, then follow the overhang right to join **12**

**12 R+D Dubz** 6a* (15m)
The easy angled pillar on the right

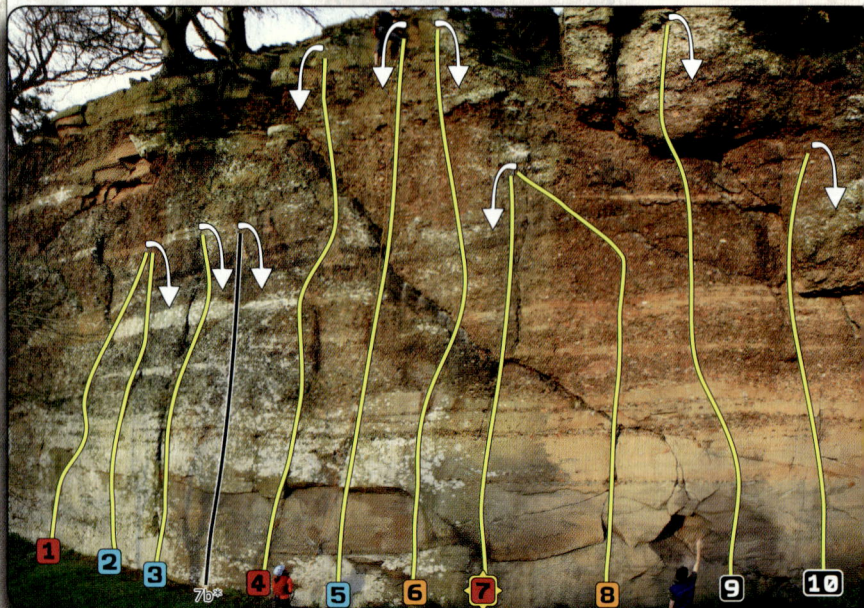

# THE PEN

A small quarried area about 150m right of the main cliff. More recently developed, so watch out for loose pebbles.

**13** **Spider Pig** $7a+*$ (12m)
The left wall, thin and sustained

**14** **Swine Flew** $6b$ (12m)
Follow the groove (may be loose at top) then move left to lower-off

**15** **Harry Trotter** $6c$ (9m)
The wall and arête

Koon Morris ponders the roof of
**Grand Theft Auto** (7a+) - p191
Photo Fraser Harle

## 8 MAIN WALL LEFT

The continuation of the wall, left from Forfaraway and behind the trees, holds a good concentration of harder lines around a couple of chossy corners.

### SECTOR SIZE ISN'T EVERYTHING

Short, steep, technical routes on the small wall just right of the cave.

**1 Grasping the Nettle** 6c* (10m)
A thin start gains the blunt rib and a shared lower-off. Easy at the grade

**2 Welcome to the Big Pocket**
6c* (10m) A hard bouldery start via the eponymous pocket

**3 Get Shorty** 6c+ (7m) A hard dynamic start involving a square mono, thankfully easier after

**4 Short Haul** 7a+ (7m) Start by traversing in from the right and make a long reach to get established in the sandstone band

**5 Sold Short** 6c* (7m) The short hanging arête is no pushover

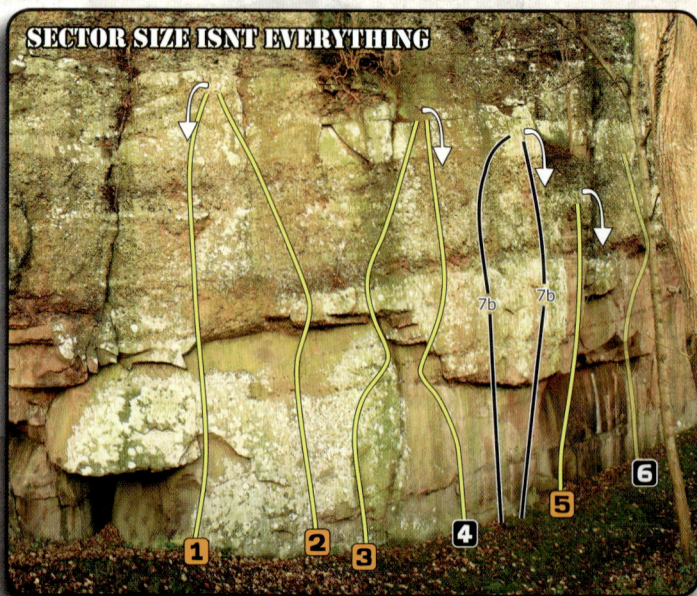

SECTOR SIZE ISNT EVERYTHING

## ELDER WALL

To the right of the corner, the routes are longer, but continue to be fiercely technical.

**6 The Uninvited** $7a+$* (12m)
The starting moves may be hard for the tall, but lead to a good jug

**7 One Foot in the Door** $7a$* (12m)
Start direct to a pocket over the lip

**8 Gatecrashers Galore** $7a+$ (12m)
High in the grade. Pass the overlap with difficulty to gain the jug

**9 Grand Theft Auto** $7a+$** (12m)
Through the small roof into the crack that splits the upper sandstone band

**10 Autobahn** $6c+$** (15m)
The prominent lower crack and the twin cracks in the upper band

**11 Need for Speed** $6c+$* (15m) The thin crack and groove eases with height

**12 Fretting Over Nothing** $7a+$** (15m) Tiny holds, long moves and a high mantel make this a testing number

**13 No Respect for your Elders** $6c+$** (15m) Thin and puzzling wall climbing leads to a good jug

**14 Pitscandly Chainsaw Massacre** $7a$* (15m) Low in the grade. Thin but good moves. Keep left out of the loose corner

**15 Deer Hunter** $6c+$* (14m) Hard moves at the 'shield' lead into the groove and a pumpy headwall

**16 Leonardo da Pinchy** $7a$* (15m) Move up into the pod then up rightward through sustained pebbles, before finishing right to **17**. Low in the grade

**17 D.i.v.o.r.c.e.** $6c+$* (14m) An extremely thin start leads quickly to easier ground

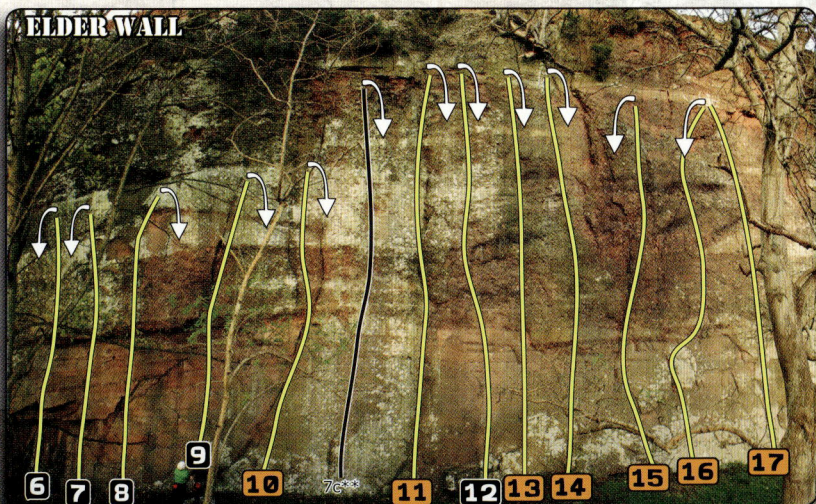

ELDER WALL

# Rob's Reed

## C CAVES AREA

### DIRTY HARRY'S CAVE
The leftmost end of the crag is dominated by a deep cave containing some of the hardest routes on the crag.

**1 Little Bo Peep** *6b* (8m)
Follow the hanging crack/flake line

**2 The Sheep of Things to Come** *6b+* (11m) The obvious corner line, with a low crux

**3 Skullduggery** *6c*** (12m) A good warm-up for its harder neighbour, with a similar steep start and technical headwall

**4 Car Pit Baggers** *7a+*** (12m)
A fine line. Steep, sustained and technical climbing on good cobbles.

To the right there is a deep cave, containing some savage test pieces, including '**Climb and Punishment**' (7b***).

**5 Dirty Harry** *6b** (12m) Start up the slab at the right end of the cave, into a groove, then break left

**6 Make My Day** *6a* (10m)
The right hand arête, finish right

### SECTOR CARAVAN
A shallower cave to the right produces a series of savage roofs that guard the start to most the routes in this sector.

**7 Good Boy Jo-Jo** *6b+** (10m)
A technical start then good pockets. Finish as for **6**

DIRTY HARRY'S CAVE

**8** **Towed in the Hole** $7a$** (12m)
A bit squeezed in, but provides thin technical interest with blinkers

**9** **Head of the Queue** $6c$+* (12m)
The crackline leads to a good rest before sustained moves through the pebbles

**10** **Snail's Pace** $7a$* (12m) The thin seam / crackline at the left end of the roofs provides a technical challenge

**11** **End of the Road** $7a$+* (12m)
A slightly smaller roof than Dennis Caravan, but no easy tick. If the crucial pebble falls out, it will get much harder

**12** **Dennis Caravan** $7a$+* (12m)
A long reach through the roofed corner leads to sustained climbing up the wall above

Topher mid-crux and perplexed on
**Car Pit Baggers** (7a+)

SECTOR CARAVAN

# Legaston

56.62735 -2.670736

56.62979 -2.670596

This open quarry was home to some of the earliest bolt-protected climbing in Scotland, but not without its share of controversy. Driller Killer, the first 'sport' line in 1984, originally had only a single bolt. Hangers were removed, replaced, stolen wholesale, until finally the quarry was accepted as a sport/training venue thanks to the equipping efforts of Neil Shepherd and friends. The rock is very compact sandstone and lends itself to quite reachy climbing between horizontal breaks - being taller is helpful here! Most of the quarry faces north, making it fairly grim in the winter, although some routes stay reliably dry.

If driving, Legaston lies just off the A933 north of Arbroath. Between Friockheim and the junction with the B961 (Dundee), at the bottom of a long hill, turn into a small track leading to a cottage. To keep the owners of the cottage happy, park as close to the road as possible keeping access clear. It is also preferred that dogs are not brought to the quarry. Walk down the track past the cottage and a wooden gate to reach the quarry (5mins). The nearest train is Arbroath, from where one can cycle along the A993 (10km), or take the bus #27 to Friockheim and walk south (1km).

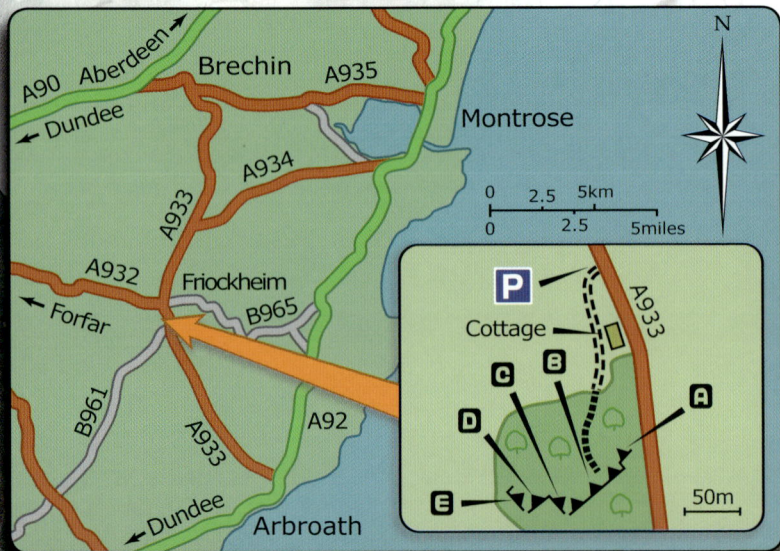

2 mins  30 mins

## Ⓐ RING BUTTRESS

The small clean wall on the left side of the quarry contains one of the first recorded sport climbs in Scotland.

**1** **The Killing Fields** *6a* (10m) An eliminate. Climbs the face avoiding the cracks either side

**2** **Armygeddon** *5+\** (10m) Follows the crack

**3** **Driller Killer** *6c\*\** (10m) One of the country's first bolted routes, and with an old-school grade. Technical, crimpy and reachy, this remains a tough test-piece

**4** **Trial by Dimension** *7a* (10m) Even more reach-dependent than **3**

**5** **Flight of the Mad Magician** *6b\*\** (10m) A good companion to Driller Killer, but with better holds. The iron ring lower-off is not UIAA rated!

**6** **Seconds Out** *6a* (9m) Retro-bolted trad crack (E15b). A bit scrappy at the top

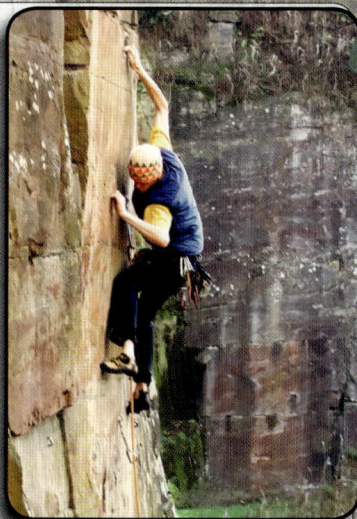

Seb crimping through **Driller Killer** (6c)

ANGUS & NORTHEAST

# Legaston

## Ⓑ MAIN WALL

The long bay at the back of the quarry holds some good clean routes on the left end, but deteriorates to the right, becoming both broken and vegetated.

⚠️ The quarry was partially filled after many of the routes were bolted, so there is sometimes a risk of decking while clipping the 2nd bolt.

**1** **Ratbag** *6a* (12m) Starting on the small ledge, climb up past the flake and through reachy horizontal breaks

**2** **Hunt the Ratbag** *6b** (12m) Directly up the wall. Reachy and hard for the grade

**3** **Death is the Hunter** *6b+** (12m) Not to be confused with its Auchinstarry namesake. Long moves on pockets leads to a very crimpy crux. Stiff!

**4** **Sweet Revenge** *6a+*** (15m) Retrobolted trad (E15b). Follow the left-slanting crackline, finishing right

**5** **Junk Man Blues** *6a+** (12m) The line running parallel to **4** on the right, and sharing its lower-off

**6** **Between the Lines** *5+** (12m) A popular route, starting as for **5** and then breaking right through steep ground

**7** **Bomber** *6a+** (14m) Start up the slab to stand on the flake, then make tricky moves to get through the roof

**8** **Brian the Snail** *6a* (12m) Start up the easy ramp before stepping right onto the flake and climbing the headwall directly. The direct start is 7b

**9** **The Rocking Stone** *4* (15m) Also previously a trad line (Severe) following the diagonal fault. May be loose

**10** **March of the Dimes** *6a* (14m) The awkward bulging wall

**11** **Shoot to Kill** *5+** (13m) Follows the shallow scoop, with only 2 bolts

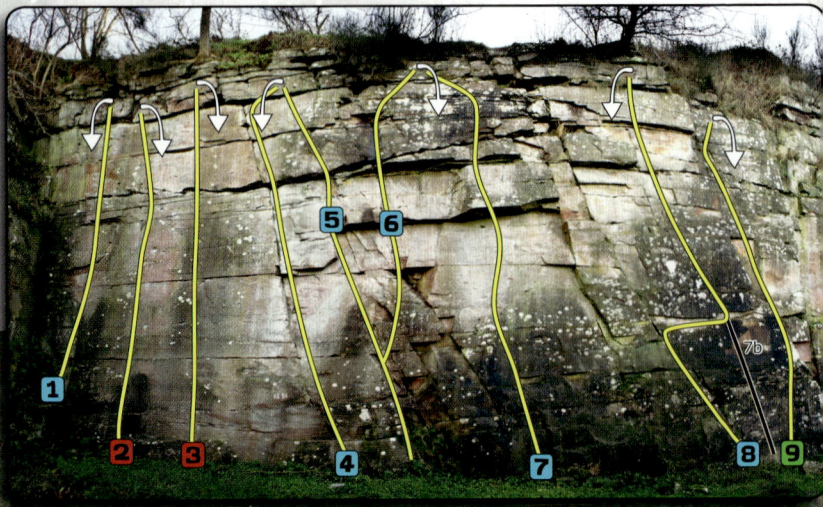

Topher pulling through the roof of **Bomber** (6a+)

**12** **Overkill** *6b** (13m) The left-hand of two cleaned lines through the tiers, with the crux on the middle tier

**13** **Desperate Measures** *6b* (13m) Start just left of the corner and stay left of the bolt-line. Moving right to better holds reduces the grade to 5+

**14** **Fire at Will** *4+* (13m) Directly up the wall passing through the stepped ramp

The right end of the bay holds four slabby routes, which quickly accumulate moss if un-climbed. If you can find them, they are:

**15** **Walking the Straight Line** *4+* (13m)

**16** **Ain't No Rolling Stone** *4+* (13m)

**17** **The Rack** *4+* (14m)

**18** **Lemon Squeezy** *4+* (14m)

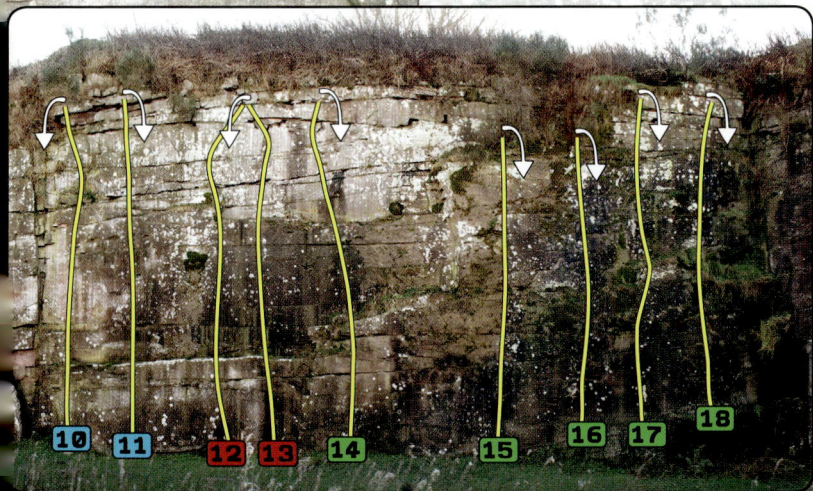

# Legaston

## C ROTTEN WALL

Better climbing than the name suggests, although the rightward routes are still a little friable.

**1 The Golden Shot** *6b+** (13m) Start on the small ledge in the corner, pull right onto the face and ascend direct to the lower-off. The direct start is 7a

**2 The Hunting Swan** *6b+* (13m) An indirect start to **3**, avoiding the crux

**3 First To Fall** *6c** (13m) A fierce fingery start forms the crux, with easier ground above

**4 Hell's Bells** *6c** (15m) Starting in the 'Pit', this also has a very hard start

**5 Fire Down Below** *6a+** (15m) Starting in the 'Pit', this is hard for the grade and contains some dubious rock

**6 Demolition Man** *5+* (13m) Climb loose rock up the groove, if you must!

**7 The Big J** *6b* (13m) Climb up to and use the carved "J" to reach the break and join the next route

**8 Rocket's Secret Machine** *7a+** (13m) A bouldery start and a tricky finish, perhaps spoiled by a good rest

**9 Everything Must Go** *6a* (13m) Just left of the arête, crumbly

**10 Edge of Darkness** *6a** (16m) Start up the face then swing onto the arête at half-way. Topout to belay stakes

## D FORBIDDEN BUTTRESS

The left side of the square recess contains perhaps the best lines in the quarry.

**11 Direct Access** *6c*** (15m) Climb the flake to the ledge, move up right to a flat edge (shared with **12**), then left to a broken flake and steep finish

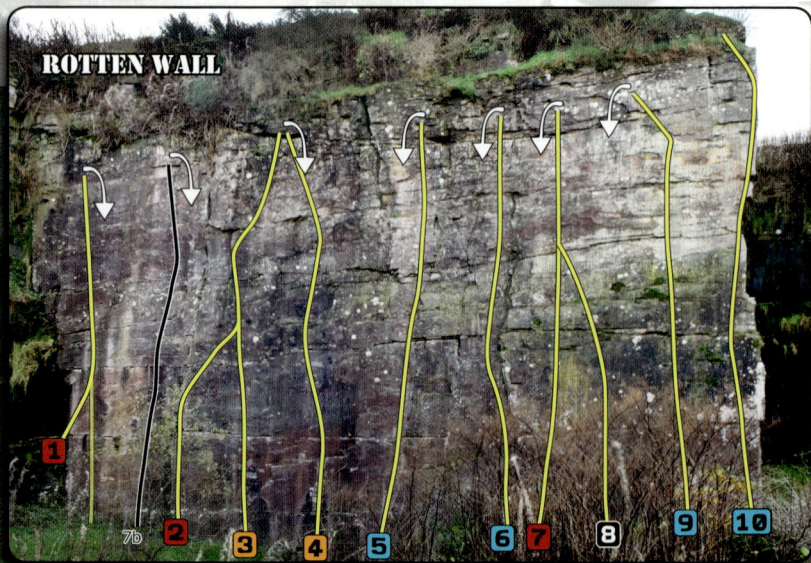

ROTTEN WALL

**12 No Remorse** 6c+*** (15m)
Sustained technical wall climbing. Climb to the overlap and through to the shared flat edge and a rest. Move up right to another overlap and finish

**13 Spandex Ballet** 7a+*** (15m)
Probably the route of the crag, but desperate for the short! Awkward moves gain a sloping ramp, then stretch between the breaks on pockets to the final overlap

# E BABYLON BUTTRESS
The back of the recess is almost always wet and vegetated. In times of drought some gardening may reveal:

**14 She Conceives Destruction** 7a (12m)
**15 Lymphomaniac** 6a (12m)
**16 Roxanne** 4* (20m)
**17 Diss!** 6b (12m)
**18 Nymphocyte** 6b+* (12m)
**19 Playing with Fire** 6c** (12m)
**20 Les Mort Dansant** 7a* (12m)
**21 Necrosis** 6a* (12m)

FORBIDDEN BUTTRESS

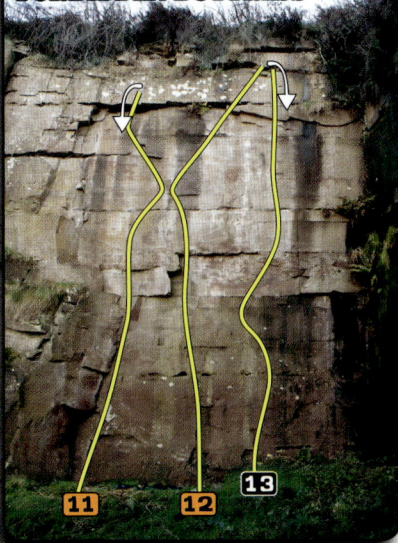

To the right of Babylon Buttress is **ROSE WALL**. It holds (L-R) **Exodus** (5) **The Weasel** (6a+*) and **Remain in the Light** (6b+). Often vegetated.

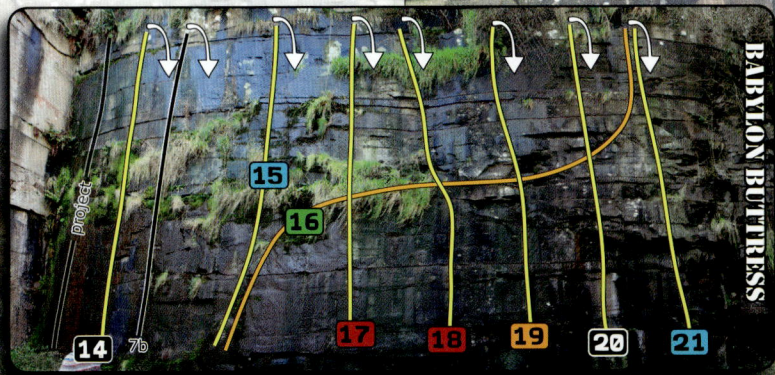

ANGUS & NORTHEAST

BABYLON BUTTRESS

# Balmashanner

56.62617 -2.890591
56.62669 -2.898037

The infamous 'Shanner' with its ferociously leaning right wall is home to some of Scotland's harder sport routes. There are however several more amenable lines for us lesser mortals! The rock is a compact sandstone similar to Legaston, but typically steeper and with interesting features. This quarry is north facing and sits in a hollow, so while it may offer shelter from the wind it can be cold. The right wall often seeps and needs a prolonged dry spell to come into condition – needless to say, not a winter venue!

From the A90 take the A932 (Dundee road) north towards Forfar for just over half a mile. Just before the town, take a concealed road on the right named Glencoe cottage. Park considerably about 50m up this road. The Dundee-Kirriemuir bus #10 will stop at Westfield on Dundee Road. Continue on foot directly up the hill onto a good footpath. After 400m, the path turns left into an avenue of trees; at this point leave the path and follow the fence line on the right along the edge of a field. After 50m cross the fence and the quarry will come into view.

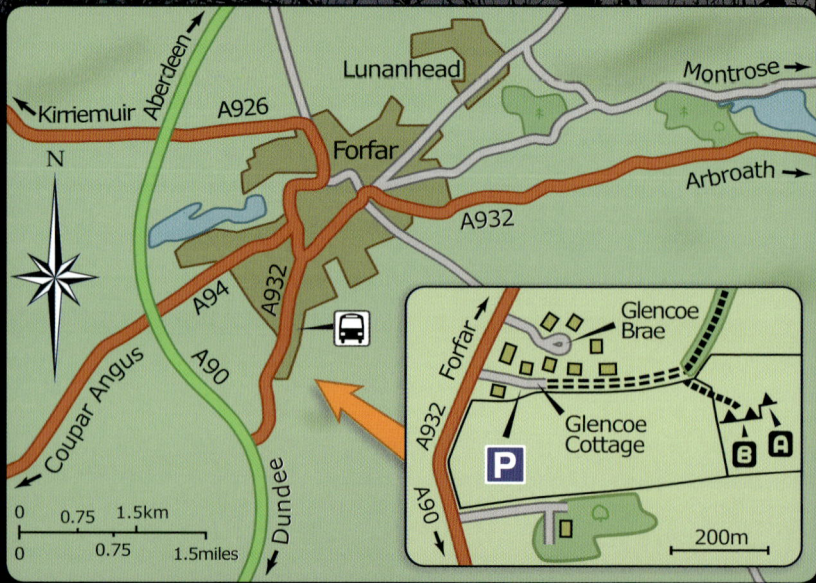

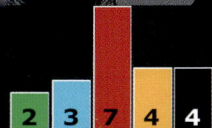

5 mins   10 mins

ANGUS & NORTHEAST

Sophie finding out that
**Syes Don't Matter** (6b)

# Balmashanner

## A. LEFT WALL

The smaller wall is easier but not of the quality of its neighbour, with some loose rock.

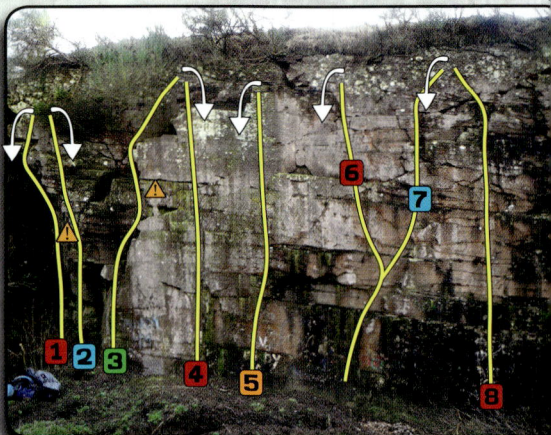

**1** **Dennis the Menace** *6b* (8m) The corner and capping overhang (loose)

**2** **Desperate Dan** *6a+* (8m) The cracked arête may feel desperate indeed (loose)

**3** **99 Flake** *4\** (8m) Climb the huge flake to a fingery finish - don't pull too hard!

**4** **Ice Scream Wall** *6b\** (8m) The thin seam gives a hard start before easing up

**5** **Balmashanner Bombshell** *6c* (9m) Another hard bouldery start before easing off further up

**6** **One Can Dan** *6b* (9m) Start up the shallow stepped corner and then break leftwards

**7** **Mini the Minx** *6a\** (10m) Follow the stepped corner in the centre of the face with a crux at half height

**8** **Rat Race Face** *6b* (10m) Hard and sustained for the grade. Take care with the clips

RIGHT WALL

# B. RIGHT WALL

The deep bay starting at the steep arête.

**9** **Syes Don't Matter** 6b (8m) Dyno up the left arête of the bay and traverse right to the lower-off

**10** **Sye of Relief** 6b+ (8m) Climb up through the niche and break out left to finish. Used to be E2

**11** **Firestarter** 6a+* (12m) The cracked groove, passing a large ledge, finishing at chains

**12** **Delivery Man** 7a+* (12m) The smooth, pale wall is short but powerful

**13** **Start the Fire** 6b+** (12m) A good warm up route! Follow the corner at the left end of the main steep wall to a lower-off on the left - pumpy!

The face now turns the corner to reveal the classic '**Savage Amusement**' (7b***) on the steep Main Wall.

**14** **Rat Attack** 6c+ (13m) Follow a thin flake-crack to step left into the base of the big flake. Finish up this. The direct start is '**Manfestations**' - a test piece 7b

**15** **Hell Bent for Lycra** 7a** (12m) The obligatory 'Shanner entrance exam! Climb the pumpy groove to a high crux

**16** **Le Bon Vacance** 7a* (13m) More technical than the previous route, but less sustained. Finish up the groove

**17** **Half the Battle** 7a* (14m) A popular training route with a crux at the top. Climb the wall to the left of the cracked cave

**18** **The Comfort Machine** 6c+* (15m) Start up **17** to the cave, then traverse right across its lip to finish up a right-trending ramp

**19** **Off the Couch** 6c (14m) A direct start to the **18**, but the rock in the cave is poor

**20** **Balamashanner Buttress** 4+ (14m) An enjoyable route up the corner that bounds the main face. Look left onto the slopers of '**The Merchant of Menace**' (8b+**) and wonder...

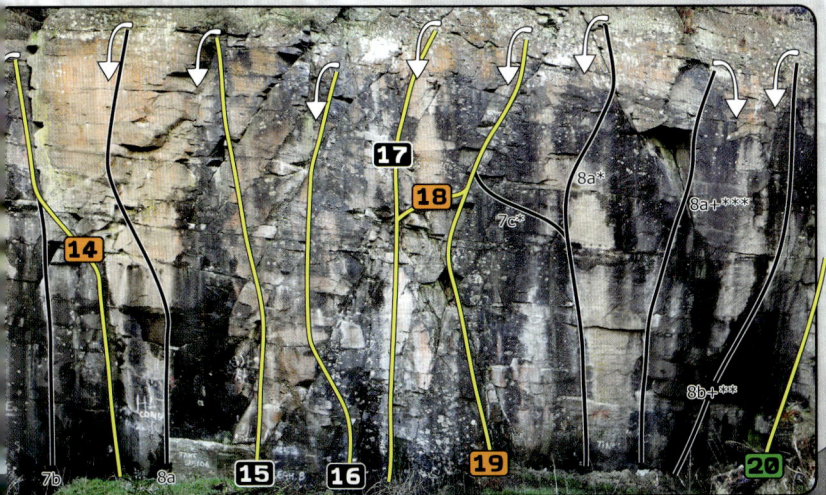

# Ley Quarry

56.52579 -3.208798

56.52500 -3.211416

While on first sight Ley Quarry is a manky hole in the ground, it contains a good range of sport routes, and is a seepage-free sun-trap. The ambience has been described as 'French' although we are unsure of what part of that country is being referred to! It's certainly not a place to take the family for a picnic, unless they have strong fingers. Please do not bring dogs.

The rock is a hard and compact sandstone. Routes tend to be reachy in character, and in places holds have been manufactured, and some even modified with resin to create shallow pockets and crimps. The routes often rely on good crimp strength and this may be the deciding factor in success or failure. Apart from a few old fixtures, the routes have been well equipped with resin bolts and lower-offs. The quarrymen left a useful ledge from which all the climbs are accessed…just be careful to not fall into the pond!

Approach from either Dundee or Coupar Angus via the A923 and take the small road signed for Newtyle (second crossroads from Coupar Angus). Bus #59 (Dundee-Blairgowrie) takes you to this point. After 1/2 mile turn right up a very narrow dirt lane to park by a small reservoir. From here follow the path leftwards past a gate.

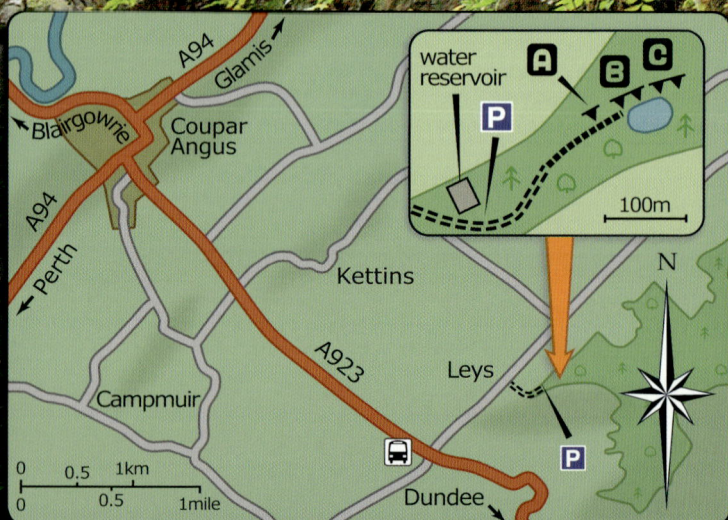

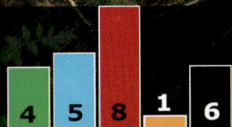

2 mins

15 mins

ANGUS & NORTHEAST

Sophie seeking out the **Nectar** (6a+)

# Ley Quarry

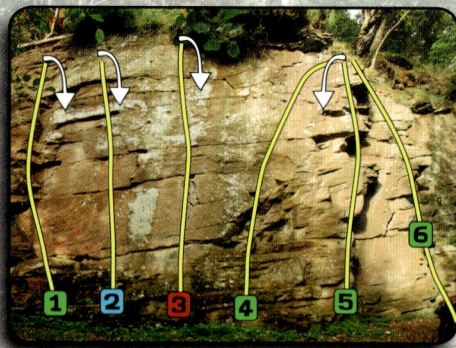

## A. SMALL WALL

**1** **Rottweiler** 4+ (7m)

**2** **Scarred for Life** 6a* (7m)
Very dependent on height

**3** **Magic Pockets** 6b* (7m)

**4** **Pit Bull** 4 (7m)

**5** **Cat Scratch Fever** 4 (7m)

**6** **April's Arête** 3+ (10m)
Start part way down the slope

## B. POOL WALL

Scramble down the bank using the fixed rope and traverse right over the pool to a narrow belay ledge.

**7** **Easy Ley** 6a+ (10m)

**8** **Nectar** 6a+* (10m) Sustained, varied and reachy to finish

**9** **Dropping Like Flies** 6b (20m) A girdle traverse running along the break from the 2nd bolt of **8** to finish up **13**

**10** **Nirvana** 7a+*** (11m) A crimpy, reachy test-piece with a vicious mono!

**11** **Five Magics** 6b+** (11m) Sustained, with a big move half-way

**12** **Footfall** 6a* (10m) The first route to be opened here, using an old quarry bolt for protection (take a sling or wide gate carabiner)

**13** **Not the Risk Business** 6c (11m) Follow the curving flake before finishing directly up the wall

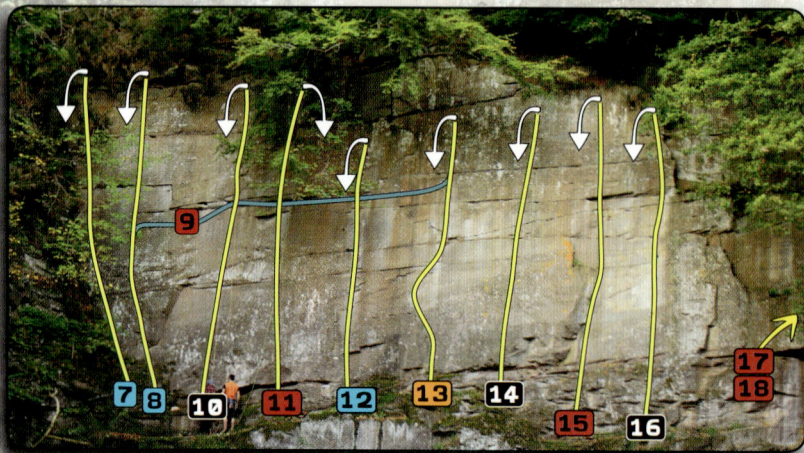

**14** **Drowning by Numbers** $7a*$
(12m) The slab with a hard start

**15** **Darkmoon Rising** $6b*$ (12m)
Starting from a lower ledge, follow the groove to committing high crux

**16** **Twilight Zone** $7a$ (10m) Thin moves up the pale wall are harder than they look. Take a brush

There is then a gap of a few metres before:

**17** **Fishing for Complements** $6b$
(10m) Hard for the grade - often dirty

**18** **Caught in the Act** $6b$ (10m)

**19** **Traditional Imperfections** $6a*$
(10m) Climb directly over the nose of the overhang and up the easy slab

WATERFRONT LEFT

## C. THE WATERFRONT

Continue along the ledge system or walk around the pond to the right. The first set of routes are usually started from the high ledge to avoid a sandy start.

**20** **Pool of Despair** $7a+*$ (9m)

**21** **Leyed to Rest** $7a$ (9m)

**22** **Barrel of Laughs** $7a**$ (9m)
A popular training route, but largely artificial

The final routes are over the land.

**23** **Life's a Beach** $6b*$ (14m) The shallow groove is sustained and, unusually for the quarry, requires more technique than sheer finger strength

**24** **Fat Man Starts to Fall** $6b*$ (11m) Start as for **23** but trend right to a tenuous, fingery and sandy headwall

ANGUS & NORTHEAST

# Other Crags

**RED HEAD** (56.61741 -2.488175. Map p137) This 90m basalt outcrop lies north of Arbroath and is the highest point on the coast. It holds Scotland's most outrageously positioned sport route; a head for heights is essential. The route can be lichenous though, so bring a brush!

**Cock O' the North** *6c*** (25m). Abseil approach (30m). From a chain belay on a ledge in the main groove, traverse left to the hanging arête. Climb this, keeping left of the bolts, then pull through the bulge to gain the headwall

Approach via Inverkeilor, off the A92 between Arbroath and Montrose. Opposite the Chance Inn, turn down Station Road. After just over a mile take a right signed 'Ethie 1 mile', then immediately left. After 500m turn left for Ethie Mains and continue straight on to Ethie Barns. At the farm continue straight on a track, turn left after 400m and park on the cliff top (P 56.61545 -2.488945). Walk north in the field, going through a break in the wall to the headland (5 mins). Just back from the edge a bolt and staples will be found on a rock slab for the abseil. Consider leaving a rope in place here in case escape is required.

The dramatic profile of Red Head, with the line of **Cock O'the North** (6c) in the shade

**ORCHESTRA CAVE** (57.06959 -2.093442) lies slightly further north than the Portlethen crags by Findon village. Its back wall includes some of the country's best hard routes. For those not climbing grade 8s, four 10m routes surround a groove left of the cave with a single lower-off (L/R): **Time Will Tell** *7a*; **Mad Cows** *6a+\** (the groove); **Start a Revolution** *6b\**; **Moonlight Sonata** *6c\**. When not greasy, the excellent **Bassoon** *7a+\*\*\** (20m) climbs the left of the cave proper. At the northern end of the village, park at the end of Old Inn Road, the last right turn (**P**1: 57.07037 -2.103651. Map p142). From the last house, head towards the sea on a good track. After 300m a fainter track heads right becoming a path over heathery ground to a dry-stone wall. Follow this to take the second perpendicular wall heading to the sea. Just NE of the end of this wall is an abseil from a block well back from the cliff. Leaving a spare rope in place helps with the exit at the end of the day. Access is tidal.

**JOHNS HEUGH** (57.02448 -2.147403) Just south from Boltsheugh, this is largely a (good) trad venue, but holds a single bolted line on the right - **Warmup** *6b\**. Turn immediately right after the railway bridge in Newtonhill and park at the Bowling Club. (**P**6: 57.03041 -2.148881. Map p142) Walk south past the buildings and a football pitch then to a large field. The crag is in a bay just north of the bridge over the railway seen on your right. Partially tidal.

Seb climbing into the sun up **Arrol's Arête** 6b
Blantyre Towers (p222)

Despite being home to the bulk of Scotland's population, the Scottish Lowlands are not overly endowed with sport climbing venues. This is largely due to the fact that the area's dolerite quarries and sea-cliffs offer good trad climbing. Rock suitable for sport is limited but some has recently been developed at Balgone, Craigpark and Ratho, the latter being controversial when it encroached on established trad climbs! Most of the Lowland's sport venues are on quarried rock; natural outcrops such as Dunglas and Balgone are few in number. Even the extracted stone itself is climbed, such as is found at the esoteric Blantyre Towers. Although not offering sport to the extent of the northern Highlands or Angus, there are enough routes to train on or while away a summer's evening.

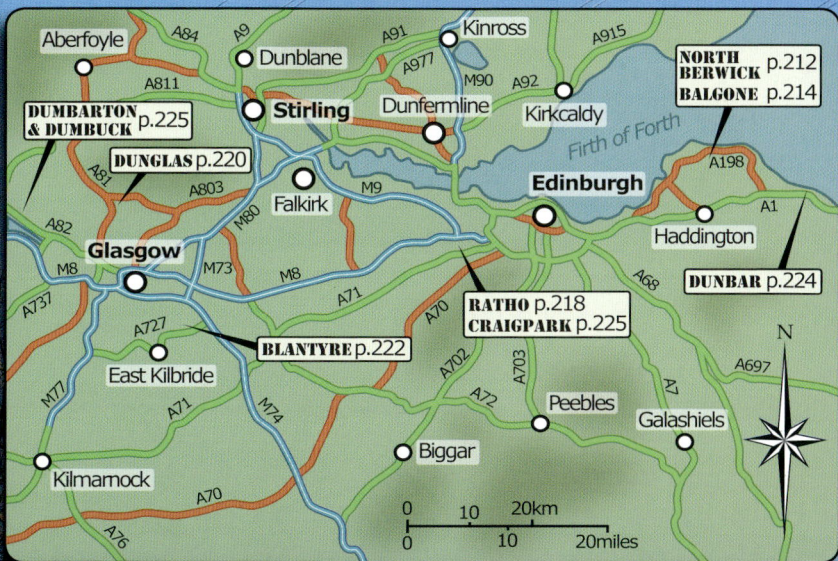

Aberfoyle
A84 A9
Dunblane A91 A977 Kinross A915
A811 M90 A92
**NORTH BERWICK** p.212
**BALGONE** p.214
**DUMBARTON & DUMBUCK** p.225
**Stirling** Dunfermline Kirkcaldy
*Firth of Forth*
**DUNGLAS** p.220 A803 M80 M9
Falkirk **Edinburgh** A198
A82 A81 A1
**Glasgow** M73 M8 A71 Haddington
M8 A70 **DUNBAR** p.224
A737 A727 A68
**RATHO** p.218
**CRAIGPARK** p.225
**BLANTYRE** p.222
East Kilbride A702 A703 N
M77 A71 M74 A72 A697
Peebles A7
Galashiels
Kilmarnock A70 Biggar
A76
0 10 20km
0 10 20miles

**SOUTHERN LOWLANDS**

# North Berwick Law

56.04655 -2.717385
56.04911 -2.719100

This small quarry is a popular sun-trap due to its easy access from Edinburgh and good quality, quick drying rock. It lies at the base of North Berwick Law, a striking volcanic remnant that affords fine views of the coastline. The town also offers the Bird Life Centre, boat trips, and beaches for non-climbing family. Most of the climbing is concentrated on two faces that form an open book at the left end of the quarry. There is limited scope for bouldering further right.

## LEFT WALL

**1 Left Hand Route** 6a+ (6m)
A short crimpy route on the upper-left tier

**2 Necktie** 6b+** (10m)
The left arête, keeping to its right side

**3 Fogtown** 7a** (10m) A bouldery start to lower-off as for **2**. It's better but harder to finish up right to the ledge (no arête) before lowering off (7a+)

**4 Law of Gravity** 7a*** (12m)
Reachy and fingery. Starting off the block to the right is easier and much less satisfying

**5 Jaws of the Law** 6c** (12m) A reachy start, but then good holds, and a no-hands rest if you can find it!

**6 Law of the Flies** 7a** (10m)
Technical and often requires a dyno, but about a grade easier for the tall

**7 Law and Disorder** 6a+* (10m)
The niche and short corner at the right end. Requires a dynamic start or good footwork!

**8 Law of the Rings** 7a* (25m)
A left-to right-girdle at mid height, starting up **2** and finishing up **7**

Approach North Berwick from the A1 via the A198, then in the town turn south onto Law Road (B1347). Pass the school and at a right hand bend, turn left to the Law car park. The train is very convenient from Edinburgh. If walking or cycling from the station, head rightwards uphill by the same route. From the parking it is a gentle five minute walk round the base of the hill, past the summit path, before the quarry comes into view on the left.

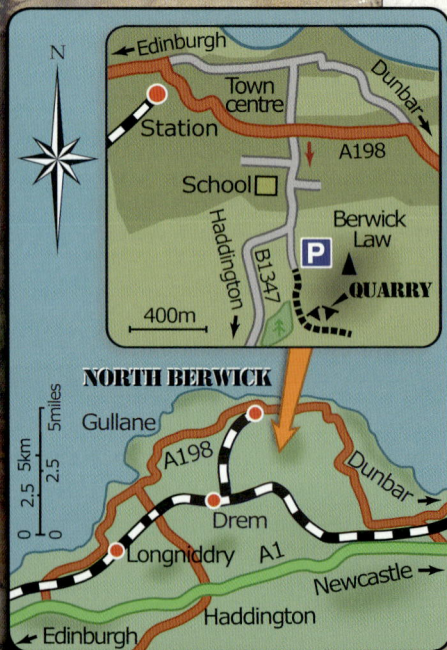

| 0 | 5 | 3 | 2 | 5 |
|---|---|---|---|---|

10 mins

15 mins

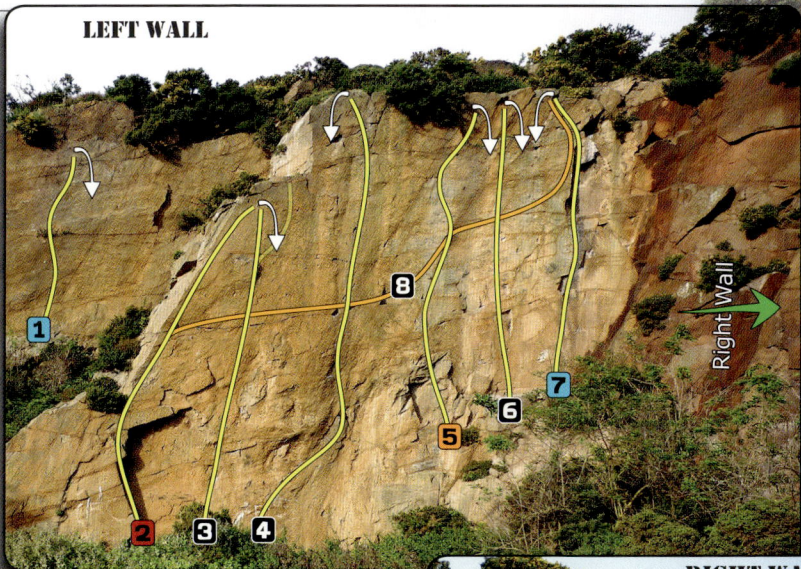

**LEFT WALL**

1 · 8 · 5 · 6 · 7 · 2 · 3 · 4

Right Wall

# RIGHT WALL

**9** **Darkness Falling** $6a+$* (10m)
The corner and slab

**10** **Igneous Intruder** $6c+$** (12m)
The central line up the slab. Technical

**11** **Dosage** $7a+$ (12m)
Very crimpy, finishing as for **10**

**12** **Old Law Breaker** $6b$** (12m)
The right hand slab route, justifiably
popular, has a tricky move at the bulge

**13** **Wild Iris** $5+$* (12m) The blocky
right arête of the slab

At the very far right end of the quarry, some
200m away, there are two short bolted lines:

**14** **Solitary Soul** $6b$* (6m)
To earn the tick, don't use the spike!

**15** **Anarchic Law** $6a+$ (8m)
The arête is out!

**RIGHT WALL**

9 · 10 · 11 · 12 · 13

SOUTHERN LOWLANDS

# Balgone Heughs

56.03194 -2.702964

56.04911 -2.719100

This recently rediscovered crag, situated on the quiet Balgone estate, provides a valuable addition of sport routes in the Central Belt. The escarpment has a pleasant position overlooking well-established deciduous forest and the man-made Balgone Loch; an important curling pond during the 1800s. The rock is a hobnobite lava of variable quality and is somewhat reminiscent of limestone, with cracks, pockets and overhangs. Being surrounded by trees the crag is very sheltered yet dries surprisingly quickly. Typical with basalts, any dampness makes the crag rather slippery.

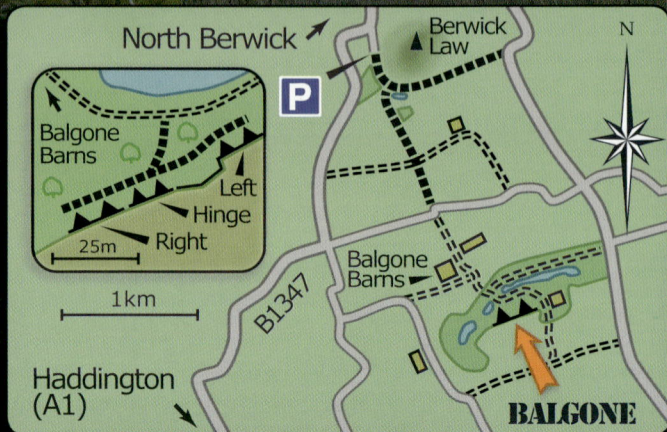

North Berwick

Berwick Law

N

P

Balgone Barns

Left

Hinge

Right

25m

1km

B1347

Balgone Barns

Haddington (A1)

BALGONE

25 mins    25 mins

⚠ **The landowner has stated that NO CARS are to be taken into the estate** – please respect this so that access is maintained! There is also an access ban during the bird shooting season - 1st Oct until 1st Feb.

Approach from North Berwick Law car park (map page 212). Take the John Muir Way on the right in the direction of East Linton. After ~1km a chicane on an asphalt road is reached. Straight ahead is a straight track signed 'Balgone Barns'. Take this track through the farm leftward and then down the hill to the loch. Immediately after the left turn in the track, take a 'faint path' on the right up to the crag.

**Balgone Heughs Overview**

**LEFT BUTTRESS**    **HINGE BUTTRESS**    **RIGHT BUTTRESS**

SOUTHERN LOWLANDS

# Balgone Heughs

## LEFT BUTTRESS

**1** **Heuthanasia** *7a+*** (13m) Climbs straight up the blank looking wall - crimpy and bouldery!

**2** **Heugh Know Nothing (Jon Snow)** *6c+*** (13m) Start as **1** then trend right up a faint ramp to a flake before heading left to the shared lower-off

**3** **The Entheughsiast** *7a** (17m) Start up **4** then move left at the roof to join **2**

**4** **Statement of Heuth** *7a+*** (15m) Gain the roofed corner with difficulty, pull out onto the face and up to a tricky finish!

**5** **Heugh and Cry** *7a** (17m) Start up the groove, pull through the overlap to a ledge, then crimp up the head wall

## HINGE BUTTRESS

**6** **The Wanderer** *6b+*** (17m) A fun meander through the overlaps. Start up the rib and groove on the left, exit right and up through the overhang to a slab. Finish more easily on the left of the arête

Just to the right of the main hinge buttress is a just off-vertical wall:

**7** **Ivy wall** *5+* (15m) The left route. A tricky start using holds to the left then climb straight up to the lower-off

**8** **The Curling Pond** *6a** (15m) A better right hand start to Ivy Wall. Nice moves for four bolts lead to the previous route

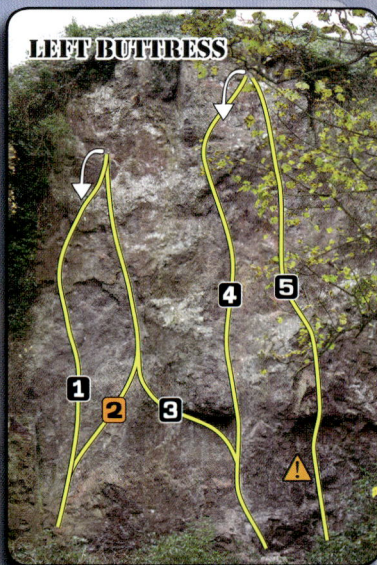

LEFT BUTTRESS

⚠ As this is a newly (re)developed crag, and some of the rock a little soft, it is advisable for belayers at least to wear helmets.

## RIGHT BUTTRESS

**9** **The Wasp** *6b*** (17m) Climb the overhang and right-slanting groove to a boss beside the corner. Go up then left under the overhang to a LO just above. Directly through the bulge left of the boss is *6c*.

**10** **Pheasant Corner** *6a+** (17m) Tackle the overhang gymnastically to gain the corner which is followed to a lower-off under a small roof

**11** **Mr Fox** *7a** (17m) Start in the groove on the left joining **12** at the top of the rib

**12** **Heughvenile Antics** *6c+**** (16m) The obvious rib up the centre of the buttress leads, via a crux on a slight bulge, to a hanging corner. A good sustained and technical route

**13** **Bullrush** *6c*** (16m) Follow a rib to a niche and overhang. Surmount this to gain a second niche. Pull through the bulge (crux) to gain holds right of the slab above. Exit left via an undercling to easier ground

Seb cruising the headwall of **The Wanderer** 6b+

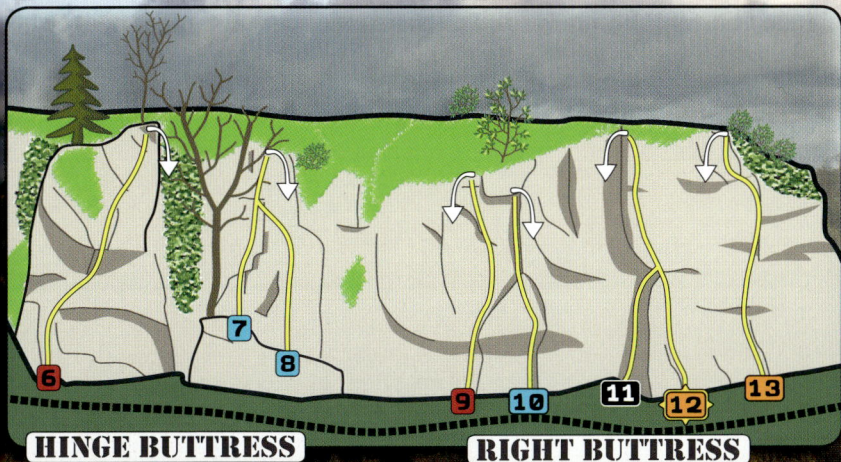

HINGE BUTTRESS

RIGHT BUTTRESS

SOUTHERN LOWLANDS

# Ratho Quarry

55.92391 -3.396574

55.92325 -3.399878

The dolerite quarry that houses the Edinburgh International Climbing Arena (EICA) also holds some fine outdoor routes. Most are traditional routes, for which the venue is justifiably well-known, but recent cleaning and bolting activity led to the development of several neglected areas. The bolted sections face east and southwest, catching sun throughout the day and drying quickly. Some holds, however, particularly in the Kamikaze area, may be covered in a little sand after rain.

Take the A8 west from Edinburgh to the Newbridge roundabout (M9 Junct. 1 from Glasgow) then the B7030 past the petrol station and follow signs for the EICA. Or, ride Lothian Bus 26 to Ratho village and walk pleasantly west along the canal for about 2km. This approach has the additional benefit of a pub at the end of your session! Walk round the right side of the EICA and down external stairs to access the quarry, or take the internal stairs down and out the back door. The car park is locked when the centre closes so park outside the gate if you are planning a later session!

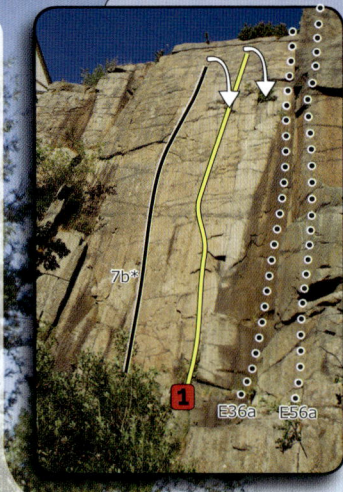

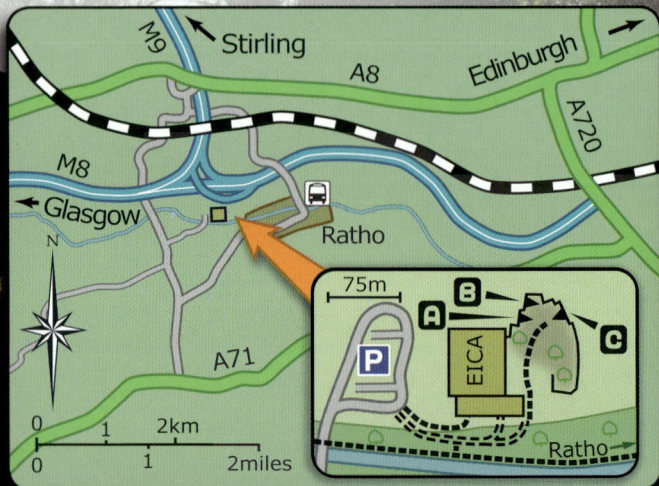

7b*

**1** E36a  E56a

1 1 5 1 1

3 mins   25 mins

**A.** The first routes are on your left as you enter the quarry, starting from a big ledge. The leftmost is **The Plums of Ratho** 7b.

**1** **The Grapes of Ratho** 6b+** (18m) A fine route up the crimpy wall left of the big corner. Continuously technical but rarely strenuous

**B.** The next, and most developed area is the large slabby promontory 10m further right.

**2** **Slow Strain** 6b+** (25m) Retro-bolted E2. A fantastic outing weaving up the left arête with interesting and varied movement

The capped groove is taken by the sustained slab test-piece **Buzooka** 7b**

**3** **Kamikaze** 6c+** (24m) Crimpy and delicate. Climb the lower wall and make tricky moves left then back right and up to gain the upper wall to the lower-off

**4** **John McCain** 6b* (12m) Manu-factured but worthwhile. Start from a scramble up right. Make balancy moves up left, then trend right on good incuts

**5** **Panzer** 6a+ (10m) Climb the tricky thin crack, then trend leftwards to a balancy finish

There is a lone route, made for beginners, on the buttress 20m right of **Panzer.**

**6** **Peashooter** 3+* (15m) Follow the cracked rib on big steps. A good route for learning trad protection whilst still on bolts!

**C.** The final three routes are on the east face opposite the EICA, left of the fire escape and a boulder-filled bay.

**7** **Impure Allure** 6b+** (20m) The stepped crackline left of the Shear Fear flake, ending atop a square cut block

**8** **The Corrieman** 6b+** (15m) Grovel into the base of a slim curving groove, then follow this more el-egantly to a ledge

**9** **Wounded Knee** 7a+* (12m) The right arête of the wall, starting on the right

SOUTHERN LOWLANDS

# Dunglas

55.98214 -4.285544

55.98559 -4.303525

The west face of the otherwise loose basalt plug of Dunglas has in its midst a steep wall of good quality rock, hosting a selection of short punchy sport routes that stay fairly dry in the rain. The routes are closely spaced and many link-ups and variations have been devised, so once you have ticked all the listed routes, just use your imagination!

Park by Strathblane Parish Church or take bus 10/C10 from Glasgow (50mins). Walk or cycle along the old railway path opposite, towards Lennoxtown. The crag becomes visible on the right. Please do not park at the farm, and avoid the lambing season (Feb-March) to maintain good access relations.

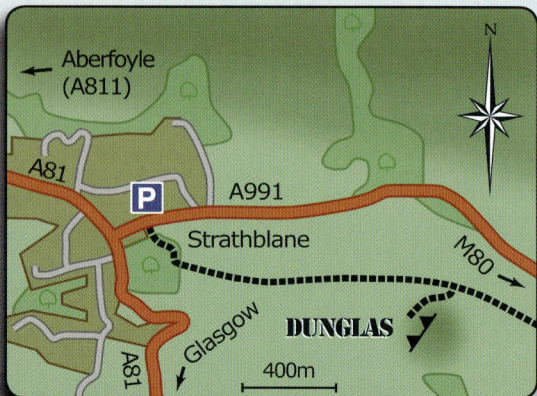

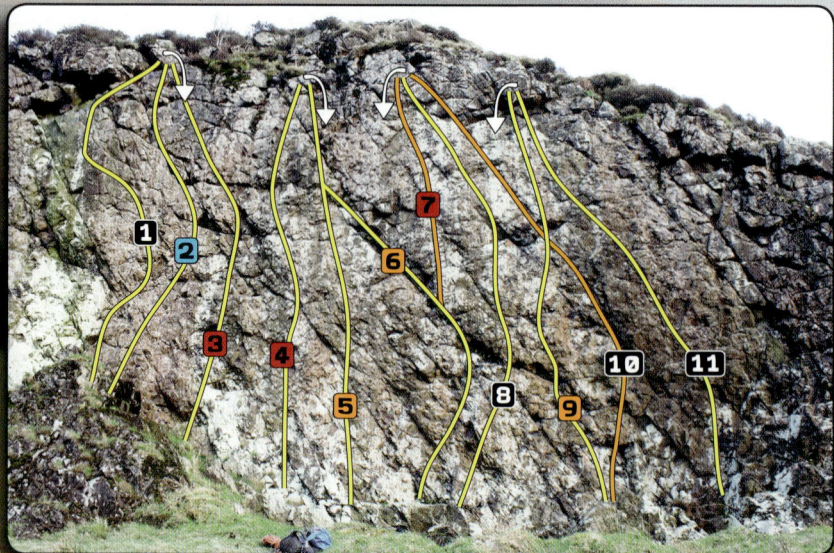

**0** **1** **3** **3** **4**

🚗🚶 10 mins   🚌🚶 15 mins

The routes are based around four lower-offs, and there is one bolt above the crag to allow access to set up a toprope.

**1** **Imodium Wall** $7a+$** (9m) Starting at the pillar, climb the green wall, step left at the second bolt and back right to the apex

**2** **Imodium Crack** $6a+$* (9m) Trend right to gain and climb the R-L slanting crack. Finish as for **1**. A direct finish is $6b$

**3** **Whiplash** $6b+$* (12m) From the base of the pillar step right and up to a triangular recess, then tackle the crimpy black headwall to finish as for **1**

**4** **Mister Poops** $6b+$** (15m) Starting just right of the pillar, step off the shelf and make hard moves to jugs and turn the roof on its left

**5** **Poop Deck** $6c+$ (15m) Climb the shattered wall directly above the shelf to reach the top of the 'Bahama' crack and an exciting finish

**6** **Bahama Breeze** $6c+$* (15m) From the right of the shelf, follow the crack diagonally left to a crux through the cracked bulge

**7** **Negotiations with Isaac** $6b+$** (15m) Start as for **6** and follow the crack to resting jugs, then finish direct to the 3rd lower-off

**8** **The Tanning Salon** $7a$** (15m) Start just right of the shelf. Pass the crack rightward to a niche, a bouldery crux and direct finish

**9** **The Beef Monster** $6c+$*** (12m) The original and best line. Start on the right hand pedestal, climb direct through the orange bulge to the niche, and finish on the 4th lower-off

**10** **The Seam** $7a+$* (15m) Step off the pedestal to the right and follow the crack leftward past an old peg to jugs and the 3rd lower-off

**11** **Airhead** $7a$** (15m) Pass through a low crux bulge to a series of flat holds, which take you left before returning right to the 4th lower-off

The **Ring Cycle** ($7b$***) is a right-to-left rising girdle starting up the **Seam** and ending as **Whiplash**

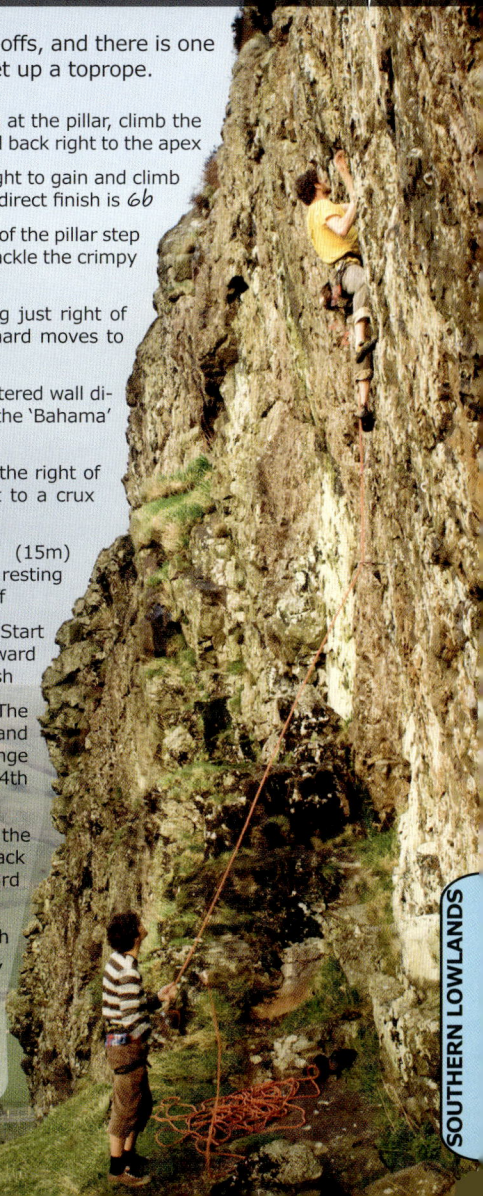

SOUTHERN LOWLANDS

# Blantyre Towers

55.78692 -4.113675

P 55.78515 -4.121566

This unique venue is located on the sandstone towers of the abandoned Greenhill railway viaduct, a project of the late Willie Arrol, a well-known local. While urban in feel, the climbing is enjoyable and technical, the sandstone lending itself to interesting features, both from the stonemasons' chisels and natural erosion. The routes tend to be sustained and notoriously difficult to on-sight, and so are graded for a red-point. Several of the routes are also graded separately for arête-avoiding eliminates, which are recommended and maximise the area's potential as a training venue. Note, however, that the legality of climbing on these structures is currently un-tested!

Heading west on the A725 dual carriageway, take the turn-off signed 'High Blantyre B758'. Go under the bridge at the roundabout. Take a left at the traffic lights down Hamilton Road until a right (no entry ahead) onto Stoneymeadow Road. Go down the road immediately off to the right for ~100m to find a parking area just after the 15mph signs. From here a path leads downhill to the river which, from over the bridge, is followed rightwards (5 min). Blantyre rail station is 20mins from Glasgow Central, and 2.5 miles from the towers.

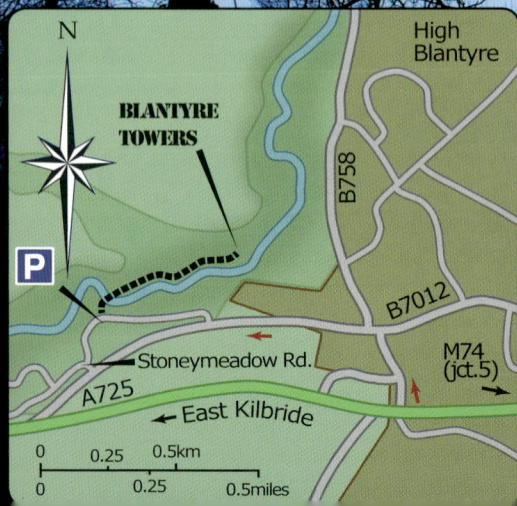

Map showing Blantyre Towers, High Blantyre, B758, B7012, M74 (jct.5), P (parking), Stoneymeadow Rd., A725, East Kilbride. Scale 0–0.5km / 0–0.5miles.

5 mins    20 mins

**1** **Allouette Arête** $6a$ * (10m) A short route up the arête with a distinct crux. If you stick to the face on the right, **2** **Allouette Eliminate** provides interest at $6b$

**3** **Tetris** $6b+$* (13m) Pushing through a hard and technical crux is rewarded with some big holds, and a bolt to clip, but it's not over yet!

**4** **Cheap Talk** $7a$* (15m) A tricky, sometimes dusty, start leads an unrelenting pump-fest

**5** **Jaqueville** $6c$* (16m) A tricky start leads to generous 'resting' holds at half height. Low in the grade

**6** **Arrol's Arête** $6b$** (18m) This soaring arête just screams to be climbed. Start up the face and then slap and hook your way up the arête. **7** **Arrol's Eliminate** ($6c+$*) uses neither arête and provides some thin moves

**8** **Andy Pandy** $6c+$** (18m) Sustained difficulties with thin, rather than powerful, climbing

**9** **Kop Out** $6b+$ (18m) Start on the left then the right arête via a deep hueco. Avoiding either arête gives the better **10** **Teeny Weeny Way-Co** ($6c$*)

**11** **Livingstone** $6c$** (20m) One of the tower's more varied climbs featuring a fine assortment of jugs, slopers and crimps

**12** **Vuvuzela** $6c$** (20m) Sustained and very hard to on-sight

**13** **Orion** $6c$ (22m) The original line, initially protected with pegs, and using either arête as required, or avoid both to tick the more spicy **14** **Orion Eliminate** ($6c+$). 12 quickdraws required

The tower nearest to the river holds the test piece **Ivy League** 7b*** and a closed project.

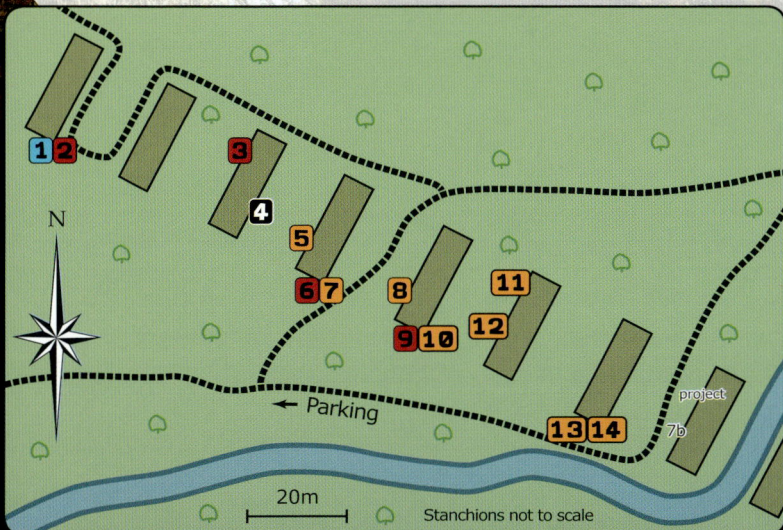

0  1  4  8  1

N

N

20m

← Parking

Stanchions not to scale

project

7b

# Dunbar

56.00511 -2.522255

**P** 56.00372 -2.521719

2 mins     5 mins

This small coastal sandstone crag offers a handful of accessible routes, some of which may be deep-water solos at high tide! Take any of several turn-offs from the A1 signed for Dunbar. From the north end of the High Street, follow Bayswell Rd 200m to park just after a garage. Across the road, steps lead down to the shore.

**1 Hoochie Coochie Man** *5+* (8m)
The obvious corner

**2 Flown Back from Boston** *5+\** (8m)
The left-hand pocketed wall

**3 Reaching for the Pilot** *6a+\** (8m)
Fewer pockets, so requires longer reaches than its neighbour

**4 Aching Arms and Dragging Heels**
*6c\*\** (10m) The most entertaining route of the bunch. Traverse the roof with heel-hooks and a hard crank to get established on the headwall

The steep sandy overhang holds an unfinished project, a 7b+ and an 8a.

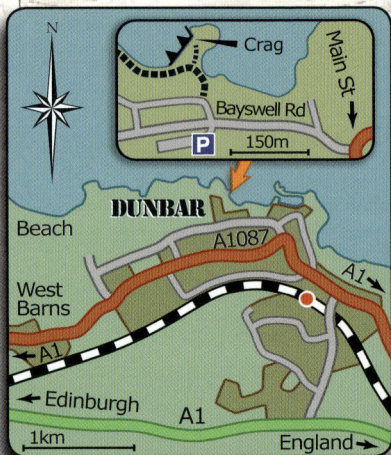

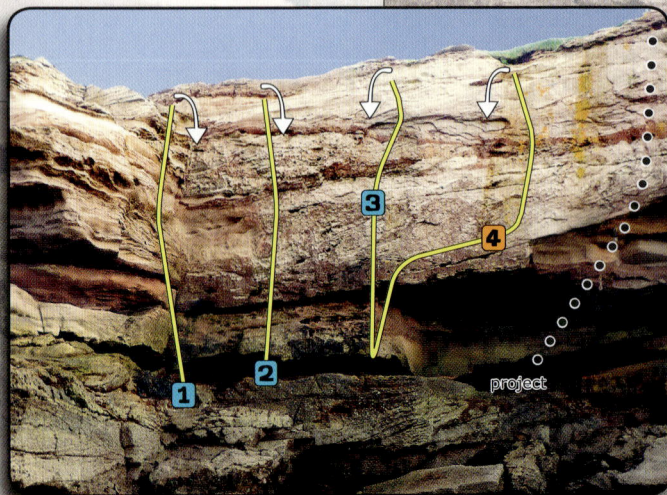

# Other Crags

## DUMBARTON ROCK (55.93752 -4.563012)

Dumbarton a.k.a. 'Dumby' is perhaps best known for its hard-core basalt bouldering, and Dave MacLeod's E11 route '**Rhapsody**'. Climbing here requires a specific technique, and first time visitors can be disheartened, but perseverance is recommended as there are a handful of good sport lines. On the steep slab below the Rhapsody face are (L/R): **Persistence of Vision** $7a+$\*\*\*-*Top30*, **First Movement** $6b+$\*\* and **Abstract Art** $6c$\*\*. The black overhang to the right sports some fiercely crimpy routes at 7c+ and above, while round the seaward side further right the two last routes are (L/R): **Natural Born Drillers** $7a$\* and **Casanostra** $6c+$. Take the A82 west from Glasgow to Dumbarton (A814) and follow the 'Dumbarton Castle' sign down Victoria St and Castle Rd. (**P** 55.93641 -4.561035)

## DUMBUCK (55.93855 -4.533423)

Just north of Dumbarton, is a short 45° overhanging wall of basalt. The greatest number of routes are 7c-8c test pieces. On the far left of the crag is **Filth Infatuated** $5+$ and the last three routes on the right of the crag are (L/R): **Twister** $7a+$, **Tragically Hip** $6c+$\*\* and **Breathe the Pressure** $6b+$\*. Turn off the A82 for Dumbarton (A814), park by the Dumbuck Hotel, and follow a path past the hotel back to the A82. Walk east and jump the fence at a grey signal box. (**P** 55.93767 -4.540274)

## CRAIGPARK QUARRY (55.92171 -3.398258)

The large open quarry across the canal from Ratho Quarry is being landscaped for housing at time of writing, but there are some bolted lines in the gully leading to the canalside that should survive. In the leftmost bay there is a cracked groove, **Circus Trick** $6b$\*\*. The central slabs hold three 9m lines (L/R): **Park Life** $6c$\*\*, **Slab LH** (open project), and **Keeping the Spark Alive** $7a$\* which features a hard technical start before a more delicate conclusion. The rightmost buttress contains three 10m routes, the first two of which share a lower-off. (L/R): **Parkin Ride** $6a+$\*, **Cakewalk** $6a+$\*, **The Pie-d Piper** $6a$\*. There is room for further development, for those willing to put in the cleaning. Park at the EICA climbing centre (p226) or in the small layby just outside its gate (**P** 55.92169 -3.400855). From the layby, step through the fence, follow the slope up right to the col and down the other side to meet the left end of the gully. Alternatively hop the fence at the last bus stop in Ratho Village (#20 from Edinburgh) and walk down a good path that emerges at the right (canal) end of the crag.

SOUTHERN LOWLANDS

# Indoor Climbing Walls

Unfortunately there are times when the infamous Scottish weather just doesn't play fair. Fortunately there are always the indoors to keep the tendons in shape for the next sunny excursion. Below is a list of the best indoor walls across the country. Price ranges are as of December 2014 for adult single entries, call for up to date information.

# ABERDEEN

## TRANSITION EXTREME
Links Road, Aberdeen, AB24 5NN
15m Lead / toprope / boulder
plus ropes course and skatepark
Mon-Fri 10:00-22:00
Sat-Sun 10:00-20:00
£6.80 - £10
01224 626 279
**www.transition-extreme.com**

# DUNDEE

## AVERTICAL WORLD
Blinshall Street, Dundee, DD1 5DF
10m Lead / toprope/ boulder
Mon-Fri 12:00-22:00
Sat-Sun 10:00-19:00
(May be reduced May-Aug)
£6.00 - £9.00
01382 201 901
**www.averticalworld.co.uk**

# STIRLING

## THE PEAK
Stirling Sports Village
Forthside Way, Stirling, FK8 1QZ
11m Lead / toprope / autobelay
Mon - Fri 06:00-22:00
Sat - Sun 08:00-20:00
£7.50
01786 273 555
**www.the-peak-stirling.org.uk**

# EDINBURGH

## ALIEN ROCK 1
8 Pier Place, Edinburgh, EH6 4LP
10m Lead / toprope / boulder
Summer Opening May-Sept
Mon-Fri 11:00-22:00
Sat-Sun 10:00-19:00
Winter opening Oct-April
Mon-Thurs 11:00-22:30
Fri 11:00-22:00
Sat-Sun 10:00-19:00
£6.00 - £8.80
0131 552 7211
**www.alienrock.co.uk**

## ALIEN ROCK 2
37 West Bowling Green Street,
Edinburgh, EH6 5NX
300 m$^2$ Bouldering
Mon-Thurs 16:00-22:00
Friday 15:00-21:00
Sat-Sun 11:00-19:00
£5.80 - £7.50
0131 552 7211
**www.alienrock.co.uk**

## EDINBURGH INTERNATIONAL CLIMBING ARENA (RATHO)
South Platt Hill
Edinburgh, EH28 8AA
25m Lead / toprope / boulder
Mon-Fri 10:00-22:00
Sat-Sun 09:00-18:00
£7.00 - £9.90
0131 333 6333
**www.eica-ratho.com**

# GLASGOW

## GLASGOW CLIMBING CENTRE (IBROX)

534 Paisley Road West, Ibrox
Glasgow, G51 1RN
12m Lead/ toprope / boulder
Mon-Fri 11:00-22:00
Sat-Sun 10:00-18:00
£5 - £8
(registration £10/life £1.50/day)
0141 427 9550
**www.glasgowclimbingcentre.com**

## THE CLIMBING ACADEMY (TCA)

124 Portman Street
Glasgow, G41 1EJ
1100 m$^2$ Bouldering
Mon-Fri 10:00-22:00
Sat-Sun 10:00-18:00
£4 - £8.00
(registration £10/life £2/day)
0141 429 6331
**www.tca-glasgow.com**

# THE HIGHLANDS

## CLIMB CALEDONIA

Bught Park, Inverness, IV3 5SS
9m Lead / toprope / boulder
Mon-Fri 15:00-22:00
           (10:00-22:00 school holidays)
Sat-Sun 10:00-17:00
£3.40 - £6.55 (plus registration £1 - £4.35)
01463 667 500
**www.invernessleisure.co.uk**

## GAIRLOCH LEISURE CENTRE

Low Road, Gairloch, IV21 2BP
8m Lead / toprope
Mon - Fri 17:00-22:00ish - call to check
(13:00-21:00 during school holidays)
Sat - Sun 10:15-16:30
01445 712 345
www.highlifehighland.com

## GLENMORE LODGE

Glenmore Lodge, Aviemore,
Inverness-Shire, PH22 1QU
Lead wall / dry-tooling / courses
Currently being redeveloped - call for details
01479 861 256
**www.glenmorelodge.org.uk**

## THE ICE FACTOR

Kinlochleven, Lochaber, PH50 4SF
15m Lead / ice / boulder
09:00-18:00 (22:00 Tues/Thur)
£7.00 - £9.50 (£27.50 for ice)
01855 831 100
**www.ice-factor.co.uk**

And coming soon....

## THREE WISE MONKEYS

Old Macintosh Memorial Church
Fassifern Road, Fort William
Phase 1 opening Summer 2015
13m Lead / Boulder / Training room
09:00 - 22:00 daily
Prices TBC
**www.threewisemonkeysclimbing.com**

# ACKNOWLEDGEMENTS

First and foremost we owe our gratitude to the many dedicated sport climbing activists across the country who developed and maintain our sport routes. Without these individuals and their hard labour, there would be no sport climbs! Installing and maintaining in situ equipment is a time consuming and expensive pastime. If you enjoy climbing Scotland's sport routes and have benefited from the hours of cleaning, drilling, and route finding, then consider making a donation to one the bolt funds, or even better getting involved in ongoing maintenance.

By no means an exhaustive list, but thank you Neil Shepherd, Rab Anderson, Murray Hamilton, Dave Cuthbertson, Duncan MacCallum, Graeme Livingstone, Cameron Phair, George Ridge, Jeff Ross, Neil Morrison, David Pert, Isla Watson, Janet Horrocks, Scott Muir, Colin Miln, Paul Tattersall, Colin Meek, Paul Thorburn, Andy Wilby, Murdoch Jamieson, Ken Edwards, Ian MacDonald, Derek Armstrong, Willie Arrol (RIP), John Watson, Calum Mayland, Simon Nadin, Andy Nisbet, Jamie Sparkes, Gregor Callum, Danny Laing, Tim Rankin, Tom Ballard, Dave Macleod, Ian Taylor, and Andy Cunningham.

The production of **7a Max** would not have been possible without all those who have helped with mileage, legwork, lost weekends, donation of photographs, route information, proof reading, the website, generator portage, couches and the general anti-social obsession involved in the production of this guide. Heartfelt thanks go out to: Emily Nicholl, Sofia Makieva, Sophie Buckingham, Paul Tattersall, Colin Miln, Gregor Callum, Stuart Stronach, Fraser Harle, Jamie Sparkes, Danny Laing, John Sharples, Chris Wilson, Will Roper, Chad Harrison, Davide Cassol, Lasma Sietensone, Malcolm, Mathilde, Roland, Conrad, and the Arbroath fisherman-come-photographer who asked how to wind-on our digital camera!

## ABOUT THE AUTHORS

**Sebastien Rider** enjoyed university so much he is still found there researching in the field of biomedical science. His climbing started at home in the mountains of the Highlands, but with several years away in the south of England and France he inevitably found the joys of sport climbing. When not climbing it is any excuse to get back north for adventures of any kind, be it snowboarding, paragliding, caving, or simply just being there!

**Topher Dagg** is a circus rigger by trade, and a monkey-botherer by training, both of which prove quite compatible with a life of climbing around the world. Having rarely touched a bolt until 2011, his trad exploits left him recovering from a broken femur, and an appreciation for the safer rehabilitation that sport routes would provide. While exploring sport venues as part of his 'physiotherapy', he and Seb realised the lack of any Scottish Sport climbing guidebooks. Both no strangers to a project or two they embarked on the 7a Max journey.

# INDEX

# INDEX

# INDEX

# INDEX

# INDEX

## NOTES

Sophie getting flexible with **Psychopomp (6b)**
Creag nan Luch - p.63